PERGAMON INTERNATIONAL LIBRARY
of Science, Technology, Engineering and Social Studies

The 1000-volume original paperback library in aid of education,
industrial training and the enjoyment of leisure

Publisher: Robert Maxwell, M.C.

The Manufacture of Knowledge

An Essay on the Constructivist
and Contextual Nature of Science

D1302579

THE PERGAMON TEXTBOOK
INSPECTION COPY SERVICE

An inspection copy of any book published in the Pergamon International Library will gladly be
sent to academic staff without obligation for their consideration for course adoption or
recommendation. Copies may be retained for a period of 60 days from receipt and returned if
not suitable. When a particular title is adopted or recommended for adoption for class
use and the recommendation results in a sale of 12 or more copies, the inspection copy may be
retained with our compliments. The Publishers will be pleased to receive suggestions for
revised editions and new titles to be published in this important International Library.

Other Titles of Interest

AGASSI, J.
The Philosophy of Technology

ANGEL, R.
Relativity: The Theory and Its Philosophy

BUNGE, W.
The Logical Foundation of Mathematics

SIMPSON, G.
Why and How: Some Problems and Methods in Historical Biology

WILDER, R.
Mathematics as a Cultural System

The Manufacture of Knowledge

An Essay on the Constructivist and Contextual Nature of Science

by

KARIN D. KNORR-CETINA
Department of Sociology
University of Pennsylvania, Philadelphia

Preface by
Rom Harré

PERGAMON PRESS

OXFORD · NEW YORK · TORONTO · SYDNEY · PARIS · FRANKFURT

U.K.	Pergamon Press Ltd., Headington Hill Hall, Oxford OX3 0BW, England
U.S.A.	Pergamon Press Inc., Maxwell House, Fairview Park, Elmsford, New York 10523, U.S.A.
CANADA	Pergamon Press Canada Ltd., Suite 104, 150 Consumers Rd., Willowdale, Ontario M2J 1P9, Canada
AUSTRALIA	Pergamon Press (Aust.) Pty. Ltd., P.O. Box 544, Potts Point, N.S.W. 2011, Australia
FRANCE	Pergamon Press SARL, 24 rue des Ecoles, 75240 Paris, Cedex 05, France
FEDERAL REPUBLIC OF GERMANY	Pergamon Press GmbH, 6242 Kronberg-Taunus, Hammerweg 6, Federal Republic of Germany

First edition 1981

British Library Cataloguing in Publication Data

Knorr-Cetina, Karin D
The manufacture of knowledge.
1. Science - Social aspects
2. Research
I. Title II. Series
301.24'3   Q175.5   80-40996
ISBN 0-08-025777-1

Printed in Great Britain by A. Wheaton & Co. Ltd., Exeter

To
Dietrich
and
Berkeley

Preface

IT IS NOW some eighty years since the idea that there is a relation between scientific knowledge and the social order in which it developed, was first proposed. We have seen this general thesis elaborated in three directions. There have been those who thought that there was a causal relation between the taken for granted socio-political structure of a period and the content of scientific theories, for instance the individualism of protestant capitalism was thought to have engendered physical atomism. This idea of a relation between the social order of a period and the content of the scientific theories popular at a time has been revived in recent years by the Edinburgh school (for instance in the recent work by D. Bloor, 1976). This is a very strong thesis, and there have been serious objections raised to it. The most fundamental is perhaps that there is no way of telling whether there is a causal relation between the social order and the scientific ideas of a time, or whether there is some third thing, the "zeitgeist", whatever that might be, that engenders both. Correlation, it might be argued, is not causation, unless one adopts the dubious causal theories of Hume.

More recently there has been a tendency to invoke social explanations when epistemological accounts of science run out, a kind of "God-of-the-gaps" argument. Historians and philosophers of science, such as Kuhn (1962) and Feyerabend (1975) have pointed to what they take to be an underdetermination of theory by the available data, both as to content and as to grounds for belief. How is it then, that scientists do make quite clear cut decisions as to which theory to prefer at some time? The alleged weakness of the epistemological account of theory choice is remedied by pointing to the power of the scientific elite and the social processes by which it is recruited, modified and sometimes overthrown, to influence what it is taken as rational to believe. Some have gone as far as Toulmin (1972) to propose that we should think of scientific elites as setting up "institutions of rationality". While it is no doubt true that the urge to demonstrate publicly that one is a rational being is socially based and socially promulgated it would be a gross example of the naturalistic fallacy to identify grounds for belief with social pressure. Not least because it might be that the scientific community maintains by social pressure, just those criteria for theory choice that best embody the practices that experience has shown are the best ways of judging theories for their truth.

Both these developments, and their defects, could be explained if one sees them as footnotes to Mannheim's original derivation, from Marx, of a sociology of knowledge. However, there has recently emerged a much more sophisticated mode of analysis. Suppose that instead of approaching the scientific community with Marx or even Goffman in hand, one were to adopt the stance of the anthropologist coming into contact with a strange tribe. At first, since one did not share their language, the tribe's own theories as to the grounds for and even the nature of their activities, would be unknown. The relative significance of those activities would be opaque. Entering the laboratory and watching with amazement the things that go on there, what would one be inclined to say? One notices with some interest that most people seem to spend most of their time writing and correcting writings. What is one to make of this? What are they doing it for? Soon enough one grasps that certain important hierarchical relations between members of the tribe develop through the public use of the writings. A steeply graded social order x, marked by the adoption of symbolic clothes and other accoutrements such as slide rules or pocket calculators, is borne in upon one.

The anthropological approach, as one might call it, is the central focus of this study. Laboratories are looked upon with the innocent eye of the traveller in exotic lands, and the societies found in these places are observed with the objective yet compassionate eye of the visitor from a quite other cultural milieu. There are many surprises that await us if we enter a laboratory and study a group of scientists in this frame of mind. The idea that the enterprise can be defined in terms of an idealized epistemology, whether that of experimentally based inductions or of the conjectures and empirical refutations of the logicist philosophers of science, is quickly refuted. Logic, it seems, is not among the "idols of the tribe". Where it appears it is as an insert in the pursuit of rhetorical advantage in debate. The experimental control of thought, the official philosophy of science, is demonstrably remote from the considerations of those who actually practice science as a way of life.

In earlier versions of this approach the power of the vision to bring out aspects of the scientific enterprise that were both surprising and in need of explanation was vitiated by an almost unacknowledged adherence to an old, and indeed exploded philosophy of science, instrumentalism. Happily the sociological work has been made more sophisticated, and in this study no *a priori* hostages to fortune by way of positivistic skeletons in the cupboard, any longer take away from the effectiveness of the study. Of course science only makes sense as a realist enterprise, an attempt, using the means at hand, to truly represent physical reality as it is. Indeed this very study is a realist enterprise, an attempt to truly represent the social order of life in laboratories and institutes of research, just as they are. By bringing the philosophical issues to the surface as matters not of prejudgement but as matters of concern, Karin Knorr has developed the first really positive challenge to the philosophy of science since the days of paradigms and internal definitions of meanings.

Rom Harré
Linacre College, Oxford

References

BLOOR, D. (1976) *Knowledge and Social Imagery,* London: Routledge & Kegan Paul.
FEYERABEND, P. K. (1975) *Against Method,* London: New Left Books.
KUHN, T. S. (1962) *The Structure of Scientific Revolutions,* Chicago: Chicago University Press.
TOULMIN, S. (1972) *Human Understanding,* Oxford: The Clarendon Press.

Acknowledgements

THIS WORK was made possible by my stay as a Ford Fellow in Berkeley, California, and by the support of the Jubiläumsfonds der Österreichischen Nationalbank in Vienna. The work was done at the Institute for Social Change, University of California, Berkeley; the Institute for Advanced Studies, Vienna; and the Department of Sociology, University of Pennsylvania, Philadelphia, which facilitated the research.

I have drawn from the ideas and help of many during the past years, including Aaron Cicourel, Gerald Cole, Rom Harré, Eric van Hove, Roger Krohn, Bruno Latour, John Searle, and Hans Georg Zilian. I am grateful once again to Richard Ogar for his editorial work, and to my husband, whose endurance I continue to exploit. I am heavily indebted to the scientists in the laboratory observed, whom I spied upon and quoted ruthlessly, and to Berkeley, which provided a beautiful and congenial environment.

Contents

Mike Peyton, The *New Scientist*.

Chapter 1

The Scientist as a Practical Reasoner: Introduction to a Constructivist and Contextual Theory of Knowledge

My lord, facts are like cows. If you look them in the face hard enough, they generally run away.
Dorothy L. Sayers

1.1 Facts and Fabrications

Dorothy Sayers' analogy between cows and facts hides both a philosophical and a methodological point. Since both will guide us throughout this book, I will begin by discussing each at some length. The philosophical point is that facts are not something we can take for granted or think of as the solid rock upon which knowledge is built. Actually, their nature is rather problematic—so much so that confrontation often scares them off. The methodological point is that the confrontation has to be long, hard and direct. Like cows, facts have become sufficiently domesticated to deal with run-of-the-mill events.

That facts are indeed problematic has been known to philosophers for quite some time. Indeed, the quest for the nature of facts—the core of the quest for the nature of knowledge—is a major reason for the proliferation of epistemological theories. The key dispute is where to locate the problem, and how to approach it. Kant, for example, saw the quest as a search for the conditions of possibility of pure science, and found his answer in the categorical make-up of the human mind. In marked contrast, one of to-day's much discussed concepts sees the core of the problem not in the human mind, but in social history. Its proposal is to search out the social relations of production from which the nature of knowledge is thought to originate.[1]

Recent theories of knowledge have tended to transfer the problem from a knowing subject's constitution of the factual to a variety of other locations. Most influential, perhaps, is the shift toward the logic of scientific inference advocated by what some have called objectivism.[2] To the objectivist, the world is composed of facts and the goal of knowledge is to provide a literal account of what that world is like.[3] The empirical laws and theoretical propositions of science are designed to provide those literal descriptions. If empirical laws and theoretical propositions literally *describe* an external world of facticity, then an enquiry into the meaning and connection of "facts" becomes an enquiry into the meaning and connection of laws and propositions. If the knowledge of scientific accounts *is* reality represented by science, then an enquiry into the nature of the "real" becomes an investigation of how the logic of scientific accounts preserves the lawlike structure of the real.[4]

1

But there are other positions. To the anti-realist, for example, it is precisely this last question which needs to be reversed.[5] Why should our interest-geared, instrumentally-generated world order mirror some inherent structure in nature? The problem of facticity is not external to science, but internal to knowledge itself. Science, says Feyerabend, is nothing but one family of beliefs equal to any other family of beliefs.[6] Systems of belief develop within social and historical contexts. Thus, the study of facticity is the study of history and social life. But if science, like the magic of the Azande, is merely a belief system, the objectivist might argue, can we not infer that the two are interchangeable? And if this position is unthinkable, does it not imply that the argument itself is a naïve form of scepticism, inconsistent with itself in the sense that it disregards the very social and historical context it otherwise postulates to establish the relativity of knowledge? According to Marx, the mark of idealism is to forget that reality is constructed neither accidentally nor under conditions of free choice.[7] In view of what can be explained by positions like the scepticist's "anything goes",[8] realism has been called the only concept "that doesn't make the success of science a miracle".[9]

Can we say, then, that the problem of facticity is to be located in the correspondence between the products of science and the external world, and that the solution is to be found in the descriptive adequacy of scientific procedure? There is more than one negative answer to such a proposal. To begin with, while objectivism (in accordance with Marx) stresses the constraints (here identified with nature) which limit the products of science, it is itself oblivious to the constituted character of these products. Peirce has made it the point of his work to argue that the process of scientific enquiry ignored by objectivism (its "context of discovery") is itself the system of reference which makes the objectification of reality possible.[10]

Thus, the problem of facticity is as much a problem of the constitution of the world through the logic of scientific procedure as it is one of explanation and validation. While the work of Bohm, Hanson, Kuhn and Feyerabend may not have resulted in a satisfactory model of scientific success, it is generally credited with pointing to the meaning variance or theory dependence of scientific observation. This meaning variance is another aspect of the active constitution of facticity through science, and one most disturbing for objectivism.[11]

Equally relevant here is the fact that models of success which do not require the basic assumptions of objectivism are both thinkable and plausible, and have been proposed within the sciences themselves. Psychiatrists, for example, have often used behavioural therapy to successfully treat both major and minor psychic disorders for which they claim not to have nor to need any descriptively adequate explanation.[12] A better illustration, perhaps, is the mouse that runs from the cat.[13] Must we assume that the mouse runs because it has in its mind a correct representation of the natural enmity inherent in the cat? Or is it not more plausible to say that any species which fails to run from its natural enemies will cease to exist, which leaves us only with those that did run? Like the progress of evolution itself, the progress of science can be linked to mechanisms which do not assume that knowledge mimics nature.

Finally, objectivism has been criticised within its own ranks for assuming a factual world structured in a lawlike manner by the constant conjunction of events. According to this critique, constant conjunctions of events result from laboratory *work* which creates closed systems in which unambiguous results are possible and repeatable. But in practice, such constant conjunctions are the rare exceptions—as is predictive success.[14]

Consequently, the laws proposed by science are transfactual and rule-like, rather than descriptively adequate. Thus, the practical success of science depends more upon the scientist's ability to analyse a situation as a whole, to think on several different levels at once, to recognise clues, and to piece together disparate bits of information, than upon the laws themselves. As with any game, winning depends less upon the rules than on what is done within the space created by those rules.

Bhaskar's analysis suggests that there is no necessary link between the "success of science" and the assumptions made by empirical realism, and that, indeed, the success of science may have to be explained on grounds very different from the thesis of symmetry between prediction and explanation. His "transcendental realism" adds another aspect to the constitutive role which both pragmatism and scepticism attribute to scientific investigation, i.e. that the experimenter is a *causal agent* of the sequence of events created, and that conjunctions of events are not provided for us but *created* by us.[15] At the same time, he holds that the questions which man puts to nature must be phrased in a language that nature "understands" and takes the instruments of science as "devices designed to decipher the vocabulary of nature".[16]

The purpose of the present study is to explore how those constant conjunctions are *created* in the laboratory (suspending for the moment any assumptions about the vocabulary of nature). Rather than view empirical observation as questions put to nature in a language she understands, we will take all references to the "constitutive" role of science seriously, and regard scientific enquiry as a process of production. Rather than considering scientific products as somehow capturing what is, we will consider them as selectively carved out, transformed and constructed from whatever is. And rather than examine the external relations between science and the "nature" we are told it describes, we will look at those internal affairs of scientific enterprise which we take to be *constructive*.[17]

The etymology of the word "fact" reveals a fact as "that which has been made", in accord with its root in the Latin *facere,* to make.[18] Yet we tend to think of scientific "facts" as given entities, and not as fabrications. In the present study, the problem of facticity is relocated and seen as a problem of (laboratory) fabrication. Clearly, then, we step beyond philosophical theories of knowledge and their objectivist (or anti-objectivist) concerns. But I would argue that once we see scientific products as first and foremost the result of a process of construction, we can begin to substitute for those concerns, as some have suggested, an empirical theory of knowledge.[19]

1.2 The Constructivist Interpretation I: Nature and the Laboratory

How do we defend the contention that scientific enquiry ought to be viewed as constructive rather than descriptive? And what exactly do we mean by this particular qualification? The first question can be answered rather simply. Even the briefest participation in the world of scientific investigation suggests that the language of truth and hypothesis testing (and with it, the descriptivist model of enquiry) is ill-equipped to deal with laboratory work. Where in the laboratory, for example, do we find the "nature" or "reality" so critical to the descriptivist interpretation? Most of the reality with which scientists deal is highly preconstructed, if not wholly artificial.

What, after all, *is* a laboratory? A local accumulation of instruments and devices within a working space composed of chairs and tables. Drawers full of minor utensils, shelves loaded with chemicals and glassware. Refrigerators and freezers stuffed with carefully labelled samples and source-materials: buffer solutions and finely ground alfalfa leaves, single cell proteins, blood samples from the assay rats and lysozymes. All of the source-materials have been specially grown and selectively bred. Most of the substances and chemicals are purified and have been obtained from the industry which serves science or from other laboratories. But whether bought or prepared by the scientists themselves, these substances are no less the product of human effort than the measurement devices or the papers on the desks. It would seem, then, that nature is not to be found in the laboratory, unless it is defined from the beginning as being the product of scientific work.

Nor do we find in the laboratory the quest for truth which is customarily ascribed to science. To be sure, the language of scientists contains innumerable references to what is or is not true. But their usage in no way differs from our own everyday use of the term in a variety of pragmatic and rhetoric functions which do not have much to do with the epistemological concept of truth. If there is a principle which seems to govern laboratory action, it is the scientists' concern with making things "work", which points to a principle of success rather than one of truth. Needless to say, to make things work—to produce results—is not identical with attempting their falsification. Nor is it the concern of the laboratory to produce results irrespective of potential criticism. Scientists guard against later attacks by anticipating and countering critical questions before publications. The scientists' vocabulary of how things work, of why they do or do not work, of steps to take to make them work, does not reflect some form of naïve verificationism, but is in fact a discourse appropriate to the *instrumental manufacture* of knowledge in the *workshop* called a "lab". Success in making things work is a much more mundane pursuit than that of truth, and one which is constantly turned into credits in scientific everyday life via publication. Thus, it is success in making things work which is reinforced as a concrete and feasible goal of scientific action, and not the distant ideal of truth which is never quite attained.

But "truth" and "nature" are not the only casualties of the laboratory; the observer would find it equally difficult to locate those "theories" which are so often associated with science. Theories adopt a peculiarly "atheoretical" character in the laboratory. They hide behind partial interpretations of "what happens" and "what is the case", and disguise themselves as temporary answers to "how-to-make-sense-of-it" questions. What makes laboratory theories so atheoretical is the lack of any divorce from instrumental manipulation. Instead, they confront us as discursively crystallised experimental operations, and are in turn woven into the process of performing experimentation.

In place of the familiar alienation between theory and practice,[20] we find an action-/cognition mesh to which the received notion of a theory can no longer be adequately applied. According to the scientists themselves, theories in research are more akin to policies than creeds.[21] Such policies blend interpretation with strategic and tactical calculations, and are sustained by methodological "how-to-do-it" projections. Like the concern with making things work, policies are necessarily tied to an interest structure. Pure theory, then, can be called an illusion the sciences have retained from philosophy.[22]

1.3 The Constructivist Interpretation II: The "Decision Ladenness" of Fact-Fabrication

The inadequacy of those concepts associated with the descriptive interpretation of scientific enquiry is not surprising, given the framework in which they developed. It is no less surprising that a shift in the framework of analysis to the actual process of research brings new conceptions into being. We have said that this process should be seen as *constructive* rather than descriptive. Let us be more specific. The thesis under consideration is that the products of science are contextually specific constructions which bear the mark of the situational contingency and interest structure of the process by which they are generated, and which cannot be adequately understood without an analysis of their construction. This means that what happens in the process of construction is *not* irrelevant to the products we obtain. It also means that the products of science have to be seen as *highly internally structured* through the process of production, independent of the question of their external structuring through some match or mismatch with reality.

How can we conceive of this internal structuring of scientific products? Scientific results, including empirical data, have been characterised as first and foremost the result of a process of fabrication. Processes of fabrication involve chains of decisions and negotiations through which their outcomes are derived. Phrased differently, they require that selections be made. Selections, in turn, can only be made on the basis of previous selections: they are based on translations into further selections.

Consider a scientist sitting at an electronic table calculator and running a regression programme on texture measurement data. The machine automatically selects a function along which it plots the data. But in order to choose among the eight functions at its disposal, it needs a criterion. Such criteria are nothing more than second order selections: they represent a choice among other potential criteria into which a first order selection can be translated. In our case, the programme actually offered a choice between two criteria, maximum R^2 and minimum maximum absolute residuum. The scientist had opted for a combination of the two.

He obtains an exponential function for his data, which he says he doesn't like. He reruns the programme, asking for a linear function, which he finds to be "not much worse" (than the exponential one). The idea, he says, is to get one type of equation, and eventually one size Beta coefficient for all runs of the problem, because it would be totally confusing to have different functions in every single case.

From observing the scientist, we might also conclude that the goal must have been to get a linear function. In order to reach a decision, the original task of the programme was to select a function translated into the selection between one of two forms of the statistical fit of the curves. In a stepwise procedure, the scientist added translations into other criteria, such as uniformity over comparable data and linearity. He eventually chose the latter because it offered greater ease of interpretation and presentation.

Callon has recently illustrated how the relationship between supply and demand in regard to information can be seen as a symbolic operation of translation (Serres, 1974) which transforms one particular definition of a problem into another particular statement of a problem. For example, the problem of reducing urban smog may be translated into the problem of reducing the amount of led in petrol, or of transforming the affected area into a pedestrian zone. This implies that the solution of problem A requires the solution of problem B, into which A has been translated.[23] In the present case, this kind of translation is seen as an inherent feature of decision-making, or—to borrow an expression from Luhmann—of selectivity in general.[24] It allows us to see scientific products as internally constructed, not only with respect to the composite laboratory selections which give rise to the product, but also with respect to the translations incorporated within those selections.

In other words, the scientific product can be seen as structured in terms of *several orders or levels of selectivity*. This complexity of scientific constructions with regard to the selections they incorporate is interesting in its own right because it does seem to suggest that scientific products are unlikely to be reproduced in the same way under different circumstances. If a scientific product is characterised by several levels of selection (or constellations of selections), it seems highly improbable that the process could be repeated, unless most of the selections are either fixed or made in a similar fashion.

Given that scientists working on a problem are related through communication, competition and cooperation, and often share similar educations, instruments and interest structures, the latter situation is not really unusual.[25] But this translation of selections not only points to scientific products as complex constructions incorporating layers of selectivity, but also (as we shall see in Chapter 4) provides the threads with which laboratory selections and the products they compose are woven into the relevant contexts of research.

In order to reach some form of closure, selections are translated into other selections. To break up that closure, the selections can be challenged on their own grounds. Selections can be called into question precisely because they *are* selections: that is, precisely because they involve the possibility of alternative selections. If scientific objects are selectively carved from reality, they can be deconstructed by challenging the selections they incorporate. If scientific facts are fabricated in the sense that they are derived from decisions, they can be defabricated by imposing alternative decisions. In scientific enquiry, the selectivity of the selections incorporated into previous scientific work is itself a *topic* for further scientific investigation. At the same time, the selections of previous work constitute a *resource* which enables scientific enquiry to proceed: they supply the tools, methods, and interpretations upon which a scientist may draw in the process of her own research.

The "artificial" character of the scientist's most important tool, the laboratory, lies in the fact that it is nothing more than a local accumulation of materialisations from previous selections. The selections of previous investigations also affect subsequent selections by modalising the conditions of further decision-making. Thus, the products of science are not only decision-impregnated, they are also decision-impregnating, in the sense that they point to new problems *and* predispose their solutions.

Briefly, then, a scientist's work consists of realising selectivity within a space constituted by previous selections, and one which is essentially overdetermined. In more economic terms, we could say that scientific work requires the re-investment of previous work in a cycle in which the selections generated by scientific work and their material equivalents are themselves the content and the capital of the work. What is reproduced in this cycle is selectivity *per se*. This form of auto-capitalisation in regard to selectivity appears as a precondition for the accumulation of scientific results. It can be multiplied by increasing the number of scientists and through increased financial resources. The conversion of scientific products into research money as described in recent economic models as discussed in Chapter 4 refers to this aspect. We can also say it refers to scientific productivity rather than to scientific production.

1.4 The Laboratory: Context of Discovery or Context of Validation?

To view scientific investigation as constructive rather than descriptive is to see scientific products as highly internally constructed in terms of the selectivity they incorporate. To study scientific investigation, then, is to study the process by which the respective selections are made. Does such a study simply shift the focus of analysis from the philosophers' context of justification to that of the generation of ideas? Or from the sociologists' realm of consensus formation to the origin of the discoveries about which an opinion is formed?

Unfortunately, such distinctions as that between discovery and validation tend to embarrass, rather than help, the social scientist who actually begins to look at scientific investigation. But why should this be the case? Are we not actually leaving the context of justification to study the process of scientific result fabrication when we enter a laboratory? Are we not justified in assuming that discovery and validation are separate processes, each independent of the other? The social scientist is embarrassed because the answer is no.

Let us begin with the philosopher's contention that validation is in practice a process of rational consensus formation within the scientific community.[26] Since the validators who form this community are presumably independent of the producers of knowledge, their critical judgement constitutes an objective basis of validation. However, if we look at the process of knowledge production in sufficient detail, it turns out that scientists constantly relate their decisions and selections to the expected response of specific members of this community of "validators", or to the dictates of the journal in which they wish to publish. Decisions are based on what is "hot" and what is "out", on what one "can" or "cannot" do, on whom they will come up against and with whom they will have to associate by making a specific point. In short, the discoveries of the laboratory are made, as part and parcel of their substance, *with a view toward* potential criticism or acceptance (as well as with respect to potential allies and enemies!).

At the same time, one finds that validations are made with an eye toward the genesis of the results being validated. Whether a proposed knowledge claim is judged plausible or implausible, interesting, unbelievable or nonsensical, may depend upon *who* proposed the result, *where* the work was done, and *how* it was accomplished. Scientists speak about the motives and interests[27] which presumably gave rise to the "finding", about the material resources available to those who did the research, and about "who stands behind" the results. They virtually *identify* the results (and we will come back to this soon) with the circumstances of their generation. Thus, it is the scientific community itself which lends crucial weight to the context of discovery in response to a knowledge claim.

On a more general level, we must recognise that both the producers and the evaluators of knowledge claims are, according to those who favour the distinction between discovery and validation, generally members of the same "community". Thus, they are held to *share* a common stock of knowledge and procedures, and presumably common standards of evaluation, professional preferences, and ways of making a judgement. Furthermore, the validators of a knowledge claim are, at the same time, clients who potentially *need* a scientific result in order to promote their own investigations. We have already said that the selections of previous research become a resource for continuing scientific operations, as well as being a topic of problematisation in further research. So the validators of a knowledge claim are often the most "dangerous" competitors and antagonists a scientist has in the struggle for credit and scientific authority.

What else does it mean when the head of a widely recognised research group says that his grant proposal has been rejected because "there are only two strong groups in the area, ourselves and MIT. So we get every one of their important proposals to review, and they get ours. Of course they don't want me to go ahead, because money is scarce."[28] The point is that the producers and validators who share methods and approaches, the producers and clients who need each other's services, and the competitors engaged in a struggle for credit or money cannot at the same time be assumed to be independent and, in that sense, objectively critical. Any separation between discovery and validation along these lines is not borne out if we look at scientific practice.

There is a second critique of the separation which should be made clear. We have heard that validation or acceptance, in practice, is seen as a process of consensus formation qualified as "rational" by some philosophers, and "social" by sociologists of science. But whether rational or social, the process appears to be one of opinion formation, and as such, located somewhere else than within scientific investigation itself. Hence, the usual classification of studies of investigation as enquiries into the context of discovery, with little or no concern for problems of validation, leading to the well-known thesis that studies of the production of knowledge in the laboratory are irrelevant to questions of acceptance.

But where do we find the process of validation, to any significant degree, if not *in* the laboratory itself?[29] If not in the process of laboratory decision-making by which a previous result, a method or a proposed interpretation, comes to be preferred over others and incorporated into new results? What *is* the process of acceptance if not one of selective incorporation of previous results into the ongoing process of research production? To call it a process of opinion formation seems to provoke a host of erroneous connotations.

We do not as yet have science courts for official opinion formation with legislative power in the conduct of future research. To view consensus as the aggregate of individual scientific opinions is misleading, since (a) short of regular opinion polls we have no access to the predominant, general or average opinions of relevant scientists, and (b) it is a commonplace in sociology that opinions have a complex and largely unknown relationship to action. So even if we knew what scientists' opinions were, we would not know which results would be consistently preferred in actual research. What we have, then, is not a process of opinion formation, but one in which certain results are solidified through continued incorporation into ongoing research. This means that the locus of solidification is the process of *scientific investigation,* or in the terms introduced earlier, the *selections* through which research results are constructed *in* the laboratory.

To be sure, scientists do express opinions *about* the results of others in a variety of contexts: lunchtime chats, discussions following a speech, or in regard to an article which someone has just read and found reason to comment on. But these opinions are arguments which depend on the context of articulation. They are not necessarily consistent within different contexts, nor do they always reflect the selections which will be made in the laboratory. It is these latter which, over time, will be transformed into the "confirmed facts" and the "technical achievements" attributed to a science. Consequently, it is the process of production and reproduction of research in the laboratory we must look at in order to study the very "context of justification".[30]

1.5 The Contextuality of Laboratory Construction

Let us dwell for a moment on the idea that to study the process of production of research in the laboratory is in fact to study part of the context of justification, or acceptance. The incorporation of an earlier result into the ongoing process of investigation is seen as a potential step toward solidification. The selection of an available method or interpretation extends its presence (for example, into one more publication) and prolongs its duration. It thereby increases the chances of its further selection and incorporation. An important question, then, is how these selections are made.

Let us first consider what the scientists themselves say when asked such a question. Much as in the case where one scientist evaluates another's work, we are referred to the specific situation in which the decision was made. When we ask, for example, why a particular instrument was chosen for a certain purpose, the response may range from "Because it's expensive and rare, and I want to get to know it", to "It's more economical in terms of energy"; from "John suggested it and showed me how to use it", to "It happened to be around, so it was the easiest thing to do"; from "What I had in mind didn't work, so I tried something new", to "They asked me to use this because it's just been bought and we have to show that we needed it"; from "It always works, according to my experience", to an astonished stare and the question, "Well, what else *could* you do?"

From the few examples above, it is obvious that these factors have different roots and different implications, that they rise from different points in the scientists' problematisation preceding a decision, and that they reside on different levels of generality. Taken together, they refer us to the varying situations which the scientists recall as grounds for their decisions. The existence of an energy crisis, or of the presence of a friend with a suggestion; a failure which triggers a variation in procedure, or a purchase which needs to be justified; a personal "experience" composed of the particulars of a scientific career, or official practice at a given point in time. It seems clear that we cannot hope to reduce these situations to a small number of criteria, much less a principle of rationality, which will allow us henceforth to predict a scientist's laboratory selections. Rather, we will have to take these selections as the product of the co-occurrence and interaction of factors whose impact and relevance they happen to constitute at a given time and place, i.e., of the circumstances within which the scientists operate.

Historians have long portrayed scientists' decisions as contingent upon the historical context in which they are situated, and some recent arguments in the philosophy of science also point in this direction.[31] If we take the idea of contextual contingency one step further to suggest that acceptance is a form of environmental selection analogous to the model of biological evolution, we have a plausible alternative to the model of (rational) opinion formation. Like adaptation, acceptance can be seen as the result of contextual pressures which come to bear on the scientists' selections in the environmental niches provided by the laboratories. If such an interpretation is take for granted in biological evolution, why is it not an equally plausible characterisation of the process of selective "survival" of scientific results? It certainly has the advantage of specifying as potentially relevant the larger social context in which science is embedded and of which the scientists' decisions form a part.

But it also has a disadvantage. If we cannot name, once and for all, the criteria according to which scientific results are chosen or eliminated, we are unable to say which selections scientists are most likely to make.[32] If the context of selection varies over time and place and as a function of previous selection, the rationale for scientific selections will likewise vary. If we add to these variable contextures the chance interactions of circumstantial variables from which selections crystallise, we cannot hope to arrive at generally valid observations about these crystallisations. In short, we are left with the somewhat disheartening picture of an indeterminate contextual variation and a social scientist who cannot provide any definite specification of it. Consequently, those who have advocated this direction in the recent past have been accused of handing science over to the reign of irrationality, and ruling out the idea of directed or progressive scientific change.[33]

1.6 Contextual Contingency as a Principle of Change

Perhaps surprisingly, this indeterminacy need not have such disquieting implications for the social scientist, let alone implications of irrationality in regard to the selections of science. Recent developments in the theory of self-regulating systems (as well as in thermodynamics) suggest the opposite interpretation—that is, that such indeterminacy is a necessary prerequisite for progressive, organised adaptation, and thus for survival and reconstructive change.[34] In other words, the effect of indeterminacy is no longer viewed as purely disruptive as is the "noise" of information theory which prevents correct transmittance of a signal, the "errors" in the genetic code which prevent normal biological replication, or the "perturbations" in a thermodynamic system. Rather, it is seen as the *sine qua non* for a progressive organisation of the system toward increasing complexity, in spite of local error or loss of information.[35]

To expound this thesis, let us look at an example by Von Foerster as reinterpreted by Atlan.[36] A certain number of cubes, some of whose surfaces have been magnetised positively and some negatively, is placed in a box which is then shaken. When the box is opened, the cubes are seen to be arranged in complex, stable geometric figures which seem to have been consciously devised by an artist. However, the shaking was nothing but chance intervention, unpredictable and independent of any preceding or future arrangement of the cubes. For anyone who did not know that the cubes were magnetic, they would seem to have organised themselves in response to a chance intervention which was itself disruptive, since it destroyed the original stable, orderly pattern of the cubes.[37]

A somewhat different example—and one which points more clearly to the levels of organisation involved—is that of biological reproduction. We know that an "error" in the transcription of the genetic code is thought to be the cause of mutations. Yet this random event on the (strictly repetitive) genetic plane can benefit the species by creating a variation which is better adapted to changing environmental conditions than the original population. The species "reorganises" itself by integrating a random mutation which has disrupted the orderly pattern of straightforward reduplication.

In the language of communication theory (which is perhaps better suited to questions of social organisation), the issue can be reformulated following Atlan (1979: 47). Suppose we have a communicative link between two subsystems A and B within a certain system. If there is no error in a message transmitted from A to B, then B will be an exact copy of A and the total information of both will be identical to that of A. If the number of errors is such that the ambiguity is identical to the amount of information A transmits, this information will be lost to such a degree that we cannot even talk about transmittance. This means that the structure of B is completely independent of that of A, and that the total information of both corresponds to that of A plus that of B. To the degree that the system depends on the communicative link between these subsystems, this total independence will amount to a destruction of the global system. With regard to the amount of information of the global system, the optimum is to have a non-zero transmission of information between A and B and a certain amount of error in this transmission.[38]

What does the claim that a certain amount of indeterminacy is constitutive for progressive self-organisation suggest in the case of science? A minimal definition of scientific development seen as directed change would assume that scientific knowledge is progressively reconstructed knowledge based upon the integration or elimination of earlier results, and that this reconstruction is a process of complexification. Complexification here means that the system is able to construct and reconstruct itself in new ways.

In common terminology, there are two correlates of this process. On the one hand, there is the ability of science to construct "new" information; that is, to produce "innovation." On the other hand, science is apparently increasingly able to construct and reconstruct itself in response to problem challenges by providing solutions to the problem,[39] which, I suppose, is what we mean when we talk about the success of science. Both abilities are aspects of the process of complexification, which in Shannon's sense corresponds to an increase of information.[40] But, as we have seen, without indeterminacy there could be no such increase of information. This indeterminacy seems to be nothing more than the degrees of freedom utilised by the system for a problem-absorbing reconstruction of itself. It becomes manifest in the observer's inability to specify in detail a small set of criteria or a principle of rationality according to which this reconstruction proceeds.

How does the idea of such a complexity-increasing reconstruction relate to the notion of contextual selection emphasised earlier in this section? System theory cannot conceive of self-organising systems, without assuming an environment to which a system responds.[41] Deprived of this notion of context, the argument introduced here makes no sense. It is the context which orients, through the selections it promotes, the process of reconstruction and development. We have introduced the notion of context here to refer to the fabric of situated variables on which the scientists base their decisions. These variables appear as the constraints upon which the scientists hold their selections to be contingent, and as the constraints they impose through decision-translations in order to reach closure in an essentially open and expanding sequence of events. Without indeterminacy with respect to these constraints, there would be no problem of closure. And, it seems, without indeterminacy there would be no new constellations of selections.

1.7 The Constructivist Interpretation III: Innovation and Selection

I have drawn upon the analogies of systems theory and biological evolution to argue that the constructivist interpretation of scientific enquiry can be plausibly extended into a contextual model of scientific change in which indeterminacy (or contextual contingency and openness of selections) does not run counter to the idea of scientific success. Let us now examine the negative side of those analogies.

The idea of laboratory selections was introduced here as the link between what is normally separated into the process of acceptance and the process of investigation. I have defined investigation as constructive in order to emphasise the selectivity embodied in scientific results. But the notion of constructiveness not only points to the "decision-laden" fabrication of scientific products, but also alludes to the products of fabrication as purposefully "new" products. We have said that the selectivity of selections is itself instituted in scientific investigation. Previous scientific selections become a resource for further selections, and thus give rise to both a selective solidification and a *diversification* of scientific products. In biological evolution, the origin of diversification is clearly identified as a mutation. The first difficulty we face, then, is to find the equivalent of such mutations in the process of scientific construction and reconstruction.

Toulmin's model of scientific change is the closest application of the analogy of biological evolution to the process of knowledge production of which I am aware, and he asks us to take it as a literal description.[42] According to Toulmin, at any given time we have a pool of scientific innovations and an ongoing process of natural selection among those innovations. The former rests with the creative individual scientist, the latter with the community of experts who judge the innovations.[43] Mutations are the variants produced by individual innovation, and their number depends on the degree of freedom of design at a particular time. The decisive factor in biological mutations is that they produce chance variations. With Toulmin, the element of chance is located in the freedom and creativity of the individual scientist.

It is precisely this location of chance which creates a major problem when the biological model is carried over to scientific (or, more generally, to societal) development. In Toulmin's adaptation of the model, special parts of this development—the individual and innovation—are carved out and given over to chance operations. Left unaffected by chance are the actions of the scientific *group* and the process of *selection* of innovation. Of course we recognise in this separation the classic distinction between discovery and validation. What is highly questionable is the rationale for such a separation. Why should the individual suffer (or profit) from chance while the group does not? Or why is the selection of innovation a process which makes sense and has direction while innovation itself is not?

Moreover, what do we count as innovation? In Toulmin's model, the published *but not yet accepted* products of scientific work constitute the pool of variations.[44] As we have seen, however, these products are themselves the result of a complex process of selection in the laboratory. More specifically, they are the result of a *directional* process *oriented toward* the production of the new, or of innovation. This is obviously implied when we say that the diversification of scientific products (or the selectivity of selections) is itself instituted in scientific investigation. From the point of view of the individual scientist as well, innovations are the result of intentional, directed work, and not merely chance happenings. It is the scientists' knowledge of what is a problem and what counts as a solution, educated guesses about where to look and what to ignore, and highly selective, expectation-based tinkering with the material that guides them toward an "innovative" result.

Once a result has been obtained, the careful selection of a publisher (and therefore, an audience), as well as various marketing strategies, can turn a laboratory product into something which may be widely accepted as "new". Nor should we forget that, to a great degree, scientists select areas of work which have not been covered by previous research; thus, their results are almost guaranteed to pass as new. Moreover, scientists constantly strive to secure personal access to resources which are not readily available to others (e.g., highly expensive or otherwise scarce technical instruments), thereby improving their own chances for being "first" with an innovation. In short, there is nothing non-directional or purely random about the individual scientist's efforts toward innovation.

One consequence of the directed and constructed character of scientific "mutations" is that the scientist's socially defined being can be seen as the result of a process of individuation which consists of the identification of a person with the differential particularities of the work associated with the person's name.[45] Such identifications appear to suppose that a person is somehow more responsible for the products she produces than would be a random generation mechanism.

A second consequence is the relation between the production of the new and the selection of the previously available; that is, between innovation and acceptance. We have already said that, to a significant degree, the locus of selection is the laboratory itself. In the terms used above, it is part of the process of innovation; and we know that, to a significant degree, it draws upon the resource of previous scientific selections. It is tempting to interpret this literally and suggest that the process of "natural selection" in the laboratory will favour those previous results which aid in the production of relevant "mutations", and at the same time further the scientist's interest in individuation. In this way, the solidification of previous results through continued laboratory selections can be seen as leading at the same time to an accelerated diversification of scientific knowledge. Note that the reference to the resource-character of selections within this accelerated diversification yields a purely formal specification: it says nothing about the substantial properties or degree of usefulness of the results. The substantial translations from which selections emerge will depend upon the context in which they are taken. In this sense, "natural selection" becomes contextual reconstruction.

Apart from the purposive, directed character of scientific "mutations" and their consequences (which point more to Lamarck than to Darwin), one other aspect of the present conception of research calls such analogies into question: for here, the selections of the laboratory are not linked to *individual* decision-making, but seen as the outcome of social *interaction* and *negotiation*. Consequently, we must reject such equations as that between the individual and innovation on one hand, and between the social group and validation on the other. In a trivial sense, we know that most laboratory work in the natural and technological sciences is conducted by groups and not by individuals. The far less trivial implication is that both the products (including those considered innovative) and the "ideas" of the laboratory are social occurrences which emerge from interaction and negotiation with others, as we shall illustrate in Chapter 2.

Consider now the individual scientists' laboratory manipulations. What they read are the results or proposals of others; what they hold in their hands are the crystallised products of previous scientific and non-scientific work; and what they obtain from measurement are figures and graphs that are only meaningful within a specific context of communication. In the case of controversy, what the scientist constructs from these activities is an argument to be inserted into a field of discursive interaction with others. More generally speaking, scientific operations can only be conducted and only make sense within a discourse whose crystallisation is found in the scriptures (the authoritative writings) of an area, but which is also constituted by the exegeses and symbolic manipulations in the laboratory.

It need not be emphasised here that science has often been tied to the possibility of a special form of discourse, i.e. written communication. For example, Husserl considered writing to be the condition for the possibility of ideal objects, and therefore of scientific concepts.[46] Peirce argues that manifestation does not reveal the presence of an object, but the presence of a sign, and reduces the logic of science to semiology.[47] Derrida reminds us that the very idea of science was born in a certain epoch of writing.[48] Latour and Woolgar have recently illustrated the importance of writing in the laboratory,[49] and the sociology of science has long focused on specific aspects of the scientists' written communication.[50]

To say that without writing (in Derrida's wide sense of the word), science could not continue to exist is a commonplace. But the point here is that, first and foremost, the communicative foundation of science constitutes the scientists' operations as a form of *discursive interaction* directed at and sustained by the arguments of others.[51] In fact, the indeterminacy which the analogy of biological evolution seeks to locate in the individual origin of innovation is rooted in the interpretative basis and the social dynamics of such interaction. This social and symbolic foundation becomes most visible in the concrete negotiations of the laboratory, in the bargaining which marks the highly selective construction and deconstruction of scientific findings and leads to the continuous reconstruction of knowledge.

The point is that the social character of such discursive interaction cannot be limited to some separate context of acceptance through group consensus formation, nor can indeterminacy be isolated in individualised innovation. Innovation and acceptance are temporary stabilisations within a process of reconstruction of knowledge that is at base a social process. The origin of indeterminacy lies within the social, with its symbolic and interactional qualities, and not, as Toulmin appears to suggest, outside. The decisions which mark scientific products are locally achieved closures of this indeterminacy. It is *within* their social location that scientific facts can be seen as selectively constructed and reconstructed.

1.8 Sources of Reconstruction: The Internal and the External

The lack of any simple equivalent to chance mutations throws up an analogical stumbling-block when we consider scientific development as a process of reconstruction of knowledge. The distinction between system and environment also raises difficulties when we consider the rationale for such a progressive reconstruction. For systems theory, progressive reconstruction (or an increase in complexity) is the system's response to a hypercomplex environment to which it adapts by increasing its own degree of complexity. More specifically, the internal reconstruction of a system results from a difference in complexity between system and environment.

But in scientific investigation, the accelerated reconstruction of scientific products is itself the issue of work—it is *endogenous* to scientific production. As we have seen, it results from the purposive and directional effort of scientists oriented toward the production of new information as defined relative to discursive problematisations. Where, then, do we locate the environmental challenge we need?

Systems theorists would probably choose to see science as a subsystem of society specifically designed and "differentiated" (in Luhmann's sense)[52] to solve the problems of complexity in some more global system, say an industrialising society. Science, in this view, becomes the instance of modern society in which a certain kind of complexification (technological?) is institutionalised, in which complexification is manufactured for modern society, with the social sciences perhaps specialising in human organisation. The reconstruction and diversification of scientific knowledge becomes a system goal to be distinguished from questions of adaptation. However, if the reconstruction of interest here is endogenous to the solution, the role of the environment with respect to this reconstruction becomes obscure.[53]

The difficulty remains even if we switch from the notion of environmental adaptation to that of environmental selection, as required by the biological analogy. In Toulmin's model, the distinction between system and environment seems to correspond to the distinction between the "internal" world of science and the "external" affairs of a wider social context. Yet the logic of events is reversed: we do not get, first, a science-internal production of variants (innovations), and then a societal selection of those variants most well adapted to the social context. According to Toulmin, the production of innovations is influenced by external factors through various channels, whereas their selective survival is regulated by the internal decisions of the scientific community (at least under normal and ideal conditions).

It is absurd, of course, to assume an opposite division of labour in which innovations are internally produced by scientists and externally selected by the non-scientific members of a society. Yet it is not clear why the former distinction, in which selective power is limited to scientists while external influences are limited to the process of research production, should necessarily be more compelling—if for no other reason than that the locus of selection is itself in the laboratory where it cannot be separated from the process of production. Thus, factors which influence the production of new information will also influence the selective solidification of previous information from which the new, to a significant degree, is derived. If the model of an evolutionary development of science emphasises (correctly, I think) that the *content* of a pool of cognitive variants at a given point in science is the product of "internal" and "external" factors, it cannot claim simultaneously that the selection of these variants—which largely occurs during the production of the variants themselves—is an exclusively "internal" matter.

The idea of environmental adaptation, and the distinction between system and environment it presupposes, create difficulties within the system theory analogy of science because complexification appears less as a response of the system to an external context than as a constitutive characteristic of scientific work itself. In the evolutionary analogy, the idea of environmental selection—and the separation it creates between the process of production and the process of selective survival of innovations—brings about difficulties because production and selective survival are hopelessly intermingled in the laboratory; consequently, *each* must be affected by the model's "internal" factors *as well as* by the environmental (or "external") ones.

Apart from these specific problems, we must deal with the more general fact that, unlike organisms, social systems do not have clearly defined boundaries with regard to some social environment of the system.[54] Social studies of science have long suffered from this difficulty, as demonstrated by the varying use of the internal/external dichotomy in analogy to a system/environment distinction. As noted by Kuhn, the distinction has been "lived with rather than studied",[55] and occasional controversies over the meaning of the distinction make it clear that different authors have lived with it in very different ways.[56] System theory makes a partial recognition of the difficulty by emphasising that boundary maintenance itself is at stake in social systems.

The fights among professional interest groups for legally sanctioned boundaries to define their professional authority and set conditions of access to the profession immediately come to mind as an example of such boundary regulating endeavours. Along with individual scientists' everyday distinctions between "we" and "they", or between matters of "science" and matters of something else, there are degrees of freedom involved in these disputes, just as there are in the social scientist's various re-generations of the distinction. Yet I see no reason to assume *a priori* that the degrees of freedom between one disciplinary speciality and another are necessarily less than the degrees of freedom between scientists who work in a field and non-scientists who represent a social (or political, or economic) interest in the field. Indeed, if we counted their respective interactions and communications, and if we considered the interests invoked in laboratory selections, we would most likely get the opposite impression.

Degrees of freedom as manifest in perceived borderlines are seen here as a function of the self-organising process itself. They interest us only with respect to the selections of the laboratory, leading (in Chapter 4) to the notion of transscientific—rather than scientific—fields. Putting aside the distinction between an internal scientific system and an external social environment (or between an environment-influenced process of production and an internal scientific process of selection), we shall consider the undifferentiated context from which the constructions of the laboratory emerge. Rather than seek the origin of indeterminacy in the individual and that of directional change in the decisions of the social group, we shall place the root of indeterminacy within the social context with its symbolic and interactional quality, and leave the origin of purposive and directional behaviour with the individual to whom it belongs.[57] We will see the symbolic and the interactional manifest themselves in the selections of the laboratory, which marks the process of scientific investigation as constructive rather than descriptive.

The decision-translations through which the selections of the laboratory are produced refer us to the context in which they are embedded. The selective interpretations of the laboratory are situationally and contextually contingent. In this way, the process of "natural selection" can be reconceived as one of contextual reconstruction in which the internal and the external are *not* analytically separated. In the chapters which follow, I shall attempt to establish the symbolic, contextually contingent and constructive character of the scientific manufacture of knowledge I have introduced here. The analogies of neo-systems theory and biological evolution have given us a plausible argument for a contextual interpretation of scientific change and for the role which indeterminacy plays in the process. In so far as these analogies tend to lead us into the trap of predetermined distinctions that prove inadequate to the actual analysis of scientific practice, my recourse to them is at best half-hearted.

1.9 Sensitive and Frigid Methodologies

It is time to return now to the second implication of the epigraph to this chapter. "Facts are like cows" Dorothy Sayers tells us: they generally run away if we look them in the face hard enough. The methodological point here is that we have to look hard, and we have to adopt an approach which gets us close enough to the phenomena to allow us a glimpse of their true character. Let us call such an approach a *sensitive* methodology. To show how it differs from its more frigid alternatives, let me sketch several distinctive feature of the sensitivity I have in mind:

1. First of all, it requires a methodological engagement rather than detachment; contact rather than distance; interest rather than disinterest; *methodological intersubjectivity* rather than neutrality. The most prevalent techniques of data collection in sociology and psychology tend to proceed like a motor-car with a disengaged clutch—that is, without a necessary point of contact between the measuring instrument and the object of examination. As a result, the engine may operate at high speed, but there is no motion in the vehicle itself.

    Complaints about the validity of common social science data have been lodged not only by the critics of their ruling methodologies, but also by their proponents.[58] By methodologically keeping the clutch in, the observer remains safely out of touch with the subject, no matter how the gears themselves are manipulated. In such a case, the question of sensitivity cannot even arise.

    Of course, such disengagement is part of a deliberate strategy of non-interference presumably designed to guarantee the very neutrality we have been talking about. But this neutrality is built upon the questionable assumptions that the meaning of utterances can be taken at face value among speakers of a language, that they do not depend on the pragmatics of concrete situations, that there is no temporality of meaning, and that the observer can reach, preserve and transmit an understanding from a distance as well as from a perspective close at hand. In short, it assumes that intersubjectivity can be safely presupposed and need not be worked at through concrete interaction.

    Yet virtually every close inspection of various segments of our social world shows that intersubjectivity is not merely a problem for the anthropologist who goes off to study a foreign culture, but for the everyday interactions of everyday life as well. It is an emergent and continually accomplished property of all communication.[59] As a result, the first requirement of a sensitive sociological approach is the achievement of an intersubjectivity which does not as yet exist. Given the emergent and achieved nature of such intersubjectivity, we cannot save ourselves the trouble of direct, unmediated and prolonged confrontation of the situation under study. If we are interested in the production and reproduction of scientific facts (which, as Whitley has so aptly noted, is still a black box to social studies of science[60]), we may be well advised to seek intersubjectivity by letting out the methodological clutch—that is, by the use of close observation at the site of production.

2. Can we say, then, that a more sensitive sociology is to be found in a return to the anthropological method of participant observation? The history of anthropology itself involves progressive attempts to establish the intersubjectivity at the core of the ethnographic encounter, beginning with the armchair anthropologists of the

19th century (who relied mainly on travel reports from others), leading to the insistence (by Malinowski and others in the early 20th century) on direct ethnographic observation and, most recently, to the criticisms levelled against ethnographic reporting by ethnoscience.

The ethnoscientists argued that ethnographers ought not (as had been their practice, and to some extent, still is) describe a culture (solely) according to their own preconceived categories, but should investigate the ways in which people construe the world of their experience, and then describe it in categories inherent to those structurings. The critique is interesting because it shows that up to this time anthropology either had not achieved the intersubjectivity it sought to establish through direct participant observation, or had not been able to preserve it through ethnographic reporting, or both.

We can conclude, then, that it has not been enough to place the social scientist in the field of investigation to study it "from within"; that is, to engage in a kind of *methodological relativism* (as opposed to objectivism) which gives maximum control over the information obtained to the subjects under study rather than to the scientist.[61] Consequently, ethnoscience has tried to "decentre" or translate as many of its categories as it can into those of the actor, developing a series of techniques designed to elicit and represent the actors' knowledge.[62] Sociological ethnomethodology has taken a similar path by decentring its language and interests, and even refusing certain common sociological objectivist concepts and concerns. These have been replaced by an interest in everyday practices, expressed in terms invented or modified to match their everyday features.[63]

The procedures of ethnoscience (and, to a lesser degree, ethnomethodology) give us a clue as to why it is not enough to substitute a qualitative, in-depth procedure for a more macroscopic approach in order to allow the field of study to exert the desired constraints on the information obtained. The problem of a sensitive methodology is not simply to get the observer to better "understand" the field of study, in the sense emphasised by hermeneutics or phenomenology,[64] but also to control the conceptual constitution given to this understanding in representing or transmitting the constraints.

In other words, the problem to which I have referred by invoking a methodological relativism is not just to understand, but *to let speak*. The ethnographic reports criticised by ethnoscience were not necessarily marked by a lack of understanding, but by a failure *to give voice* to that about which a story was told. To make good this failure, ethnoscience has engaged in a form of systematised lexicography,[65] and ethnomethodology has taken some steps toward developing a subject-relative speech of its own designed to capture the voice of that about which is speaks.

The case-study approach in sociology has virtually ignored these problems. But the difficulty may lie in the fact that it is not interested in lexicography and may resent the illocutionary and perlocutionary consequences of subject-centred speech.[66] A relatively simple move with significant results is the attempt to record the phenomena of investigation with greater precision through the use of optical and acoustic instruments. Clearly, only the sort of pre-summarisation material provided by tape- and video-recorders can be subjected to the level of micro-process-analysis one would want to accompany a sensitive methodology.

However, while this material has the advantage of not being summarised, it is *not* unconstructed: the techniques of transcription and categorisation of non-verbal behaviour, the partial recording obtained by a camera, or the change in behaviour provoked by the presence of a recorder all point to the selectivity incorporated in such material. As in the case of scientific products, the results of social science have to be seen as selectively constructed. The point of a sensitive sociology is not to remedy constructivity, but—to borrow the term introduced above—to *decentre constructivity* such that it becomes an intersubjective endeavour. That we must go to extreme lengths to allow the field of study to *actually exert* the desired constraints on the information construed is demonstrated by the development of anthropology, which long ago denounced societal ethnocentrism, only to find itself continuously engaged in its own professional ethnocentrism.

3. Methodological engagement was seen as the first prerequisite of the sensitive sociology I have in mind. Methodological relativism decentres that sociology so that it approaches an *ethnography* similar to the anthropologists' respective enterprise. The third distinctive feature to be specified here is *methodological interactionism,* which guarantees that this ethnography remains interested in the practice, rather than the cognition, of its subjects. It is also distinctively different from the methodological individualism and wholism which has divided sociology up to now.

Methodological individualism has been variously described as a doctrine which holds that social (and individual) phenomena are explicable in terms of human action, and that an explication of human action must revert to individuals because only they set responsible, intentional action.[67] In different disguises, such individualism appears in many sociological methods and theories. Its long-standing antagonist has been a wholism which contends that society as a whole is greater than a collection of individuals, and that society both affects and constrains individual behaviour.[68] Our commitment to a sensitive methodology compels us, at least temporarily, to go beyond aggregate data and summary descriptions of social phenomena. However, it does not commit us to taking the individual as a natural unit of analysis.

In fact, I have argued against the individualism found in the evolutionary model of scientific innovation, and in favour of viewing innovation as the product of context and interaction. Microsociological research has pointed to the emergent (temporal), actor-bound and setting-bound properties of human action. If the actions of an individual depend on who else is present and on how the dynamics of their interaction develop, it is obviously not enough to consider individuals and their intentions.

The point stressed earlier was that the dynamics of interaction between individuals contain an element of indeterminacy in the sense that the course of the interchange cannot be deduced from knowledge of the individual actors' intentions or interests. The point to be stressed here is that a sensitive methodology cannot ignore the existence of such dynamics, or of the temporal, actor-bound and setting-bound character of human action. It is clear that our units of observation and explication must allow the temporal, contextual and interactional features of action to emerge. Thus, the focus can no more be upon individuals than upon society at large. Methodological interactionism considers interaction to be a more adequate form of explication, and the one from which the contextual and temporal features of action arise.[69]

1.10 From the Question Why to the Question How

Methodological reorientations are usually accompanied by problem shifts and displacements of the goals of investigation. Having turned their back on the more frigid tools of social investigation in order to move toward a sensitive sociology, some microsociological approaches have also eschewed various established questions of the social sciences. On the most general level, they seem less interested in the question of "why", than in the less conspicuous notion of "how". For example, cognitive sociology is less interested in why social order exists than in how the members of a group acquire the sense that it exists. The symbolic interactionist cares less about why the members of a group invoke certain meaning-frames than about how they negotiate and monitor a definition of the situation. The ethnomethodologist seeks not to explain, but to learn how we proceed when we convince ourselves to have something explained in everyday life.[70]

We may argue that explanation is needed to understand a social phenomenon and arrive at practically relevant conclusions, but some of the above approaches are not interested in practical conclusions. Others might contend that answers to the how are often a prerequisite for sensible answers to the why. If we know, for example, how the child acquires a sense of social order, we may already have learned something about why a social order "exists".[71]

Furthermore, the thesis which proclaims a symmetry between explanation and prediction (in the sense that practical conclusions depend on preceding explanations) is more uncertain than ever among those who investigate such questions.[72] Practical experience has demonstrated that the gap between predictions derived from social explanations and actual courses of action is as yet unbridged.[73] On the other hand, how people do social things is of immediate practical interest: by exploring customary lines of action, it proves crucial to social learning, and by opening up new lines of action, it proves crucial to social change.

To ask "how" often requires that we take the radically naïve stance promoted by Lofland and turn the obvious into the problematic.[74] In fact, it is exactly this stance which Dorothy Sayers has challenged us to take. The question of *how* scientists produce and reproduce their knowledge in the laboratory is the major interest of this book, and has already been extensively introduced under the guise of my remarks on the constructivity and contextuality of the scientific enterprise. "How" is the first question that an ethnography of knowledge as advocated here will have to face.

The methods I have outlined in Section 9 represent a first step toward the sensitivity necessary to answer the question, and the present study is one of the first to make this attempt with regard to the production of knowledge.[75] The reader should be forewarned that it will manifest all the insufficiencies inherent in the partisan character of such studies.

1.11 The Scientist as a Practical Reasoner

From what we have said earlier, it is clear that the question of how scientists produce and reproduce their knowledge refers us to the site of scientific action. It prompts us to look (and as closely as possible) at the process of manufacture of knowledge on the spot. In other words, we must dismiss the battery of intermediary tools normally used to negotiate with social reality, and immerse ourselves directly in the stream of scientific action.

Strictly speaking, it is not really scientific action we have to confront in direct observation, but the *savage meaning* on ongoing events *for and by* the scientists. To get at this meaning, we must rely on talk. Without it, not even prolonged visits to the laboratory and training in the discipline at stake will make the rationale behind laboratory moves apparent. As I have said before, scientists operate in a space that is essentially overdetermined. The major task of the laboratory is to rule out possibilities, manipulate the balance of choices so that one becomes more attractive than the others, and to up- or downgrade variables with respect to alternatives.

An understanding of these processes cannot be gained from observation alone. We must also listen to the talk about what happens, the asides and the curses, the mutterings of exasperation, the questions they ask each other, the formal discussions and lunchtime chats. We must read the laboratory protocol books and rely on answers supplied by the scientists. For the scientist, the savage meaning of things is contained in their laboratory reasoning; and the talk which centres around this reasoning must be our major source of information.

The closest we can get to a description of the formal features of this reasoning is to draw upon Alfred Schutz' conceptual clarification, found in Garfinkel's work on the rational properties of (symbolic) action.[76] However, it would be misleading to take this clarification at face value, because it presupposes a difference between scientific and everyday reasoning which I do not accept. Garfinkel suggests that there are in fact two kinds of rationalities: those which occur as "stable properties and sanctionable ideals" of scientific action alone, and those which occur in everyday life. The former are considered detrimental to the stable flow of everyday practical action.

The five rules of interpretive procedure which characterise scientific reasoning are constituted in contrast to everyday reasoning. The rule of unlimited doubt, for example, guarantees that scientists will not limit their scepticism by the kind of "practical considerations" which govern everday practice. The rule of "knowing nothing" allows scientists to suspend their own knowledge in order "to see where it leads", while testing in everyday life proceeds on the basis of what can be taken for granted. Scientific problems are solved by reference to a rule of standard time, while everyday interactions are paced in accord with reified time slices that have a beginning, duration, and end. A rule of universalised others offers the scientist a chance to trust the findings of colleagues, while practical action supposedly gains credence from the natural facts of life. Finally, a rule of publicisability assures that all matters relevant to scientific depictions of possible worlds are made public, whereas everyday situations are conceived against a background of private motives and interests.

Except for the principle of standard time, these rules are surprisingly similar to the norms of organised scepticism, disinterestedness and communism that Merton once postulated for science—and are subject to the same kind of criticism.[77] More relevant than this attempt to identify the scientific ethic with a specific form of reasoning is Garfinkel's summary of the unspecific properties of common sense rationalities, for these are what we actually find in laboratory reasoning. Among these are a concern for making things comparable, for a "good fit" between observation and interpretation, for timing, predictability and correct procedures; a search for previously successful means, a conscious analysis of the alternatives and consequences of action; an interest in the planning of strategies; and an awareness of choices, as well as the grounds upon which these choices can be made.

But a complete characterisation of the formal properties of laboratory reasoning is not the point here. In fact, part of the thrust of this book is to demonstrate that there are no rationalities unique to laboratory action. The formal features of reasoning show the scientist to be a *practical reasoner*. Therefore, to examine the meanings which sustain the manufacture of knowledge in the laboratory is to look at the *content* of the scientists' practical reasoning.

1.12 The Cognitive and the Practical Reasoner

The closest approach to a description of the practical concerns of scientific action can be found in the literature of the cognitive sociology of science. Ever since the debates which followed Kuhn's theory of scientific revolution, social studies of science have emphasised that the cognitive (or technical, scientific) aspects of science must be included in its empirical investigation; to look simply at the social aspects of scientific organisation and communication has been considered insufficient. Scientific practice is marked by cognitive concerns, and we cannot hope to understand it without giving them due consideration.[78]

The most influential line of research developed since is the study of speciality institutionalisation, whose cognitive components can be traced back to the paradigm-ingredients noted by Kuhn (1970). For example, Whitley (1975) states that these components consist of the research practices, techniques, explanatory models, speciality concerns and metaphysical values or beliefs which underly an area's research activities. Weingart (1976) forms a hierarchy of relevant cognitive elements from conceptual schemes, artifact paradigms (or classical problem solutions), acknowledged scientific achievements, metaphysical paradigms and values.

Subsequent studies have tended to define their goals in accord with Whitley (1972), both in terms of how the social and cognitive components interact in the production of knowledge, and in the relationship between different forms of cognitive (scientific) knowledge and society. Until recently, the former question was dominant [79] and led to a series of contemporary and historical studies of discipline or speciality formation.[80]

What we have advocated here is a second line of research which has just begun to emerge, [81] but which is equally interested in a more comprehensive study of science. It differs from the first by its choice of direct anthropological observation of scientists at work, making it somewhat akin to the microscopic studies of various aspects of scientific experimentation and argumentation advocated by Collins (1975) and Bloor (1976). One consequence of the observational approach seems to be a reaffirmation of doubts about the usefulness of the social-cognitive dichotomy.

The dichotomy can be challenged on several grounds. First, as Bourdieu (1975a: 22 f.) has argued, scientific or cognitive strategies are also political strategies. Every scientific choice (whether a method or a place of publication) can be seen as an investment strategy objectively directed at a maximisation of scientific profits, i.e., an increase in social authority and recognition.[82]

Second, as Bloor has noted, the distinction between social and scientific is used to separate the bias, fraud or distortion arising out of social influences, from what is objective or true and has cognitive roots.[83] And it is used in this way not only by investigators of science, but by scientists themselves, which implies that the social cognitive dichotomy must be considered first as a resource of strategic interaction.[84]

Third, there is the problem of separating social and cognitive factors in a situation, such as the policy field, where many areas have been "scientised" (*verwissenschaftlicht*) by the hegemony of science (Küppers *et al.*, 1978: 16). Before the mutual influence of social and cognitive variables can be determined, they must first be conceived of and measured independently.

Finally, Latour and Woolgar (1979: 32) have pointed out that the social/cognitive distinction prevents the social scientist from examining its role within scientific activities themselves. Furthermore, if some of these activities are prejudged as cognitive or technical matters, they may be spared any substantial, sociological investigation. While there is no necessary reason for this to happen, the actual practice of social studies of science seems to support the contention. For example, Weingart (1976: 51) has suggested that cognitive sociology of science has as yet to wait for a systematic (and presumably satisfactory) conceptualisation of the cognitive components of science.

But if it has not yet provided an adequate concept of the scientists' most substantial concerns, the cognitive sociology of science *has* stimulated the investigation of those concerns as part of the social study of science. Such urgings are taken to heart in the direct observation of the methods of producing and reproducing knowledge advocated here, for the focus is precisely on those activities of science called cognitive, and the methical objective is to grasp them as closely and sensitively as possible.

Realising these goals renders the social/cognitive dichotomy obsolete. Distinctions between the cognitive and the social, the technical and the career-relevant, the scientific and the non-scientific are constantly blurred and redrawn in the laboratory. Furthermore, traffic between social and technical or scientific areas is itself a subject of scientific negotiation: today's socially produced knowledge claim may be tomorrow's technical scientific finding, and vice versa.

Non-scientific matters become "scientised", not merely in areas of policy, but within the laboratory as well. In order to realise our interest in the scientists' "cognitive" concerns (rather than their social relations), we must view actual laboratory activities *indiscriminately*. To grasp the meaning of those activities, we must engage ourselves in laboratory reasoning, which reveals the scientist to be a *practical reasoner* who refuses to be split into social and technical personalities. What emerges from this reasoning is the *practices* of knowledge production, and not some abstract social or cognitive ingredients. The question of how knowledge is produced and reproduced asks nothing more (and nothing less) than a theory of such practices.

1.13 Data and Presentation

A sensitive approach to the study of science, as I pointed out earlier, forces us to dismiss the methodological intermediaries generally used for collecting data. We must renounce the services of interviewers, questionnaires and statistical offices, and expose ourselves, through direct observation and participation, to the savage meaning of the scientists' laboratory action.

However, this is more easily said than done. Having despaired of the task for the moment, Apostel *et al.*[85] have pointed out that scientists are socially less accessible to being investigated than prison inmates, factory workers, "primitive" cultures, or even students, none of whom really has the resources for a defence against the social scientist's demands. And those demands are nothing less than unreasonable. Unlike the student who may earn college credit, or the factory worker who may be paid for his time, or the prisoner who has nothing *but* time, or the native who takes the time to enjoy a diversion, scientists feel they have "no time" to lose. While this may be universally true, the problem is particularly acute in the United States where career advancement normally depends upon the number of publications and citations.

The social scientist, on the other hand, is an intruder in the laboratory, especially when armed with what I call a sensitive methodology (which is not to be confused with the "unobtrusive" measurement once proposed by Webb *et al.*, 1966). To refrain from asking questions is against the social scientist's interests, as is refusing to listen to telephone calls or personal conversations, or to check out test-results, or spy at group meetings, or follow the scientists from one scene of action to another.

Consequently, the social scientist will often prove to be a source of embarrassment to the subjects of his or her investigation, startling them by entering the room while they brood over a paper or by looking over their shoulders as they take a measurement. An unexpected question may cause them to mix up their recordings; unsolicited help may end up confusing their samples. They may be forced to apologise to their unattended colleagues for being "shadowed". In short, the social scientist may be accused, as I have been, of becoming a constant "pain in the neck".

The presence of a talkative and ignorant social scientist in small offices and cramped laboratories is somewhat different from that of an anthropologist living in a separate tent in the open "field" of a native gathering place. The anthropologist will train and eventually pay an informant, or associate with different groups and turn for help to whomever is most willing, or even disappear when it seems appropriate, leaving the little obscurities for some later date. But the social scientist in the laboratory needs to keep track of the activities of one particular group. There is no shopping around for insights wherever they are cheapest, because the process of events is an interest in itself. To withdraw for substantial periods of time would mean forfeiting any records of what happened, beyond an occasional recollection offered by the scientist.

The choice of the laboratory used in the present study was dictated by the opportunity to be accepted as an intruder (no matter how talkative or ignorant); and the choice of a group to trouble with my constant presence was determined by the willingness of one scientist in particular to serve as my informant throughout the period of observation. The observations were conducted from October 1976 through October 1977 at a government-financed research centre in Berkeley, California. In January 1977, the centre employed approximately 330 scientists and engineers (including technical and service staff), and an additional 86 students, visiting scientists, temporary employees and other collaborators.

The work of the centre was devoted to basic and applied research in chemical, physical, microbiological, toxicological, engineering and economic areas, conducted under the auspices of seventeen separate research units (the number of which has since been reduced). Two of these units were devoted to chemistry, while others dealt in plant biochemistry, plant phytochemistry, toxicology, microbiology, chemical analysis, instrumental analysis, fibre science and food technology. Two units worked in the field of food engineering, with the other six being orientated more toward general problems than specific disciplines. Several service groups (such as photographers and illustrators) were at the scientists' disposal, as were the other, reportedly excellent, technical facilities. An internal study of staff productivity (as measured in terms of citation rates and total citations per staff member) was on a par with the average rate of productivity at several large universities. A well equipped research centre engaged in normal science done by a typical aggregation of scientists of whom some were highly recognised and many were not—that was the impression.

My observations focused on plant protein research, an area which turned out to include aspects of protein generation and recovery, purification, particle structure, texture, assessment of biological value, and applications in the area of human nutrition. Note that my observations were not focused on a specific group of individuals: although the scientists and technicians I watched belonged to the same research unit, the working "group" constantly varied in size and administrative composition. At times it reached out toward the facilities, services and cooperation of other research units, while at others it withdrew into itself, sometimes to a point where no more than one scientist, half a technician, and a rarely seen "senior member" actually did the work.

During my stay, the work was conducted in at least four different laboratories of the centre (not counting service laboratories involved in routine chemical analyses). Virtually every scientist at the centre had a small lab connected with the office, as well as access to several large facilities shared by members of a unit. Various lines of research were generally conducted simultaneously, and each scientist seemed to be engaged in a host of different projects. Keeping track of these various enterprises was as much a problem for the scientists as it was for me, and there was a lot of rushing back and forth between different facilities to keep an eye on instruments or technicians, and to remedy all sorts of experimental breakdowns.

In addition to observation, I collected the laboratory protocols, drafts of papers, and published results of the relevant research. I also conducted formal interviews with scientists from five other research units, covering a variety of scientific fields, on questions which arose from the observations. Only a small fraction of the material can be analysed here. The examples presented are derived from notes I took during and after the observations, from tape-recorded conversations and interviews, and from the written materials collected. Where appropriate, this information has been verified with the respective scientists (which often led to efforts as renegotiating what was "really" meant or what should or should not be included in a publication like this).

I have tried to stick, wherever possible, to a verbatim rendering of the scientists' laboratory reasoning. But it would be absurd to claim that a participant-observer's notes can provide a literal account of what happened. Where tape-recording is impractical or impossible (and a year's observation cannot be put on tape), the observer's notes are little more than hurried, incomplete sketches in which many words spoken in the laboratory are omitted and occasionally, some have been confused. Since it is often more useful to listen than scribble frantically in one's book, the observer's notes are best described as on-the-spot reconstructions of what happened, based on the words, interpretations and corrections that emerged from the immediate situation.

As I implied earlier, this procedure does not go very far toward the methodological relativism advocated for a sensitive *ethnography of knowledge*, even when it is bolstered by abundant mechanical recording. Remember also that the most disturbing problem in any sensitive approach is not so much that of listening better or understanding more, but being able to let the situation speak. In other words, it is a problem of conserving meaning, and being able to reduce and present data in a way which remains faithful to the field of observation. Tape-recordings solve only the preliminary (yet nonetheless crucial) problem of conserving the source.

To avoid the need for excessive reconstruction, I have resisted the temptation to work part of the material into a case history of the research (although my notes do follow some lines of enquiry from the scientist's concept of a beginning to the temporary end in publication). Instead, I have selected and summarised examples from the laboratory to remind us of their source, which, as emphasised before, is the scientists' practical reasoning. Since we have taken this practical reasoning to be indicative of the decision-making process through which knowledge is constructed, various aspects of this reasoning can be used to illustrate different points about the "how" of scientific production.

I will first provide examples of the situationally contingent, circumstantial character of knowledge construction—an argument which displays the selections of the laboratory as *contextual* and the practice of science as *local*. Chapter 3 digresses into the analogical reasoning of the laboratory, which is linked less to innovation than to the *orientation* of the process of contextual selection. In Chapter 4, I argue that the contextual selections of the laboratory are also situated in a field of social relationships into which the scientists insert themselves. The chapter results in a critique of the established concept of scientific community as the unit of cognitive and social organisation in science, and of the quasi-economic models aligned with this conception. It proposes instead the idea of *variable transscientific fields,* and illustrates the relationships which traverse and sustain these fields as constituted by resource-relationships. In Chapter 5, we observe the transformation of the constructive operations of research as we move from the laboratory to the scientific paper—the single most acclaimed product of research. In other words, we will compare the savage reasoning of the laboratory with the tame (and yet interest-ridden) rhetoric through which the scientists turn their private laboratory constructions into public products. Based on what was said before, Chapter 6 will argue that we might have to reconsider a dichotomy which has become increasingly dear to us in recent years: the distinction between the two sciences, between the symbolic, decision-laden world of the humanities and social sciences, and the world of technology and nature.

Throughout the rest of the book, I shall talk about "science" and "technology" without any further qualification in the spirit of grounded theorising which proves so seductive to close observational studies. The well-disposed reader may want to remember that these observations have been conducted with a handful of scientists in one problem area at one research laboratory (the ill-disposed readers will recall this on their own). From time to time, I will attempt to exorcise "wrong" social studies of science, hoping to put the "right" ones in their place. I trust in the reader's indulgence in reflecting that it is often the exorcised with which we are most familiar, and from which we have learned most.

Notes

1. cf. Sohn-Rethel (1972). For a short presentation of his theory in English, see Sohn-Rethel (1973, 1975). A critical summary of Sohn-Rethel's theory of knowledge can be found in Dombrowski *et al.* (1978).

2. For an example of this position, see Sellars (1963). Critical discussions from differing perspectives (leading to different conclusions) can be found in Bhaskar (1978) and Habermas (1971): pp. 67 ff.

3. This is not a naïve statement of the empirical realist's position, although it may sound like one. The naïve position would hold that the picture which science gives us of the world is a true one. In contrast, the above statement emphasises an epistemic attitude, rather than the correspondence of actual results. For a further discussion of this, see B. van Fraasen (1977): Ch. 2, pp. 2 ff. Suppe's formulation is that the results of scientific enquiry are generalised descriptions of reality which must be true in order for the theory to be adequate. cf. Suppe (1974): 211.

4. cf. Habermas (1971): 69.

5. See also the definitions of the anti-realist position advanced by Lakatos in his criticism of Toulmin (1976).

6. For an exposition of Feyerabend's position, see his essays "Explanation, Reduction and Empiricism" (1962), and "Against Method" (1970). See also the more extensive discussion in Feyerabend (1975).

7. In this connection, Gouldner speaks of the "decontextualisation" upon which idealism thrives, and which Marx criticised by asking for a recovery of the class-character of social phenomena (1976: 44 ff.). See also Gidden's formulation, "if men make society, they do so not merely under conditions of their own choosing" (1976: 102, 126), used in his criticism of ethnomethodology for its tendency toward idealism.

8. In its extreme forms, scepticism implies a type of idealism. Suppe claims that none of the analysis of science which can be said to have scepticist consequences are necessarily committed to them. To affirm that the objects of observation exist and have properties independent of conceptualisation is consistent with their position. But the nature of the objects observed and the properties they are seen to possess are determined in part by the conceptual frame of the observer. cf. Suppe (1974: 192 ff.) The slogan "anything goes" is the trademark of Feyerabend's scepticism. He says that "the only principle that does not inhibit progress is that of *anything goes*" (1975: 10, 23 ff.).

9. cf. Putnam (1971: 22).

10. See "The Logic of 1873" for a formulation of Peirce's programme. Peirce (1931-35, Volume 2, paragraphs 227 ff.).

11. For example, see the symposium edited by Suppe (1974) on the question of the meaning variance of observation sentences and its implications for the philosophy of science. The thesis relies primarily on the work of Bohm (1957), Hanson (1958), Kuhn (1962, 1970) and Feyerabend (e.g. 1962, 1970, 1975).

12. cf. the behavioural therapy proposed and illustrated by Watzlawick, Weakland and Fisch (1974).

13. The example is taken from van Fraasen (1977, Ch. 2: 45).

14. cf. Bhaskar (1978), particularly Ch. 2: 118 ff. for an exposition of this critique. By way of example, Bhaskar says that to predict the next eruption of Vesuvius would require a complete state-description of an open system which is multiply determined and controlled above and beyond the constraints imposed by the laws of physics and chemistry.

15. Bhaskar's argument is based on the transcendental question of what the world must be like for science to be possible. Briefly stated, Bhaskar argues from the nature of experimental activity, which he holds to be intelligible only if the experimenter is conceived of as a causal agent in a sequence of events, but not of the causal law which the sequence of events identifies. According to Bhaskar, this implies that there is an ontological distinction between scientific laws and patterns of events. See the summary of his position in Bhaskar (1978: 12 ff.).

16. Bhaskar (1978: 54). Bhaskar calls those things which exist independent of men, but of which we can have knowledge through experimental activity, the "intransitive objects of knowledge", in contrast to the "transitive objects" which constitute the raw material of science: the artificial, antecedent objects dealt with in scientific investigations, such as established facts and theories, models, methods and techniques. Apparently, the intransitive objects of knowledge can only be characterised by the same names as those of the transitive objects. For example, Bhaskar speaks of "the mechanism of natural selection" which "had been going on for millions of years" before Darwin. cf. Bhaskar (1978: 22). For an amusing fable on the matter of real objects, scientific objects, and popular objects see Latour (1980b).

17. Preliminary statements in regard to the interpretation of science as constructive rather than descriptive can be found in Knorr (1977; 1979a).

18. This has been pointed out to me by Bruno Latour.

19. For example, in his critique of Carnap's failure to translate physicalistic discource into terms of sense experience, logic and set theory, Quine argues that it would be better to discover how science is *in fact* developed and learned; that is, "to settle for psychology" rather than "fabricate fictitious" rational reconstructions (1969: 78).

While Quine has consistently defended the rights of an "empirical epistemology", he never actually became the anthropological observer he envisioned in a mental experiment in his *Word and Object* (1960). Other philosophers of science like Toulmin (e.g. 1972) and Feyerabend (e.g. 1975), similarly disenchanted with what can be achieved by pure epistemology, were actually moved to study science historically and sociologically. Examples of more recent calls for an empirical epistemology—understood as an empirical investigation of the questions which traditionally occupy the philosophy of science—are Campbell (1977) and Apostel *et al.* (1979). Compare Böhme, van den Daele and Krohn (1977). Not surprisingly, there has been an increasing emphasis on close, observational studies—an "anthropology of knowledge"—rather than on empirical, macroscopic studies of science.

20. Most familiar, of course, from discussions of the epistemological and methodological state of the social sciences.

21. In 1907, the eminent physicist Joseph John Thomson said, "From the point of view of the physicist, a theory of matter is a policy rather than a creed; its object is to connect or coordinate apparently diverse phenomena, and above all to suggest, stimulate and direct experiment" (1907: 10). See also Bachelard (1934).

22. This is a paraphrase of Habermas (1971: 315), whose meaning differs somewhat from what is intended here.

23. See Callon (1975) and Callon, Courtial and Turner (1979) for a series of examples and for the sort of quantitative content analysis of problem networks they use. See also Callon (1980) for an English presentation of some of the material. The concept of translation is elaborated and discussed by Serres (1974).

24. For a comprehensive exposition of Luhmann's systems theory approach, see his *Soziologische Aufklärung* I and II (1971, 1975), parts of which have been translated into English and will be published by Columbia University Press (1981).

25. This explains the occurrence of simultaneous "discoveries" by scientists who in fact did not steal from one another. Note that scientific institutions and the familiar forms of social control in science can be seen as a comprehensive structure to assure that selections remain to a large degree fixed, and that the remainder are made in a similar, compatible and repeatable way. Note also that the descriptivist interpretation of enquiry can be taken to suggest that the constellations of selections which enter a scientifically produced finding are in all relevant respects constrained by nature itself.

26. cf. K. Popper (1963:216ff.)

27. See also D. Phillips (1974: 82 ff.). Phillips has pointed out that, as a consequence, we have to assume, in opposition to Mills and Merton, that the motives and social position of an enquirer are indeed relevant for the evaluation she gets from fellow scientists.

28. This scientist, a department head at a top university, implied that the reviewers even knew *whose* proposal they were reviewing. This is not surprising, even when names are eliminated from the proposal: the amount of money asked, the kind of research proposed, the resources (including instruments) mentioned, all suggest the source of a proposal in those highly specialised areas where it is a matter of survival for scientists to know very well "who" (in the widest sense of the word) is in the area.

29. Other areas relevant here are journals and publishers, or contexts in which decisions about the publication of results are made. Results which are not published or otherwise circulated effectively obviously have a much smaller chance to even enter the process of general validation.

30. It is tempting to quote Wittgenstein here: "So sagst Du also, dass die Übereinstimmung der Menschen entscheide, was richtig und was falsch ist?—Richtig und falsch ist, was Menschen sagen; und in der Sprache stimmen die Menschen überein. Dies ist keine Übereinstimmung der Meinungen, sondern der Lebensform." The English translation is: "So you are saying that human agreement decides what is true and what is false?—It is what human beings *say* that is true and false; and they agree in the *language* they use. That is not agreement in opinions, but in form of life." See paragraph 241 of the Philosophical Investigations as translated by G. E. M. Anscombe (1968).

31. I am referring here to Feyerabend's contention that the interpretations which scientists choose are relative to a cultural and historical context, and can only be understood if we look at these contexts. The thesis rules out the possibility of specifying a set of context-independent criteria according to which consensus formation proceeds. In contrast, Kuhn does not rule out the possibility of such criteria. See Feyerabend (1975) and Kuhn (1970), particularly the discussion in the postscript.

32. Note that Toulmin's model of scientific evolution (the closest adaptation of the biological model) goes to some length to avoid such consequences. First, as we shall see later, Toulmin restricts the idea of environmental selection to a form of scientific selection. Secondly, as Lakatos points out in his critique of Toulmin, he invokes a "Cunning of Reason" in history which somehow secures the final validity of the selections that have been made. For these and other reasons which will become clear later, Toulmin's model is not a contextual model as proposed here. cf. Toulmin (1972) and Lakatos (1976).

33. For a summary presentation of the whole discussion, see Lakatos and Musgrave (1970).

34. In stochastic processes on the molecular level, in which the smaller the number of interacting molecules, the greater the role of fluctuation, it has been shown that the absence of "errors" or indeterminacy corresponds not only to an absence of innovation and hence of an increase of information, but to an actual loss of information. Without chance fluctuations, the system cannot maintain itself in a stationary state. This means that without the intervention of "error", chance or indeterminacy in biological evolution, for example, all species would disappear without being replaced by others. cf. Atlan (1979: 54f.). For a propagation of the idea as a principle of order relevant to science see particularly Latour and Woolgar (1979). For the most illuminative philosophical analysis which deals with the topic see Serres (1980).

35. The second principle of thermodynamics postulates that natural systems show an evolution toward increasing entropy or maximum molecular disorder, which is identical to a distribution of equal probability. The recent developments to which we have alluded above show that self-organising systems *do* have the capacity to react to perturbations by using them as a factor of organisation, by making them beneficial to the survival of the system. As will become more clear in the examples that follow, the point is not to deny the potentially disruptive effect of noise, or indeterminacy, but to say that whether or not the effect will be disruptive depends on the reaction of the system.

36. This reinterpretation is crucial because it suggests that the point is not, as Von Foerster's terminology tells us, the construction of "*order*" out of disorder (indeterminacy, chance), but the emergence or organisation as defined by an increase in complexity or system differentiation. According to Atlan, Von Foerster envisioned an increase of repetition or redundancy with which the notion of order is associated in information theory. Only if we see indeterminacy as resulting in greater organisation or complexity, rather than in order, can we define this effect as an increase of information for the system and understand the adaptive power which derives from this organisation. cf. Von Foerster (1960) and Atlan (1979).

37. In natural language, "order" and "organisation" are often used indiscriminately, and this often occurs in philosophical treatments of the subject as well (Morin 1977). Yet it should be noted that there is one important difference to be kept in mind even if we merely use the principle of "organisation by chance" as an analogy. While order implies stability, an organisation toward increasing complexity is inherently linked to change and a system-internal increase of information. It is this part of the analogy which I take to be particularly well suited when we apply it to science, and not the interpretation of "order from disorder".

38. As a simple example, consider the leak in the communicative network of the Nixon administration with regard to the bombing of Cambodia (kept secret by the administration). While the leak was without doubt disruptive for some core members of the administration, it may well have benefited the more global system of American democracy. The implication is that we have to take into account different *levels* of organisation in order to distinguish between the disruptive and integrative (or organising) effects of noise.

39. Of course, science produces new problems at the same time, which is part of the process of reconstruction.

40. The quantity of information within a system is taken to be a measure of the improbability that the combination of the different constituents of the system is the result of chance. This is why the quantity of information could have been proposed as a measure of complexity. Strictly speaking, there are three different versions of writing the quantity of information which correspond to three kinds of complexity, all defined in relation to our knowledge. The first refers to a variety of which we do not know the distribution ($H = \log N$), the second expresses disorder ($H = \Sigma p \log p$), and the third measures a lack of knowledge of the internal constraints or redundancies of a system ($H = H\max(1-R)$), where H = the quantity of information, p = the probability that a certain sign is present, and R = the redundancy—all according to the summary by Atlan (1979: 79 f.). Note that the characterisation is formal and does not take into account the content of the signs.

41. According to Ashby, it is logically impossible that a self-organising system be closed, i.e. a system which does not interact with an environment. If the system could change its organisation solely as a function of its internal states, this change would be governed by a constant. True change has to be induced either through a program of change injected from the outside or through external chance interferences. cf. Ashby (1962).

42. See Toulmin (1967) for a short presentation of his model and of the non-metaphoric reading intended (p. 470 f.). A more extensive analysis is found in Toulmin (1972). Compare Campbell (1974).

43. Toulmin seems to suggest that this is normally and ideally the case, although he points out that historical cases do not always follow the pattern he proposes. Hence his distinction between "compact" traditions which follow his systematic pattern, and "diffuse" traditions which may not. cf Toulmin (1967), particularly paragraph 4.

44. This makes sense, since it does not presuppose that the observer holds some criterion as to what counts as an innovation. In the above case, all results counted as new by the scientists themselves would presumably be part of the "pool of scientific innovations".

45. Since change and particularisation are built into scientific products, we can also say that scientific work allows for differentiation effects, and these differentiation effects can be appropriated by scientists. It is clear that the individuation provided by scientific work need not necessarily go to individual persons. Many would argue that the increasing socialisation of science means that we have an increasing appropriation of differentiation effects by groups, and more importantly, by institutions. This tendency toward a greater anonymity for individual authors of scientific products can also be seen as an indication of a progressive "proletarisation" of scientists, to which we will return in Chapter 4.

46. In particular, see his essay on the origin of geometry (1962).

47. For a short presentation, see the chapter on "Logic as Semiotic" in the Dover edition of Peirce's selected writings (1955: 98 ff.).

48. In *Of Grammatology* (1976: 27).

49. See particularly p. 45 ff., where Latour and Woolgar introduce the notion of "literary inscription" for taking a measurement in the laboratory (1979).

50. There has been a particular focus on studies of citation, examples of which are too numerous to be listed here. For two recent reviews which point to potential new directions, see Chubin and Moitra (1975) and Sullivan, White and Barboni (1977). For other aspects of patterns of communication among scientists, see Zuckerman (1977), Ziman (1968), Studer and Chubin (1980) or Gaston (1973, 1978).

51. Böhme has concluded that a concept of the scientific community within a theory of scientific action needs to be based on a theory of the process of argumentation in science. See Böhme (1975).

52. For an exposition of Luhmann's notion of differentiation in English, see his article on the "Differentiation of Society" (1977a).

53. Another possibility would be to search for system borders somewhere within the process of research production itself. The selectivity incorporated in scientific products allows for a problematisation of constitutive decisions, and problematisation could come to be seen as a form of environment-triggered increase of complexity. The complexifying new selections of the laboratory counter these challenges of problematisation.

54. For a summary of this and other criticisms of systems theory as applied to social systems, see Habermas (1979), particularly p. 141 f. in Chapter 4, "Toward a Reconstruction of Historical Materialism".

55. Cited in Johnston (1976: 195). Johnston summarises some of the uses of the internal/external distinction which he traces back to assumptions enshrined in the history and philosophy of science that have been unquestioningly adopted by subsequent analyses of science.

56. For example, see Kuhn's criticism of Lakatos' use of the distinction (1971: 139 f.). To Lakatos, the internal seems to be coextensive with the rational part of science. Kuhn, in contrast, appears to equate the internal/external dichotomy with the distinction between the cognitive and the social, a practice he claims is shared by all historians of science.

57. The fact that in the end only individuals can institute intentional action has led to an argument for a methodological individualism, to which we shall return in Section 1.9.

58. See, for example, Galtung's critique of some kinds of survey research (1967: 148 ff.). Cicourel (1964) has provided the most comprehensive and influential criticism. See also the new methodological developments based upon this and other criticisms which are summarised in Brenner, Marsh and Brenner (1978) and Brenner (1980), particularly in the Introduction.

59. Such close inspections have primarily occurred within various microsociological perspectives, such as ethnomethodology, cognitive sociology, symbolic interactionism, ethnogenics and phenomenology. For a summary presentation of some of the studies relevant here, see Mehan and Wood (1975). Harré (1977), Cicourel (1973), Berger and Luckmann (1967), and the earlier works of Goffman (e.g. 1961), all include representative statements about the problematic character of everyday interaction.

60. Whitley's whole argument with respect to "black-boxism" and the sociology of science is found in his article of the same title (1972).

61. Ethnoscientists distinguish between an "emic" (from phonemic) structural approach, and an "etic" (from phonetic) intercultural approach which imposes the concepts and distinctions of "scientific" anthropology (Pike, 1967: 37 ff.). For recent reviews of developments in ethnoscience or cognitive anthropology, see Bernabe and Pinxten (1974) and Pinxten (1979).

62. See Schoepfle, Topper and Fisher (1974: 382).

63. The best example of the use of such terms may be Garfinkel himself (1967).

64. Consequently, it is not enough to require that the student of social science be familiar with the speciality under study, or be a trained member of the respective scientific discipline. Anthropology demonstrates that, while this may be a necessary prerequisite for a decentred analysis, it is by no means a sufficient condition for its achievement. In light of the problem concerning the decentring of scientific speech, the battle over the hermeneutic or non-hermeneutic character of ethnographic observation seems to be somewhat obsolete. My own summary presentations of the current state of anthropological methodology and of its challenges can be found in Knorr (1973; 1980).

65. The term is drawn from Werner (1969), who, like many others, believes that it is the unfortunate, but unavoidable fate of ethnography to record systematically the structuring of the world contained in the linguistic expressions of a culture.

66. By which I mean the ugly consequences to which ethnomethodologists' efforts to preserve subject-centred speech often lead: tormented language and a tormented reader who tries in vain to decipher the hidden meaning of the new professional idiom.

67. For this formulation, see Agassi (1973: 185 f.). See also the collection of essays edited by John O'Neill (1973) on *Modes of Individualism and Collectivism,* which contains many contributions relevant to these two methodological orientations.

68. One of the chief critics of methodological individualism in recent years has been Steven Lukes. See his collection of essays (1978), particularly the essay on "Methodological Individualism Reconsidered" (Chapter 9).

69. The point here is a methodological orientation relative to methodological individualism and wholism, and not a plea for carrying sociological "symbolic interactionism" over into social studies of science (which, by the way, has already been introduced into science studies). While the present endeavour is undoubtedly informed by developments in symbolic interactionism, it cannot claim to be a species of that orientation. As the reader may note, I feel a greater debt to other microscopic—and some macroscopic—orientations.

70. For a brief summary of how ethnomethodology has reinterpreted some traditional problems of sociology along these lines, see Zimmerman and Wieder (1970). For example, norms and rules interest the ethnomethodologist not as an explanatory concept for social action, but as a topic of analysis, as a resource which members use to structure and orient everyday life, and to convince themselves of the orderly structure of this world.

71. For a number of relevant analyses, see Cicourel (1973). The reason we often learn something about the "why" by answering the "how", of course, is that both questions are often connected by a series of translations. To trace "how" something came about often points to its origin, or yields a genetic "explanation". A similar relationship holds between "what" (the traditional question faced by the anthropological observer) and "why". As Lukes (1978: 184 f.) has reminded us, to identify an item of behaviour or a set of beliefs is sometimes enough to explain it: explanation often resides precisely in a successful and sufficiently wide-ranging identification of behaviour or types of behaviour. The ethnoscientist's attempt to identify cultural knowledge in the terms in which it is couched by a particular culture should teach us something about why certain patterns of behaviour exist in that culture, and about similar questions.

72. See the comprehensive discussion of the thesis of symmetry in Stegmüller (1969, Vol. 1, Part 2: 153 ff.).

73. See Luhmann (1977b: 16, 28), who argues that the binary schematisation between true and false may be inadequate for the instrumental applicability of a theoretical explanation in practical action. Luhmann refers to the example of the Coleman report which cites the racial and social composition of school classes as the most important variable in explaining educational success. Busing was widely introduced in the United States to alter that composition, but educational success did not follow, for reasons which support Luhmann's point but are not relevant here.

74. See Lofland (1976: 2) on the whole matter mentioned here.

75. Although the case study approach is widely favoured at present (not only in social studies of science, but in sociology in general), it is surprising that so few sociologists have as yet done what Lofland advocates in his codification of a qualitative methodology (1976)—that is, actually to enter the field as a (participant) observer.

76. The essay can be found in Garfinkel (1967: 272 ff.). See also Schutz (1943) on the "Problem of Rationality in the Social World", to which Garfinkel refers.

77. Merton has been attacked on this subject so often that we need not repeat the criticism here. Those unfamiliar with the subject are referred to Barnes and Dolby (1970) and Stehr (1978). Note, however, that Merton postulated norms, and not stable properties of scientific action. In this respect Garfinkel, who talks about rules which routinely manifest themselves in action, goes far beyond Merton.

78. For selected examples of such arguments, see Whitley (1972), Nowotny's call for a cognitive approach to the study of science (1973), Mulkay's argument that the sociological study of science must include its technical culture (1974a) or Weingart's specification of cognitive/technical and social variables (as well as their interrelationship) in the study of the production of knowledge (1976). Most recent "social" studies of science in Western Europe have tried to include the "cognitive" side of science. The studies published under the title *Cognitive and Historical Sociology of Scientific Knowledge* by Elkana and Mendelsohn (1981) provide the most recent example of the trend. For a relevant, general presentation and discussion of the "cognitive paradigm", see de Mey (1981).

79. There have been several recent attempts to move beyond science and explore the relationship between knowledge and society. In particular, see Barnes (1977), and Mulkay (1979). See also the work of Foucault from a historical perspective (e.g. 1975, 1977), the work of Holzner and Marx (1979) from a general, sociological perspective, and Stehr and Meja (1982) on classical vs. recent sociology of knowledge.

80. For a representative collection of such studies, see Lamaine, MacLeod, Mulkay and Weingart (1976). Other studies can be found in Mendelsohn, Weingart and Whitley (1977), particularly Parts 1 and 2. See also the studies by Edge and Mulkay (1976), Küppers, Lundgreen and Weingart (1978), or Studer and Chubin (1980).

81. Published studies based upon direct anthropological observation of scientists are still scarce. The monograph by Latour and Woolgar (1979) is to my knowledge the most extensive study of the sort within the tradition of social studies of science. See also Latour (1980a) and my earlier articles based upon the same observational study drawn upon here (Knorr, 1977; 1979a, b; and Knorr and Knorr, 1978). An interesting antecedent of such studies is the work, not of a sociologist of science, but a theologian (himself a physicist) whose observations of scientists were financed by a group of progressive Catholics not involved in academia (Thill, 1972). Preliminary results of some anthropological studies of science still in progress can be found in Jurdant (1979), Apostel *et al.* (1979) (to whom I owe the information about Thill), and in McKegney (1979), Lynch (1979) and Zenzen and Restivo (1979), whose results were presented at a conference on the social process of scientific investigation organised by Roger Krohn at MacGill University, Montreal. For the thesis that we are experiencing a general "anthropological turn" in the social sciences and in science studies, see Lepenies (1981). See also the work begun by Williams and Law (1980).

82. Note that Bourdieu is not talking about the motives for a scientist's conscious objectives, although the choice of an area of work is often consciously motivated by career considerations.

83. In delineating a strong programme for the sociology of science, Bloor has criticised the asymmetric treatment which offers a social explanation for recognised scientific mistakes, but not for scientific achievements so long as they are held to be sound. The central thesis of his book is that "objectivity is a social phenomenon", "logical necessity is a species of moral obligation" and the "ideas of knowledge are based on social imagery". Cf. Bloor, 1976: 141. In his later work Bloor returns to the distinction between a social and cognitive sphere in science by empirically correlating variables which he associates with them. See Bloor (1978).

84. For a similar argument with regard to "the supposed norms of science", see Mulkay (1976).

85. i.e., in his plea for an empirical investigation of traditionally epistemological problems (1979: 4).

Chapter 2

The Scientist as an Indexical Reasoner: The Contextuality and the Opportunism of Research

2.1 Bringing Space and Time Back In:
The Indexical Logic and the Opportunism of Research

What are the translations from which laboratory selections emerge in the process of research? How do scientists reach the closure through which an essentially open field of possibilities crystallises into laboratory selections? In Chapter 1, I hinted at the concrete research situation as the key to understanding how the decisions of the laboratory are made. A close look at the research scene shows that laboratory selections are local, depending both on the context of research and the concrete research situation. We see the idiosyncrasies involved in these selections, and how the decision criteria depend more on the process than to provide for (or govern) its closure and determinacy. In short, a close look at the research scene forces us to bring space and time back into scientific operations, and to conceive of them as locally situated operations.

In recent years, the notion of situation and the idea of context-dependency has gained its greatest prominence in some microsociological approaches, where it stands for what ethnomethodologists have called the "indexicality" of social action. The concept of an indexical expression is taken from the writings of Bar-Hillel, and was originally coined by Peirce to refer to the fact that a sign may have different meanings in different contexts, and that the same meaning may be expressed by different signs (1931-35, Vol. 2: 143).[1] Within ethnomethodology, indexicality refers to the location of utterances in a context of time, space, and eventually, of tacit rules. In contrast to a correspondence theory of meaning, meanings are held to be "situationally determined", dependent upon the concrete context in which they appear in the sense that "they unfold only within an unending sequence of practical actions" through the participants' interactional activities (cf. Mehan and Wood, 1975: 23).

In the following discussion, I will use the term "indexicality" to refer to the *situational contingency* and *contextual location* of scientific action. This contextual location reveals that the products of scientific research are fabricated and negotiated by particular agents at a particular time and place; that these products are carried by the particular interests of these agents, and by local rather than universally valid interpretations; and that the scientific actors play on the very limits of the situational location of their action. In short, the contingency and contextuality of scientific action demonstrates that the products of science are hybrids which bear the mark of the very *indexical logic* which characterises their production, and are not the outgrowth of some special scientific rationality to be contrasted with the rationality of social interaction.

Scientific method is seen to be much more similar to social method—and the products of natural science more similar to those of social science—than we have consistently tended to assume.

How can we illustrate this indexical logic in somewhat more detail? The first aspect of indexicality is an implied *opportunism* which manifests itself in a mode of operation comparable to that of a "tinkerer":

> ". . . a tinkerer . . . does not know what he is going to produce but uses whatever he finds around him . . . to produce some kind of workable object. . . . The tinkerer, in constrast (to the engineer) always manages with odds and ends. What he ultimately produces, is generally related to no special project, and it results from a series of contingent events, of all the opportunities he had—often, without any well-defined long term project, the tinkerer gives his material unexpected functions to produce a new object. . . . (These objects) represent, not a perfect product of engineering, but a patch work of odd sets pieced together when and where opportunities arose. . . ."[2]

Tinkerers are opportunists. They are aware of the material opportunities they encounter at a given place, and they exploit them to achieve their projects. At the same time, they recognise what is feasible, and adjust or develop their projects accordingly. While doing this, they are constantly engaged in producing and reproducing some kind of workable object which successfully meets the purpose they have temporarily settled on.

When we observe scientists at work in the laboratory, this sort of opportunism appears to be the hallmark of their mode of production. Referring to the opportunism of research does not suggest that scientists are unsystematic, irrational or career-oriented in their procedures. They may or may not be, depending on a variety of circumstances. The opportunism I have in mind characterises a *process,* rather than individuals. It refers to the *indexicality* of a mode of production from the point of view of the *occasioned* character of the products of research, in contrast to the idea that the particularities of a given research situation are irrelevant or negligible.

As in the example of tinkering, the occasioned character of research first manifests itself in the role played by local resources and facilities. For example, in the institute I observed, the existence of a large-scale laboratory in which proteins could be generated, modified and tested in large volumes was treasured as a valuable opportunity because it would be difficult or impossible to carry out certain kinds of research without such facilities. The laboratory was well equipped, well staffed, and supervised by an experienced older technician described as extremely reliable and "clever"—a series of additional advantages. As a result, a lot of scientific energy was spent in gaining access to the laboratory in order to "exploit" this "resource". Research which required the use of this laboratory was eagerly sought or invented. A newly purchased electron microscope utilising laser-beams exerted a similar attraction.

Needless to say, the scientists who controlled these respective resources spent a great amount of effort trying to keep others from using them, being perfectly aware of the increase of value achieved through making an already scarce resource even more scarce. In science as elsewhere, particular interests and opportunism sustain each other.

But it is not only the highly scarce—and hence, attractive—resources which orient the course of scientific research: I saw a paper on functional properties of proteins based almost exclusively on chemical determinations supplied by one of the institute's specially designed "service" laboratories. The scientist who wrote the paper made it clear to me that, if he had been forced to perform (or even supervise) the work himself, he would have selected an entirely different series of tests from those available at the service lab; but given the techniques available, he would prefer to use the service lab whenever possible.

Preference is also given to technical instruments and apparatus which the scientists know are "around somewhere". Projects take certain turns because, as the scientists explain, "We had a piece of equipment that had been developed in another project that we could use." Certain measurements are taken because "the machines were here, so it was very easy to go down and use them", and certain results are obtained because "well, we were looking for a way to get the foam off, you see, and it (*the instrument*) was there. . . ." Of course, the resources and facilities available at a certain place and time are not simply picked up and used—they are also the objects of constant negotiation and manipulation. Equipment earmarked for certain purposes is frequently converted to serve some other goal, or simply "misused".

For example, because a device for measuring density was broken, one scientist centrifuged the material to be measured, then calculated an approximate density from the difference in volume measurements before and after centrifuging. Since centrifuging provided compression under fully controlled and standardised conditions, the idea, as inconspicuous as it seemed, was in fact quite ingenious. In a similar case, a scientist borrowed a pressure meter he happened to see in one of the laboratories, and "misused" it to determine the gas absorption capacity of a substance (4-20/25). Moreover, chemicals which were in stock were routinely substituted for those which were not, so as not to impede the process of ongoing events.

Ideas may be less tangible than research products, but they are no less circumstantially determined in the research process. In part, ideas are triggered by the resources and facilities available at a given place and time. They may also emerge from the dynamics of interaction between researchers, or they may be the contingent result of other occasions. Scientists themselves refer constantly to this phenomenon: ideas "occur" to them in a particular situation, or they "run into" an idea while in pursuit of something else, or an idea is triggered by a research paper they "happened to come across". Historians of science have often demonstrated this emergence of ideas from situational contingencies, and there is little need for me to further illustrate the point.

Instead, let us examine the role the larger environment plays in setting the conditions from which new research results are bred, and in supplying the criteria upon which the selections of the research process are based. These conditions and criteria often reflect relatively short term concerns of exclusively local relevance. For example, when I asked a chemical engineer whether an interest in saving water (Northern California at that time was into the third year of a severe drought) had played a role in his efforts to use foam in place of water for certain surface treatments of plants, he said:

> "Oh yes, water savings, and pollution, or reduction. You see, first of all, water saving . . . and secondly, the less time that you expose, and the less volume of water you expose to the surfaces, the less leaching. And we were hoping that by using a replacement for water—which in this case was foam . . . that you would leach less out of the product. But I mean, the first thing was water . . .. In other words, volume of foam to volume of liquid used to generate the foam is like 20

to 1, so that you could occupy a volume or cover surfaces with a twentieth of the volume of water'' (9-28/2).

Another example arises from a local emphasis on chemical compositions which included only a few carefully selected ingredients, thus reducing adverse effects from the interaction of ingredients in complex compositions (which are often counteracted by still more complex compositions). When I asked a chemist whether I was correct in assuming that he applied this criterion, he said:

"Absolutely. Well, in the prevention of lycinolalanine formation, we started out adding systein. And From that, we thought—well, we could probably accomplish the same thing by sulphite, which is cheaper and simpler. And then we thought, well no, if we just keep the air away from it, we would do the same thing. And that's where we ended up. It was reducing the amount of treatment, really, and still reaching the same end. You know, if you control the air incorporation, I control most of the reaction'' (9-30/4).

During the period of observation, the most conspicuous examples related to the form and amount of energy used. As might be expected, energetic criteria were introduced into the "cognitive" operations of the laboratory with the emergence of the energy crisis. The emphasis placed on the energy-implications of a research project closely paralleled the apparent degree of the crisis (which was relatively pronounced during my stay in the laboratory).

For example, an important step in protein recovery is precipitating it from solution, generally by heat coagulation. One of the scientists working on proteins had come across a paper which mentioned the use of ferric chloride as an effective method of precipitating proteins from waste water at low temperature. In the context of an energy shortage, the use of ferric chloride struck the scientist as an excellent alternative to heat coagulation, which, given the low protein yield of the source material, consumed a disproportionate amount of energy. Since the scientist needed the protein in substantial quantities for bioassay tests with rats, and because he thought the method might arouse "wide interest" if it could be made to work in contexts beyond that of the original paper, he promptly began a series of experiments using ferric chloride. In the same test-series, he favoured filtration over centrifuging because of the energy-savings it implied (4-4/4).

Let me conclude this section by emphasising that scientists are well aware of the situationally contingent nature of their products. As implied earlier, they refer to these contingencies in *explaining* a particular result when it is questioned, identifying it with the very indexical selectivity which constituted it. In fact, scientists may *play directly* on contextual limitations when they are trying to expand their own horizons or opportunities in competition with others.

So the tinkerer is not merely a passive opportunist who responds to whatever strikes her as potentially interesting in a local situation. For example, during a discussion of further plans and projects, a member of the protein group told me that he had come across a Russian paper "that hopefully nobody here knows". The paper implied that the results of an experiment currently in progress could be significantly improved by using a particular plant juice. What seemed to turn this suggestion into a profitable "idea" was precisely the fact that "nobody here" knew about it. When asked if he intended to quote the source of the idea, the scientist said he would "cite the paper somewhere" (1-28/1).

Ideas need not be stolen (although they undoubtedly are at times) in a universe where particular transgressions of contextual limitations not only serve as routine strategies of resource mobilisation, but as sources of increased credit for the author. Such uses (or misuses) of the literature lie behind some scientists' boast that, unlike most of their colleagues, they "do not miss out on things published in other languages", correctly considering this to be a "major strength". Or as when scientists consider it a "tragedy" that they cannot get all the material they ask for. Consider the words of a biochemist, who told me that

> ". . . there is a certain . . . a high percentage, maybe, uh . . . 40% of what I ask for which I never get. . . . The authors don't send you a reprint, the library can't get it—for one reason or another. I don't get it. It makes me mad, but I do have the reference, so that when the time comes when it becomes real critical to know about it, I pound doors and I get it eventually. But you know, if I did this for everything that I can't get, I would be doing nothing but (this)" (9-29/9).

Unable to spend the necessary time, the scientist knew that she was missing out on much of the relevant material. But she had no choice, given the various barriers to the internationality of science in the (published!) literature itself—barriers far beyond and far greater than those posed by language. At the same time she played on these limitations by transgressing them from time to time to bolster the "originality" of her research group, or to enhance the "excellence" of her book. Actualised contextures and their borders set the scene from which laboratory meanings emerge, and impose limits within which the scientists operate. But they also constitute a resource in the scientific mode of operation.

2.2 Local Idiosyncrasies

There are many other spatial and temporal contingencies relevant to the decisions and selections which make up research results in the natural sciences. Some are such a matter of routine that they are scarcely noticed—for example, local employment regulations which prohibit testing after 4:30 p.m. or at weekends, so that freezing and storing procedures not specifically mentioned in the resulting papers must be used to compensate for these unmethodical interruptions. Perhaps more interesting for the sociologist who wants to compare procedures in social and natural science are *local idiosyncrasies,* a phenomenon almost completely ignored in the literature on science.

Like any other organisation, research laboratories develop *local interpretations* of methodical rules, a *local know-how* in regard to what is meant and how to make things work the best in actual research practice. For example, the research institute I observed had several "service" laboratories designed to perform standard but necessary analyses of chemical composition. Many of these analyses were also "official", in the sense that they had been tested, documented and recommended for use by the American Chemical Association or some other group of this sort. When one scientist who had come to the institute from another area first used these facilities, he was surprised to learn that the tests were performed without replication, apparently under the assumption that such standard routines carried no risks or uncertainties.

His own interpretation was exactly the opposite: measurements become routine, he explained, precisely because they *are* important, which means that precision is their foremost requirement. Precision without replication, he said, was "crap". He illustrated his point by saying that single chemical ingredients within a substance are reported as percentages of the dry substance. If even a relatively simple measurement (such as water content) is slightly imprecise, the error will affect all other measurements. Consequently, he said, "when I read *one* figure in the literature, I would automatically assume that I have been confronted with a mean value (based upon several replications)".

In this case, each side stuck to its own interpretation. To win his point, the scientist repeatedly asked the analytical laboratory for the same analysis twice, using different sample codings so as not to raise suspicion. The clash of two locally-developed systems of interpretation became glaringly apparent when the expectations of a scientist who had moved from one system to the other were constantly violated (2-17).

Local idiosyncrasies also bear upon questions of composition and quantification; that is, what substances are to be used in an experiment, and how much. Standard formulations exist in certain areas, but even these are not immune to local idiosyncrasies. As we have seen above, scientists often reject these standards for anything other than routine composition analyses, claiming that they "lag too far behind" current knowledge or are "too old", given the amount of time it takes for a method to become officially acknowledged. But there is also a more basic reservation. In the words of one biochemist:

> "The more basic work is usually done . . . on something similar, but not the same. You know, if it's done on what I am interested in, then it's not worth doing again. So usually it's been done on something similar. . . . And see, I think you almost always have to adapt (a method) in some way. Sure, occasionally you find something (a method) that just fits in perfectly to solve a problem—but I'd say that's the exception rather than the rule" (30-9/5).

Interest in distinctions rather than similarities in procedure promotes local idiosyncrasies, but so does the experimental material itself. This material constitutes an additional source of constant variation because it is usually locally grown (plants and organisms), bred (animals), or produced (substances prepared or isolated in the laboratory). For example, the plant protein used in the experiments under observation came from local plant varieties, as did much of the raw material used by scientists in other groups. As the head of a chemical engineering group saw it:

> "The big variability is getting the raw material. We have never been able to get the same raw material again, and this is the . . . (inaudible) . . . every researcher has to face. It's the same in microbiology. You have to scratch yourself in the same place every time you play, and everything has to be the same, or else the accounts are meaningless" (7-30/3).

Variation in the source material used by the biological sciences has often been recognised as a "nuisance" by researchers and students of science alike. But beyond its being a "nuisance", this variability enhances the differentiation and distinctiveness of research products which the scientists themselves seek. And, as I have mentioned, while it contributes to the idiosyncrasies of research, it is by no means the only constituent, contrary to what is sometimes implied by arguments dealing with the variability of results. The scientists' often treasured know-how is another factor, and one which is particularly obvious in questions of composition and quantification.

For example, before the proteins mentioned earlier were subjected to high temperature and fermentation, differently processed versions were mixed with several other substances in order to compare reactions. The number and quantity of such substances reflected each scientist's attempt to achieve control over the process, utilising prior knowledge of what quantities had been used in the past with what outcome, and educated quesses as to what might be successful in the case at hand. The procedures used in these experiments were also influenced by routinised local interpretations. For example, the time needed to manipulate the mixtures before they were placed into the fermentation cabinet was counted here as "fermentation time", while in other places it figures separately.

In the same test series, weight and volume of the samples were measured immediately after exposure to high temperature. According to the scientist who had come from another institute, this procedure was "problematic" because the volume changes during the cooling period. Thus, the results depend on *when* the measurement is taken. In general, the time during which test material was exposed to treatment was based on local knowledge as to what works best.

The treatment of substances before experimental use also illustrates local differences. In the example above, the organisms used for fermentation were stored and used for several weeks, whereas in other laboratories they are exchanged after a maximum of one week. Note that such variations do *not* indicate that storage time of a microorganism is irrelevant to the results obtained, according to the scientists with whom I raised the question. Rather, these variations indicate differences in local interpretations as to what is relevant, and why (1-26/2).

This argument could be extended to include measurement devices and instruments as further sources of potential local variation. Instead, let me stress that at least some of this potential variation is acknowledged in published papers by reference to brand names, identification of firms which supplied particular instruments, and provision of detailed descriptions of various procedures. The argument here is *not* that science is *private* or non-public, but that the information obtained in natural and technological science research is idiosyncratic. In other words, the selections of the research process reflect interpretations which are crystallisations of order in a local contingency space. Contrary to what we may think, criteria for "what matters" and "what does not matter" are neither fully defined nor standardised throughout the scientific community. Nor are the rules of official science exempted from local interpretation.

In sum, we can say that these interpretations refer to at least three areas of selection:

1. Questions of *composition,* or questions which relate to the selection of specific substances, ingredients or means of instrumentation.
2. Questions of *quantification,* or questions of how much of a substance is to be used, how long a process ought to be maintained, when a measurement or sample should be taken, etc.
3. Questions of *control,* or questions which refer to such methodological options as simplicity of composition versus complexity, strict versus indirect comparability, etc.

Given these choices, research in the natural and technological sciences cannot be partitioned into one section which is open to situationally contingent selections and contextual influences (such as that in which a research problem is defined), and another which consists of the internal, objective and standardised execution of the necessary enquiry. Since choices exist *throughout* the process of experimentation, there is no research core which, even in principle, is left unaffected by the circumstances of production. In other words, as is the case in the social sciences, natural and technological scientific research is in principle indetermined by the scriptures (authoritative writings) of a field, as well as by its tacit knowledge, if both are thought to represent generally available information. Closure of this situation is achieved locally, with the help of idiosyncratic interpretation which itself results from this indeterminacy.

2.3 Occasioned Selections and the Oscillation of Decision Criteria

If idiosyncratic interpretations and an opportunistic logic mark the selections of the research process, then what role do decision criteria play in these selections? Presumably, decision criteria hold more than local relevance, and overrule at least some local contingencies by suggesting which decisions *should* be made in regard to the indeterminate choices that scientists confront. Let us first consider the nature of a decision criterion. As suggested before, the making of a piece of knowledge involves a series of decisions and negotiations; that is, it consistently requires that selections be made. Selections in turn, can only be made on the basis of other selections. In other words, selections must be translated into further selections.

For example, a choice between a filter and a centrifuge to eliminate chemical precipitation agents from protein samples was translated by the scientists involved into a problem of energy consumption. In choosing the more energy-efficient instrument, they deferred to a criterion of energy consumption. But this criterion is nothing more than a further selection, since many other translations of the problem can easily be imagined. In fact, when it turned out that the more energy-efficient filter did not work, the scientists reverted to the centrifuge, thus invoking the criterion of the practical availability.

Not surprisingly, scientists themselves often scrutinise decision criteria as but one specific selection out of the many possible (e.g., when an earlier decision is questioned in the course of research, or when a research result is evaluated in the light of the decisions which account for its specific characteristics). Thus, decision criteria are actually translations of selections into further selections, and there can be no doubt that some of these translations appear more frequently than others. For instance, in my observations and in discussions with other scientists at the institute, I found frequent references to costs, simplicity, feasibility under local circumstances, and in particular, to whether or not something would "work".

Yet the invocation of such general criteria by no means precludes the impact of a locally contingent situation. To begin with, decision criteria are invoked in specific circumstances, with reference to a specific *aspect* of the research whose costs are considered, and with respect to a specific *equivalent* such as money, time, effort, etc. These aspects and equivalents provide the indexical meaning of the criterion. We can also say that general criteria, such as those pertaining to cost, are nothing but schematisations of specific translations which vary not only with the problem at stake (upon which the costly aspect and the equivalent of "cost" depend), but in regard to local interpretations as well (in the sense that certain specific translations will be locally preferred).

In the institute studied, it was easier to get money to buy an expensive technical instrument than to come up with equivalent sums for hiring technicians or student assistants. Consequently, scientists frequently preferred instrumental procedures to those involving additional manpower, and, judging from the number of unused technical instruments lying around, the institute was overstocked with apparatus. Other examples were brought up in the previous section, in regard to locally developed know-how concerning "what works" in certain problem-situations.

The selection of a substance, technique or composition formula "because it works" refers us to the greater relevance of *success* than truth in actual laboratory work. Successes, as suggested before, do not share the absolute quality of truth. Not only is success, as one scientist said, "a different trip for every one of us", but what works—and what consequently counts toward success—depends as much upon routine translations arising from the practical concerns at a research site, as on the dynamics of negotiation and renewal, or the modification of these translations.

If criteria are seen as schematisations of specific translations of choices which originate in local laboratory situations, we cannot automatically assume that the same criteria are consistently applied in differing situations. Not surprisingly, scientific reasoning is marked by criteria-variation. More specifically, it is often marked by an *oscillation* between diametrically opposed criteria. A good example can be found in a bit of thoroughly "applied" protein research designed to test the suitability of plant proteins for human consumption. A major tests series was conducted to explore the behaviour and effect of these proteins when used as food additives. The tests were performed in a special laboratory designed for experiments in regard to the baking qualities of various foods (to emphasise the practical relevance of the institute's research).

In the present case, one of the questions posed was how the addition of differently treated proteins of varied origins would influence the texture of test breads. In view of the fact that the experiments did not involve chemical mixtures of interest only to scientists, but actual (albeit sample size) "breads", one would expect that the basic, pre-additive samples would somehow simulate a standard bread—that is, that the criterion for the choice (and quantity) of ingredients would be based on the composition of standard bakery breads.

However, the scientist who supervised the tests chose the ingredients on the basis of experimental control rather than practical application, using only "absolutely essential" components. Consequently, he ended up testing protein as a food additive in "breads" of a kind found nowhere else, and which, except in the case of famine, could not be considered "food". Thus, the principle behind six months of research and several papers was one of basic science. He explicitly defined his project as an attempt to find out what happened to the samples under maximally controlled conditions—even though this principle contrasted sharply with the otherwise "applied" nature of the project, and despite the fact that the criterion of practical relevance had been the reason for testing the proteins in the first place (12-29).

Such shifts in criteria are nothing new. But the point here is that they are neither exceptional, nor the mark of misdirected, "subversive" research in which the scientist's personal interests overrule what is "right and proper". To the contrary, this oscillation between criteria—depending on occasioned preferences, advantages and opportunities—seems to be a common feature of scientific practice. In general, however, it is probably less visible than in the above case, since many laboratory choices are implicit rather than explicit. If the selections themselves are not the focus of attention, an implicit change of criterion emerges only from conversation and off-the-cuff remarks.

In a case referred to earlier, in which the use of ferric chloride replaced heat coagulation as a means to precipitate protein at low temperature, the choice was rationalised in terms of energy savings which would substantially reduce the cost of generating large quantities of protein. Yet after several months of successful testing, the scientist in charge of the work said that he had "no idea what the ferric chloride costs", and, furthermore, was "not interested". In this project, costs were defined in terms of energy, and largely ignored for everything else. I am not denying that, had the cost of ferric chloride been conspicuously high, the "idea" would have been discredited in the eyes of the scientists. But short of threats which might impose themselves, selections were translated *not* into terms of costs, but into questions of making things work (6-8/2).

Part of the reason that these oscillations in decision criteria are rarely noticed in the laboratory is that scientists (and participant observers as well) are more likely to ask "why" than "why not". So long as the grounds for a decision seem plausibly or an option remains unproblematic, there seems little reason to ask why something else was *not* chosen. Furthermore, in many cases the possible alternatives are not obvious, and can be discovered only by various degrees of effort. As we shall see in Chapter 5, scientific papers are not designed to promote an understanding of alternatives, but to foster the impression that what *has been done* is all that *could be done*. But it is not difficult to find conspicuous cases of criteria oscillation in the published literature, if one takes the trouble to look carefully.

To give one last example, let us consider work in the generation of single-cell proteins. The entire thrust of this research effort is the notion that protein suitable for human consumption can be isolated from the cells of certain highly abundant micro-organisms. However, the necessary disruption of the cell wall is at present accomplished by a homogenisation method using liquid CO_2 as a coolant,[3] a method which costs about $10,000 per 1,000 grams of microbial protein. Moreover, the resulting protein is chemically modified in order to become more suitable for human consumption. And before this process of modification can proceed, the protein is treated with potentially toxic organic compounds.[4]

Thus, the picture we get from these long-term research efforts is that of a "cheap" protein which is tremendously expensive to produce, and which is made "suitable for human consumption" by the use of toxic substances. It is to be hoped that the Food and Drug Administration will keep such microbial proteins from ever entering the market. Needless to say, scientists adjust their goals as they go along to suit the direction a research effort takes. Thus, if the chosen criteria rule out the intended use of a result, the effort will take a "fundamental" turn, or relate to other uses.[5]

2.4 The Neglected Research Site: Organisation vs. Laboratory Situation

Not only the manufacture of knowledge in the laboratory, but the occasioned character of laboratory selections (illustrated by opportunism, local idiosyncrasies and criteria switches) has been neglected in the relevant literature. This neglect of the occasioned character of social action is not confined to studies of science. As Goffman pointed out in an article entitled "The Neglected Situation", the implication of most social research has been that "social situations do not have properties and a structure of their own, but merely mark . . . the geometric intersection of actors making talk and actors bearing particular social attributes". Established sociological variables, such as age, sex or social class, are measured along a high-low scale, and the intersection of the respective values of these variables held to determine what happens in a situation. In opposition to this practice, Goffman and others have argued that, in terms of verbal interaction, social situations constitute a reality *sui generis* which entails constraints, organisation and a dynamics which cannot be predicted from the values which participant actors assume on a set of variables.[6] See also the concept of "milieu" developed by Grathoff (1979).[7]

The charge that the research situation has been neglected in relevant studies of science might be countered by pointing out that scientific *organisations* have been widely investigated both in sociology of science and in social history of science.[8] During the past few years in particular, cognitive sociology of science has become increasingly interested in the role that organisations play in orienting scientific research.[9] However, organisations are generally too large to allow the sort of microscopic study advocated here. But the more important question raised by Goffman concerns the indeterminacy of social action *over and above* what we can derive from locating this action within a set of organisational characteristics.

This indeterminacy was mentioned in Chapter 1 with respect to the failure of studies of science to subsume the production or acceptance of knowledge under a set of generally valid criteria. At this point, it should be emphasised that this indeterminacy penetrates into the very core of organisations, for its origin lies in situated interpretation and the dynamics of interaction within particular situations. If we choose a unit of analysis larger than the actual site of action, we remain removed from the indeterminacy which marks the situation.

Organisational theory has known for some time that one cannot assume homogeneous goals among different members of an organisation, nor that the official purpose of an organisation actually integrates the actions of its members. Even if organisational goals are based on something more than public image, they will be interpreted differently by different people at different times. Organisations are important because they provide an umbrella for various groups and occasions, but their existence as units independent of the social interactions they subsume does not rule out the need to investigate those underlying interactions.[10] Through the study of such interactions we can hope to understand the meanings and consequentiality of the formal characteristics of an organisation. In the scientific laboratory, for example, such meanings consistently point beyond the organisation to transscientific fields of interaction and communication, as we shall see in Chapter 4. The frame of reference sketched by the scientists themselves constantly criss-crosses organisational borders, becoming at once larger and smaller than the unit circumscribed by these borders.

A curious correlate of this indeterminacy is that social reality seems to become more complex, more variable and, in a sense, more disordered the nearer we get to its microlevel, and *not,* as one might assume, the closer we get to the question of societal macrostructures.[11] It is tempting to associate the "nature" of organisations with the indeterminacy of social action by conceiving of them as an everyday device to assure, through control and regulation, that the outcomes of this action are stable. This assumption seems to underlie many organisational approaches in which organisational action is thought to be effectively regulated by means of rules and formalised procedures. However, while we can often trace a rule back to an interest in controlling social action, we cannot assume that such formal rules effectively eliminate the situational logic and contingency of social action.

Nor can we rely on the equally simple assumption that contingency can be eliminated by the exertion of sheer power. Some recent studies of organisational decision-making have documented an amazing amount of interpretative activity within the structural framework of formal rules and definitions.[12] The following summary of nine months of interaction between one scientist and the leader of a different group demonstrates the slack which may remain despite the existence of unambiguous rules and clearly defined power relationships in the scientific organisation, as well as the varied outcomes and situational definitions to which this slack gives rise.

2.5 Variable Rules, and Power

The research centre maintained several large laboratories which were specifically designed to produce substances with properties which would rule out normal laboratory operations and partially simulate the conditions of industrial practice. Equipment for such laboratories is expensive, and training a group of technicians to run the operations properly may take years. According to the scientists we heard that such facilities are rare and highly valued. Since the use of such a laboratory constitutes a "rare opportunity", those scientists who did have access appeared very anxious to deny that access to anyone else.

In theory, the laboratories and other equipment supervised by any one unit or research leader had to be made available to everyone else, when needed. Thus, the private appropriation of scarce resources was ruled out: that is ruled out in "law", but not in practice. Watkins[13] was the research leader for such a lab. But in addition to his official tasks, he was interested in effectively controlling the use of the laboratory. Word among the scientists I observed was that he made it extremely difficult for anyone else to use the facility.

Moreover, he controlled the technical staff of the laboratory. Years earlier, he had hired Kelly (who was working at a job he did not like) and put him in charge of the lab technicians. Kelly would not do a thing without Watkins' orders or endorsement; Kelly himself kept the rest of the technicians in line. Watkins enjoyed a good deal of international repute, and flew to Washington every few weeks to act as a government consultant. By means of personal power, Watkins had effectively subverted the official rule intended to guarantee that resources were shared, and thereby created a state of disorder in which anything was possible—depending on individual negotiations with Watkins, and on the respective situation.

Soon after Dietrich joined the group of scientists I principally observed, he was intrigued by the idea of using Watkins' lab for protein recovery tests. The idea garnered little support from his superiors, who had once been members of Watkins' group and still harboured a grudge against him (although they didn't want to talk about it). But Dietrich persisted with his idea, and soon gained Watkins' cooperation. Since Watkins had worked in the area of protein recovery for many years (although he used other source materials than Dietrich and his colleagues), it was felt that he would be interested in observing the experiments and acquainting his staff with the procedures involved. At any rate, he granted access to "his" laboratory and "his" staff.

A few months later, Dietrich wanted to use the laboratory again, but without Watkins' direct involvement. Because Watkins was known to insist that he be co-author of any papers based on research conducted in his facilities, Dietrich tried to find some way to avoid this unwanted collaborator. To this end, he claimed that he had run out of protein and needed another round of protein generation; his *actual* intent was to add an important step to the experimental procedure which would change the colour and biological value of the recovered protein. An "official" request for access to his laboratory met with the expected roadblocks from Watkins, who claimed that his own group needed the lab.

After a long silence, he finally "agreed", scheduling the experiments for the next day, which left Dietrich too little time for proper preparation. Watkins went out of town that day, but left Kelly and another scientist in his group to make sure that Dietrich adhered strictly to the initial procedure. Dietrich said nothing to Kelly about the new step to be included in the experiments, and Kelly used the previous flow chart to guide the operations. When the time came for the new operation, Dietrich tried to smuggle it in by suggesting matter-of-factly that it was something they "obviously" had to do. While negotiating for the inclusion of the operation, the scientist whom Watkins had appointed as his "watchdog" suddenly appeared to enquire about the progress of the experiment. According of Dietrich, Kelly had called to alert him about the new step. The result was that Dietrich had to abandon his original plan.

The third round of the exchange occurred some months later, when Dietrich showed Watkins the paper he had written on the basis of the first set of experiments. Of course, Watkins was a co-author, since his laboratory had been used. After reading the results, Watkins urged Dietrich to repeat the tests. Dietrich interpreted this as an attempt to make sure the procedure worked, and that Watkins' technicians were thoroughly familiar with it. He felt that Watkins now realised the procedure's potential. After giving it some thought, Dietrich agreed to repeat the experiments. He also decided to include the additional step, but this time in a revised and sufficiently pre-tested version he thought would go unnoticed. This time he succeeded.

Watkins' attitude toward Dietrich and his interest in the laboratory was neutral at first, then highly negative and resistant, and finally positive when it was Watkins' own idea that Dietrich use the lab. These variations existed despite the fact that the same experiments were at stake each time, and despite a directly relevant official rule and a rigid power constellation. Within the indeterminacy created by Watkins' subversion of the rule, Watkins and Dietrich negotiated the outcome of their interaction with varied success, based upon their changing interests and interpretations.

The point with respect to rules is that they seem, in this process, to function more as instruments of negotiation or weapons with varied uses, than as stabilising guidelines for action heeded by the various actors. Rules are actively manipulated in the process of negotiation, which means that they may be supported, reinforced, modified, stretched, twisted, neglected or even ignored altogether. Their role is variable, and whether an existing rule can or cannot be adduced in support of one's right depends upon the specific situation. In the present example, Dietrich could not simply turn to the director of the research centre and demand his right of access to Watkins' lab. Such a move would probably have damaged his social relations (and those of his research leader), thus jeopardising the ultimate success of his project and that of any future research along those lines.

But if rules are strictly reinforced in one respect, compensatory changes in other respects may well counteract their effect. For example, the "strict" rule that manuscripts had to be reviewed by two other scientists at the research centre before they could be submitted to a journal was counteracted by the scientists' right to choose such reviewers themselves. Thus, the rule could be used to foster one's own interests. For example, if Dietrich wanted to publish a paper without further delays, he chose reviewers who were known to be "easy-going". If he or his co-authors wanted to be "on the safe side", they chose one "critical" reviewer. (Choosing *two* critical reviewers was considered risky, since it was therefore possible to get two unfavourable reviews and thereby become known as the author of a "bad" paper.) In effect, the scientists were able to render the rule ineffective whenever they wanted to, and return the control over what was published back to themselves. In sum, while we must not diminish the importance of rules as instruments of social action, we cannot assume that they *rule out* the underlying indeterminacy and contingency of such action, nor the processes of negotiation which should have been determined by those rules.

If formal rules can be said to actively structure, rather than restrictively regulate, the processes of interaction, it is also true that such regulation is achieved through the exertion of power by those who formally or informally control certain aspects of an organisation? As indicated by the dynamics of the previous example, any exertion of power presupposes at least some *potential* power on the part of those against whom it is directed. Despite a rigid power constellation which seemed to give Watkins an unbeatable hand, Dietrich was by no means a loser. As has been pointed out, the mobilisation of potential sources of power by the "powerless" can be a major strategy for social change, while the effects of an easy victory of one party over another are usually provisional and temporary.[14]

To borrow a phrase from Crozier *et al.,* power is a symmetrical, albeit unbalanced, relationship. This symmetry suggests that power must be analysed concretely and specifically in social action, as a complex social function whose effect is neither negative (a point stressed by Foucault) nor part of a definite regulation imposed on the respective relation.[15] Given that contexts and situations change constantly, power cannot secure a favourable outcome once and for all by forcing social action into automatic reproduction. Rather, *power must be played* in a constantly changing game—and, once again, this means that the indeterminacy and situational contingency of social action have not been eliminated.

2.6 Conclusion

Let us consider variable rules, oscillation of decision criteria, local research idiosyncrasies, opportunism of the process, and the scientists' play with contextual limitations to be different aspects of an *opportunistic logic* of research. It is reassuring to find that other laboratory studies are just beginning to confirm such an opportunistic logic.[16] As I have already indicated, scientific findings can be seen as complex compounds of selections which are *contextually contingent* in the indexical sense illustrated here. It is clear, too, that once the selections of the laboratory have been crystallised into a scientific result, the contingencies and contextual selections from which it was composed can no longer be differentiated. In fact, the scientists themselves actually decontextualise the products of their work when they turn them into "findings", "reported" in the scientific paper.

To restore the contextuality of science, we have had to go into the laboratory and observe the process of knowledge production. In view of the opportunistic logic we found at work in this process, "scientific method" can be seen as a locally situated, locally proliferating form of practice, rather than a paradigm of non-local universality. It is context-impregnated, rather than context-free. And it can be seen as rooted in a site of social action, just as other forms of social life are.

Notes

1. See also the related ideas by Schutz (1970), to which R. Grathoff has alerted me. Barnes and Law (1976) have reviewed indexical expressions in science. See Bar-Hillel (1954).

2. This description of tinkering is taken from Jacob (1977), who uses the image of the tinkerer to illustrate biological evolution as a non-optimal, redundant, playful chance process, rather than a well-planned, systematic one in which everything has a purpose and nothing is wasted.

3. For the description and use of this method, see Dunhill and Lilly (1975) and Cunningham, Cater and Mattil (1977).

4. Kinsella and Shetty (1978: 814) note that the "broad range of reagents" used in research on the chemical modification of protein are "mostly unsuitable for use with food proteins". For further references, see the same authors. An earlier summary is found in Means and Feeney (1971).

5. Both tendencies can be documented in the literature on microbial protein and chemical modification of protein, to which the above mentioned authors provide sufficient references.

6. cf. Goffman (1972: 63). Goffman defines situations more narrowly than I do here "as an environment of mutual monitoring possibilities, anywhere within which an individual will find himself accessible to the naked sense of all others who are 'present', and similarly find them accessible to him".

7. Grathoff discusses the concept of "milieu" with a view to a phenomenology of the typical and the normal based upon Schutz and Natanson. See also Grathoff (1975).

8. Most studies of scientific organisations have focused on the productivity of scientists or the potential problems and difficulties which arise from a bureaucratic environment surrounding scientific activities. For example, see Crane (1965), Meltzer (1965), Marcson (1960), Kornhauser (1962), Pelz and Andrews (1966, revised 1976), Blume and Sinclair (1973) and the studies collected in Andrews (1979).

9. Cognitive sociology of science has emphasised the need to include cognitive factors in the study of scientific organisations. See particularly Whitley (1975; 1977a,b; 1978). For evidence that some cognitive factors may not play the role attributed to them, see Cole (1979). For the increasing attention devoted to scientific organisations in recent years, see the two European international surveys conducted on the topic. One, coordinated by the Science Policy Division of Unesco in Paris, has been repeated in several other European countries. See deHemptinne and Andrews (1979) and deHemptinne (1979). For some recent results of these efforts, see Andrews (1979), Crawford and Perry (1976) and Lemaine and Lecuyer (1972). A summary of relevant developments in science policy is given by Salomon (1977). For the changing role of scientists in various organisational settings, see Ben-David (1971).

10. One example of a comprehensive argument in this direction is provided by Silverman's summary of the state of organisational theory (1970). For recent critiques relevant to scientific organisations, see Callon and Vignolle (1977), de Kervasdoué and Kimberly (1977) and Knorr (1979b).

11. Part of the reason for this, of course, is that macrosociology tends to rely on aggregate data and summary statistics, often neglecting not only the dynamic features of direct interaction, but also the dynamics and historicity of societal change. Compared with the simplified results of such a procedure, the microlevel of social actions appears unduly complex, leading to the impression that it constantly eludes the grasp of scientific analysis.

12. For example, studies of organisational records produced by mental health clinics, hospitals, police departments, juvenile courts, and similar institutions have shown that these interpretations result in a series of characteristics which Denzin (1969) summarises as follows: (1) Organisations perpetuate themselves

through time by generating fictitious records; (2) comparable organisations differ in the meanings they assign to the same events (birth, death, marriage, mental illness, crime, etc.); (3) the production of organisational records is basically an interactional process based on rumour, gossip, overheard conversation, discrepant information, and biographically imperfect book-keeping; and (4) in piecing together these organisational reports, members routinely rely on open-ended categories of meaning and interpretation to classify recalcitrant cases—that is, they continuously elaborate and modify the meaning of categories. It is clear that such results require the use of a sensitive methodology (as outlined earlier) in any study of organisations.

13. For obvious reasons, the names of the scientists in this and other examples have been changed.

14. This is the point of Coleman's *Resources for Social Change* (1971). The best example of mobilising unconventional (and illegitimate) power is modern terrorism.

15. The kind of concrete analysis of power I have in mind is demonstrated from a sociological perspective in Cicourel's work on juvenile delinquency and from a historical perspective in Foucault's recent work. See Cicourel (968) and Foucault (1975, 1977). Foucault's theoretical points on the matter are summarised in his "Vérité et pouvoir" (1978); see also his earlier statements (1975: 29-33; 1977: 121-135). Another recent example of the inclusion of a notion of power into a microsociological approach is Harré (1979).

16. Although they do so under different titles. I have generally used the notions of indexicality, opportunism and situational contingency to refer to the phenomenon (1977; 1979a, b). Others have also referred to the importance of milieu, to local disorder, or to the circumstantial nature of research. See particularly Latour and Woolgar (1979: 235 ff.) and the as yet unpublished papers by Lynch (1979) and Zenzen and Restivo (1979).

Chapter 3

The Scientist as an Analogical Reasoner: A Principle of Orientation and a Critique of the Metaphor Theory of Innovation

"Seven Beauties" is Miss Wertmuller's "King Kong", her
"Nashville", her "8½", her "Navigator", her "City Lights".

Vincent Canby, Sunday *New York Times*

3.1 The Metaphor Theory of Innovation

To Nietzsche, *equating the unequal* was the origin of all ideas. "The essential feature of our thought", he said "is fitting new material into old schemas . . . *making* equal what is new". Nietzsche went on to argue that truth itself is nothing more than "a mobile army of metaphors, metonymies, anthromorphisms" whose origins in "making equal" have been forgotten.[1] The metaphor theory of innovation has rediscovered the source of the new in figurative discourse, but seems to have forgotten that making equal is a process of work involving force and the potential for either success or failure. While we shall criticise the metaphor theory for its equation between the occurrence of an "idea" and the phenomenon of innovation, it will interest us here not only as the dominant theory of innovation, but as a theory which has something to say about the *circulation* of scientific selections (or ideas) among different research contexts, thus pointing to a principle of research *orientation*. Let us now review the metaphor theory as a theory of innovation, and then confront it with the process of research encountered in the laboratory.

Imagine two scientists chatting about the progress of some protein work over a bag lunch. One takes his protein samples from the shelf and shows them to the other. He says he cannot account for the different volumes obtained in a series of experiments concerning proteins exposed to different degrees of temperature. The other suggests that perhaps the hardness of the protein particles is a relevant factor, and elaborates on particle size and behaviour. "Well," says the first scientist, turning the "worst"-looking sample around in his hands, "this protein *really* looks just like sand!"

Similes like this have attracted some attention in recent literature because of the role attributed to them in scientific innovation. "If the protein looks like sand," reasoned the scientist whose samples they had been, "it must be denatured. If it *is* denatured, its effect would be to dilute the samples, and nothing else. If it does dilute the samples just like sand, it would prove the 'dilution theory' in which everybody seems to believe. But if it does *not* have the same effect as sand, I can finally disprove this dilution rubbish and propose my own interpretation." Three hours later the scientist had abandoned his

49

previous project, gone to the storage room to find some chemically pure sand, set up a "quick and dirty" experiment designed to compare the behaviour of sand- and protein-samples under heat treatment, and nearly destroyed a perfectly good blender in the process.

But he had also built a strong case for his interpretation, for the behaviour of the sand-diluted samples differed significantly from that of the protein-diluted samples. To be sure, the results were preliminary because of the slap-dash nature of the test. Nevertheless, the comparison between protein and sand eventually led to a new theory of protein additives, and to an elaborate investigation of protein particle behaviour.

The metaphor theory of innovation assumes that such figurative comparisons as that between protein and sand are the very source of conceptual innovation.[2] Through metaphor, two phenomena not usually associated with one another are suddenly perceived to have some kind of correspondence. This intimation of similarity between hitherto unrelated ideas allows the systems of knowledge and belief associated with each conceptual object to be brought to bear upon the other, and brings about the creative extension of knowledge. The example above is slightly more complicated, since the similarities between protein and sand suggested an experiment to expose a presumed underlying dissimilarity between the respective particles with respect to the property of denaturation. Yet it did so by bringing knowledge about the properties of one phenomenon (sand) to bear upon another (protein) whose properties were the subject of investigation.

In the literary use of metaphor, the same effect is achieved through systems of association combined with a conceptual object. For example, Dante's "hell is a lake of ice"[3] extends the reader's previous image of hell by including in it those associations normally restricted to the "lake of ice". This creative extension of ideas is not limited to the conceptual object under consideration, for the object will also alter the image invoked to illuminate it: not only does hell become more like a lake of ice, a lake of ice becomes more like hell. This conceptual *interaction* as a basically symmetric relationship lies at the core of the metaphor theory of innovation.

However, conceptual interaction and symmetry of influence do not merely characterise metaphoric classifications, but are part of analogical reasoning, or similarity classifications in general. Analogical reasoning is based on a logic of resemblance in which the notion of similarity is described as logically basic, in the sense that it is presupposed from the very beginnings of language learning, and primitive, in the sense that it apparently cannot be reduced to analytic criteria.[4] It appears that metaphoric classification is best differentiated from other kinds of analogical reasoning by the degree of *distance* or independence between the two conceptual systems brought together through similarity classification.

In the limiting case of "primary recognition",[5] we can no longer distinguish between the two conceptual systems. Primary recognition refers to seeing something as something; that is, to the recognition of differential segments of our natural and social environment by identifying them in either our natural language or a professional idiolect. A scientist who said, "The stuff has gone white", as he looked at his protein samples provides an example from the laboratory in which a given stimulus is identified as an instance of a certain kind. Note that the definition of primary recognition in terms of similarity lends credence to the "theory-ladenness" of observation.[6]

A second form of similarity classification is involved when we "interpret" a situation or "account for" a phenomenon. The scientist who noticed the white colour of his samples concluded that "the protein was precipitated", and this interpretation became the basis for further procedures. In a sense, when we determine that a given situation fits a particular interpretation, we are concluding that the current situation is analogous to those from which the interpretation was originally derived. In other words, the original situation serves as a kind of paradigm against which the new situation is matched.

Even more important is the fact that we are apt to make inferences about unobserved aspects of the new situation from the paradigm case. This making of inferences is in principle symmetrical, since the contexts of association surrounding the interpreting and the interpreted situations potentially influence each other. This can be seen in the laboratory when the outcome of a recalcitrant experiment suggests a modification of the interpretation that originally created the expectations governing the experiment. What is important here is that the classifications involved are intended—and used—in a *literal* way, which means that the observed situation tends to be absorbed in the similarity class that is applied to it.

Despite this tendency toward assimilation, the classified situation retains its independence as long as it is independently describable, and so does the interpretation. This becomes obvious when an interpretation is modified, revised or extended. In the above example, it was discovered that the protein had not only been precipitated, but had also been affected by the means of precipitation. Given the basic independence between an interpretation and the situation it classifies, we can also say that this kind of similarity classification involves a greater distance than primary recognition.

Metaphor can now be seen as the form of similarity classification which involves the greatest distance between the conceptual objects involved, since it would be absurd or false to take the proposed conjunction *literally*. Primary recognition recognises an occurrence as something. Interpretations classify an occurrence as "actually" an instance of something else. Metaphors classify occurrences as similar, but *not* actually the same. For example, the protein cited earlier was never actually considered to be sand. Note that a metaphor can become a literal interpretation over time, or for some specific reasons.

According to Hesse,[7] even primary recognitions do not provide "a stable and independent list of primitive observation predicates". Nor, of course, do interpretative or metaphoric classifications establish a similarity relationship which could not be disestablished or altered with respect to the degree of distance it originally implied. Needless to say, much of the scientist's work goes into demonstrating why and to what degree some object is or is not an instance of a certain kind. Similarity relationships are not merely perceived; nor are they hidden, to be discovered once and for all, as Koestler seems to suggest.[8] The scientist's suddenly recognised similarities include elements of decision and persuasion, and consequently of change as well.[9] In this sense, the similarities which underlie a metaphor or an analogy are complex rather than primitive, fragile and temporary rather than basic and stable.

Because of their figurative character, metaphors may show this more clearly than literal interpretations. But the important point about metaphor, as stressed initially, is not the figurative character of the similarity relationship established between the objects brought together, but the conceptual interaction and subsequent extension of knowledge to which it leads. However, the conceptual interaction is not limited to the use of metaphor, but seems to be a routine feature of "displacements of concepts" in general.[10]

Conceptual objects are regularly transferred to instances beyond their original range of application, and displaced into contexts which differ from their established situation. Moreover, they are extended to problems clearly distinct from those they have previously been used to solve. It is this difference of some sort which is reflected in the distinct descriptions of the two objects brought together, and bridged by analogical reasoning. Conceptual interaction emerges from the different universes of knowledge or belief associated with the distinctive descriptions brought together by a presumed similarity.

While an analogy is a prerequisite for conceptual interaction, it need not be figurative: when two situations or problems are seen as similar, the knowledge of one will be extended to the other, just as with a figurative similarity. The move toward the inclusion of a non-figurative analogy is important not only because of the dominance of analogical reasoning in the laboratory, but also because it allows us to see that the process by which knowledge is analogically extended is at the same time a process by which selections (or ideas) are *circulated* and *transformed* through the medium of recontextualisation. A perceived analogy acts as a vehicle through which a scientific object is circulated from a preceding (research) context to a new (research) one. The interaction invoked by the metaphor theory of innovation is part of the process of transformation which follows upon the recontextualisation of the circulated object. Both scientific change and that solidification of knowledge known as "consensus formation" tie into this process of circulation and transformation, and both are part of what comes to be considered as the core of innovation.

3.2 The Scientists' Accounts of Innovation

The previous section suggests that the social scientist's account of innovation in terms of metaphor must be extended to analogical reasoning in general, since conceptual interaction (and the extension of knowledge it breeds) cannot be limited to figurative similarity relationships. The argument here is that the scientists' own accounts of innovation display such a broadened perspective, since they link innovation to the making of analogies in a much more general sense than that postulated by the metaphor theory of innovation. When scientists were asked to explain the origin of an idea they considered to be innovative, they generally displayed themselves as analogical reasoners who built their "innovative" research upon a perceived similarity between hitherto unrelated problem contexts.

Let us consider the story of Holzman, a biochemist who told me about his work on the isolation of hormones in a mould—a line of research he traced back to a colleague's idea that steroids might be involved in the transformation processes the mould underwent. He explained that the colleague, a biologist named Becker, seemed to be attracted by the problem of the slime mould:

> "She is not the only one interested in this mould. Many biologists like it because it is a model of differentiation. It changes from an animal to a plant as the result of some hormonal stimulation."

Becker was aware that steroids are involved in the reproduction of many life forms.

When she became pregnant, it "occurred" to her that the as yet unknown hormone which stimulated the transformation of the mould might be a steroid:

"Her original discovery was that, while she was pregnant, her own urine (which contains steroids) would stimulate the mould to undergo this conversion. The idea that steroids are involved in the reproduction of even the lowest forms of life is not new . . . although most biologists still don't accept it. Anyhow, she, uh, tried it, and it worked. I mean, what happens is very spectacular. These bugs are like amoeba, they crawl around on a plate of agar, and one of them will make a hormone whose nature was unknown at that time. When one creature makes this hormone, the other creatures congregate around this individual. In other words, this substance acts as an attractant. And after they all get together, they undergo this phenomenal transformation from amoeboid, animal-like creatures to a regular mould, you know. . . ."

The isolation of the hormone in the laboratory was complicated by the fact that subsequent attempts to stimulate the mould with Becker's urine did not work out. According to Holzman:

"It was not a real effect. No one could ever repeat (it). She had a good hunch that steroids were involved, but she had the wrong observations."

Consequently, Holzman turned to a more direct way of trying to isolate the hormone:

"So anyhow, she brought in this pregnancy urine. I was working on, uh, steroid hormones in urine, among other things, and I knew how to isolate them. I used my methods, and what I got out of her urine didn't work at all. I had some hormones in the lab in pure form, and they didn't work either. Then I had the idea of going to the mould directly. During the time that this congregation of individuals takes place, there must be more of this hormone present. So I thought that if we, uh, go to this mould directly and then isolate from it the fraction that is biologically active, that causes this attraction, we will find out what this hormone is. So we did this, using methods that I had developed over the years . . . you have to use fractionation methods, you know. In deciding which fraction to keep and which to throw away, you have to have a bioassay method. So—after your separation, you take the individual fractions and test them and see whether they cause aggregation. We did that together, and lo and behold, one of the fractions had the ability to cause aggregation. And this happened to be a steroid. Since then, other steroids have been isolated from all kinds of mould. They also have sex hormone activity. They are not related to the sex hormone that women have in pregnancy. They are steroids, but they are in a different class of steroids" (6-18/5).

The similarity underlying Becker's attempt to stimulate the mould with the help of pregnancy urine is that between the transformation of the mould and reproduction in other forms of life. Since the latter often involves steroids, Becker had "a good hunch" that steroids might be involved in the transformation of the mould as well. In the scientist's account, the notion that the unknown hormones might very well be steroids is based on establishing a similarity between two contexts and transferring a single element from one context to another.

The following story shows a similar pattern. It was told by the same biochemist, and involves the group he supervised:

> "This happened when we already had a small group, and I was interested in find-
> ing out how steroids were synthesised in plants. These are plant steroids, and
> there are all kinds of theories on how they are made. But nobody really knew. So
> we were working away, and doing pretty pedestrian stuff, until one of my col-
> leagues found . . . a lot of radioactivity incorporated in a particular fraction pre-
> sent in such minute quantities that we couldn't identify the material. But talking
> among ourselves, we came to the conclusion that it could be cholesterol. There
> was another man in the group who was working on unrelated problems and had a
> similar observation. . . . Then they pooled their resources—and, uh, of course,
> mine too—and together we came up with the conclusion that this was in fact
> cholesterol. This opened up a whole series of experiments which culminated in the
> fact that cholesterol—which up to then was considered to be an animal product
> that wasn't even present in plants—is actually the substance from which all plant
> steroids are made. And this is, uh, very significant: we can now trace the biosyn-
> thesis of plant steroids very easily by administering radioactive cholesterol and
> seeing what transformations it has to go through before it becomes one of those
> many, many steroids that occur in plants."

When I asked how the group had arrived at its joint conclusion, he said:

> "You see, I had been working on people up to then. And, although it wasn't very
> clear at the time I started, it became increasingly evident—from my own work
> and that of other people—that cholesterol in animals and people is the key
> substance from which all other steroids are made.
>   But it was believed at the time that 'plants do not contain cholesterol'. So first
> there was my colleagues' discovery that radioactivity accumulated in a certain
> fraction. . . . *The link* (between the observation of accumulated radioactivity and
> the idea that the substance was cholesterol) *was that that's what you would expect
> in animals.* That's what we, as well as other people, had previously observed. But
> that the same thing could happen in plants was completely unexpected, because
> until then nobody even suspected that plants contain cholesterol" (14-5/2, em-
> phasis added.)

The observation of accumulated radioactivity in a certain fraction of plant material
(together with other aspects of the problem) provided a context close enough to that of
cholesterol-formation in animals to suggest the "idea" that cholesterol was also formed
in plants, despite the prevailing contrary opinion. (I should note that at least part of the
idea's attractiveness arose from its opposition to established beliefs.) Thus, we again
find the circulation of an element from one context to another which was sufficiently
similar to the original to both suggest and warrant the transfer. These two examples
can also be considered in terms of the result of the transfer: in both cases, the scientists
found an explanation for an unknown phenomenon by assimilating it with a known
one; that is, to the operation of steroids in reproduction, and of cholesterol in animals.
Other accounts of the origin of research results called "innovative" did not invoke the
context of explanation, yet implied the same pattern of circulation by analogy.
    In the following account (a summary of comments made by scientists during the
period of observation), the transposed element is an enzymatic procedure. Walter, a

technologist, found that a certain plant protein contained an expectably high amount of toxic solanine. During the latter part of my observations, he virtually ignored the problem, since it had no immediate bearing on the research in progress, nor on any projected publication. Nonetheless, he was bothered by it, and occasionally spoke of the need to eliminate or reduce the amount of solanine. At one point, he wondered if the elimination of solanine couldn't become a by-product of other, more pressing experiments.

He discussed his plan with Holzman, who had worked on solanine for many years. Holzman felt that Walter's method held no promise of success, but mentioned that his own laboratory had successfully eliminated a similar toxic compound from another plant by using an enzymatic procedure, in work that as yet had not been published.

Walter immediately picked up on the "idea" of using Holzman's enzymatic procedure to elimate the solanine from his own proteins:

> "I think I had the advantage of being the only one who got the message (*about the existence and the success of Holzman's enzymatic procedure*), and the only one who understood its implications (*for the elimination of solanine*)."

Both Scientists deemed it highly probable that an equivalent enzymatic procedure would work with the plant material, but Holzman was "not interested" in doing the necessary research himself, being "too settled on chromatography and his own projects". For Walter, Holzman's disinterest presented an excellent opportunity not only "to solve the problem", but to distinguish himself by exploiting an idea which would otherwise not be used.

Note that when Walter first heard about the enzymatic procedure, he immediately saw it as the key to solving the problem of solanine elimination, despite the fact that the procedure had been established for use with a *different* plant and a *different* toxic compound. But the contextual similarities between the problem of solanine elimination and the problem for which Holzman had developed the procedure were sufficiently appealing to suggest a transference of the "idea". Of course, the "transfer" involved both modification and adaptation, thus requiring an actual *transformation* of the procedure involved.

I encountered many cases of this sort during the period of observation. For example, one of the scientists involved in plant protein generation had been given a report written by the head of his group after visiting research groups in various industrial and non-industrial countries. The report mentioned in passing, the scientist said, that "the people at NN tried to enrich soft drinks with protein and found that the protein colour of the samples became lighter when citric acid was applied in the process". Samples had been sent to them by the head of the group for the respective protein-additive tests. Since the scientist was interested in obtaining a protein powder which was as light as possible, the idea of using citric acid as a non-polluting coagulant seemed promising enough to justify a series of experiments (3-15/1).

While the previous examples illustrate the transfer of a method or procedure from one context to another, the following account (drawn from the food engineering group at the institute I observed) involves the transfer of a type of solution. The group leader explained the origin of their current research efforts in sweet corn processing. The problem, as described by the research leader, is that:

> "The corn is cut with a knife, (and in) doing so you create a tremendous amount of effluent during the washing step and lose all of the flavour of the product. . . . This is something that everybody (who has) worked in the food industry and seen corn processing plants is aware of."

The scientists began to look at this process when "a group upstairs" suggested that they ought to be working on a "big project". The project head, whose background is in chemical engineering, continued:

> "So we said OK, we'll show you that we can do a big project. . . . We formed a group and started to look at ways of changing the process completely. . . . It is intuitively obvious that you have to keep the corn kernel intact, because if you break it open everything is leached out. So we had to go to a process that stripped the kernel off the cob without damaging the body of the kernel. We went to the literature and found the patents, plenty of them. People had frozen the cob and broken off the kernels, (there were) a number of cutting techniques, etc. . . . R. came up with the idea of splitting the cob in half and then wiping the kernels off with a belt. Well, they started out with a belt like this and went through many different types of belts before they finally ended up with one that worked. So we now have a technology, at least in its infancy, that can produce unit kernels. But right after the start of the project, after the first season, we realised that the corn cob itself was designed to frustrate the removal of kernels by a rolling or plucking action, as we called it."

The scientist was very familiar with a solution that had played a key role in efforts to solve mechanical harvesting problems, and this familiarity allowed for a transfer of the solution:

> "In the tomato industry, mechanical harvesting was successful only because they were able to develop a variety that *could* be mechanically harvested. And the thing that occurred to me to do was to check around, to find out if there (was) a corn that is loosely held and more suitable for the kind of mechanical stripping we were talking about. I made a few phone calls around the country to people I had worked with in the past who knew something about sweet corn. After two or three calls, I was directed to one of the key corn breeders in the country.
>
> It turns out that this fellow had been breeding corn for 25 years trying to get a variety that was very loosely held, for fresh market consumption. But it was a sweet corn without the little pieces of tissue at the base of the kernels that get stuck in your teeth. He had bred corn with two rows, four rows, square cobs. So he pulls out (this corn) and shows (it to) me, and it is the type of thing where, when it is at the proper maturity for processing, the kernels roll right out. He had just increased the amount of seed to the point at which he could go to Florida that winter and grow the first handful for commercial testing. We got the first handful, and this year we got the first pound of the seed. We have been able to evaluate it, and indeed it is the type of raw material that will allow . . . (mechanical) processing" (7-30).

There is no need for further accounts to illustrate the kind of analogical reasoning outlined initially. It should also be clear that the extension of knowledge based upon the interaction of similar instances is essentially a symmetrical process. For example, not only did the familiar operation of steroids in the reproduction of certain forms of life suggest a similar role in the transformation of slime mould, but the knowledge of the hormone itself changed to include a series of steroids subsequently isolated from all kinds of moulds. Similar changes occurred with regard to cholesterol, to the enzymatic procedure proposed to remove toxic compounds from certain plants, and to the bleaching and precipitating effect of citric acid. But it should also be clear from these accounts that the transformations did not result from mere *conceptual* interaction, but from a process of production and reproduction.

3.3 Analogy Relations and the Opportunistic Logic of Research

"Usually, the beginning of a piece of research is when something strikes a spark on one's imagination: something one does not know seems a particularly fascinating thing to try and find out. Partly, the thing itself seems important and fascinating in its own right, partly, one has intimations that one can find it out. That is where the spark comes in—the intimation that one actually can find it out gives one a particular thrill that is irresistible. There is a flash, and as with love one knows that one is in it" (William Cooper, *The Struggles of Albert Woods*).

Let us now look at these scientific accounts of innovation from a different angle, as accounts of events in the process of research production. What does the occurrence of an "idea" based on analogical inference mean in this process? The first thing to note is that the "ideas" which mark either an analogical transfer or the occurrence of a metaphor take on the character of *solutions*. We have already noted that the very significance of analogical reasoning in this context lies in the fact that it brings knowledge from a familiar, well-known, clear case to bear upon an unclear, less familiar, problematic situation. Thus, the analogical relation mobilises a resource which creates an opportunity for success: since the knowledge mobilised by the analogy or metaphor has already worked in a similar context, it seems likely that it can be made to work, given appropriate modifications, in the new situation.

It is precisely this *promise of success* to which Albert Woods refers in the quote from William Cooper's tale of an experimental chemist.[11] It is the intimation that one can *actually* find it out that brings the irresistible thrill. And it is this promise of success associated with the "unsatisfied capacity"[12] of the scientists' analogical transfers which lurks behind the talk of an idea's "interest".

The most immediate consequence of this line of reasoning points to a difference between the "ideas" of the laboratory and the "hypotheses" of methodological vernacular. If the "ideas" marking an analogical relation display themselves as unrealised solutions holding a promise of success, then the research associated with such ideas assumes a peculiar *post hoc* quality; that is, the investigation is undertaken only *after* the solution has been found. Seeing such ideas as unrealised solutions contrasts sharply with the notion that they are, logically speaking, hypotheses, or *ex ante* conjectures about a phenomenon subjected to test in the research process.

Hypotheses are tried against data in order to determine, ultimately, whether they are true or false, or one of their weaker substitutes such as confirmed/disconfirmed or tenable/untenable. They require that the data collected through research be independent arbiters of the propositions they contain. Ideas that are actually unrealised solutions mobilised by an analogical relation cannot assume such independence. Unrealised solutions are not tried against data, but *made to work* by scientists actively engaged in constructing the results anticipated by the solution. They can be made to work differently by different scientists, depending on practical circumstances, and they are made to work with different degrees of success.

I do not mean to suggest that realising a solution is a simple, smooth or brief undertaking, but instead, that making a solution work raises other questions than those specified by the language of hypothesis-testing. The standards against which the ideas of the laboratory are measured do not refer to the world of theoretical interpretation, but to a world of instrumentation, collaboration, publication and investment. In short, to a process of production whose products are specified by what *can* be done. Unrealised solutions do not eliminate problems, fruitless searches or outright failures from the process of research. But they do turn the open ground of unresolved research into the closed program of a production line. It is unrealised solutions—*not* problems—which take the lead in this process of production, and the power associated with unrealised capacities that drives the research process forward. And where it goes depends upon where its greatest capacities lie.

This does mean, of course, that the opportunistic logic of research has a direction, even though the direction may be only transient and temporary. The occurrence of an unrealised solution is important to scientists in that they take it as an organising principle for subsequent actions and selections. It provides a principle for reevaluating previous priorities, and introduces new equivalences. It makes some decision translations more salient and downgrades others. In a literal sense, it establishes order in the sense that it provides the very principles of selection upon which continued action is predicated.

It is interesting to note that unlike what we expect from logic in general, consistency does not seem to be an inherent part of the order created by an opportunistic logic. The selections of the research process are not validated on the basis of an impartial individual hearing, but matter primarily in relation to the practical circumstances of action as structured and organised by unrealised solutions.

This explains why it is possible to find an entire research effort built upon a dual string of decision translations that run counter to each other. Or why such factors as cost or toxicity may be considered and not considered in the very same project. Decision translations emerge from the frame of reference surrounding an unrealised solution which has taken the lead in a process of research. Given the potential of single cell proteins, the cost of smashing the cell walls by using liquid CO_2 was conspicuously neglected.

In general, we cannot explain away the discrepancy between the propagation of a particular decision translation in regard to an unrealised solution, and its neglect in the process of realisation by claiming that the scientists had no other choice. For example, several alternative coagulants were usually available in the protein research, and were actually explored in the work, as we shall see later on.

3.4 The Opportunism and the Conservatism of Analogical Reasoning

Referring to the logic of research as opportunistic not only brings space and time back into scientific procedure and dissolves a particular "scientific" rationality into situated, circumstantial reasonings, but also points to the scientists' organisation of selections in terms of perceived opportunities associated with similarity-relations. To be sure, these opportunities are actively pursued by scientists, who are not, as I encountered them in the laboratory, unconcerned tinkerers dallying with the bricolage of a work of art. The reasoning of the laboratory is personally interested, a point to which we shall return. The scientists' tendency to respond to "ideas" as "solutions" manifests this interest, as does their concern with risks.

It is clear that the *post-hoc* character of the research initiated by a solution does not rule out the possibility of failure and mistake. As suggested before,[13] solutions as problem translations are themselves problematic, in that they raise further problems to be solved. Realising the idea that steroids might be involved in the transformation of slime mould posed the problem, first, of isolating the steroids, and then, of proper identification. A scientist's hunch about how such subsequent problems can be solved is not always correct, as we have seen in the case of the slime mould. Furthermore, problems may have to be attended to even if an attractive or reasonably satisfactory solution is not in sight. To paraphrase Albert Woods,[14] scientists cannot always lay themselves open for something to strike a spark on them—they may have to strike a spark on it, and do so within a limited amount of time. This also implies a certain risk of failure.

Scientists at the centre I observed were well aware of these risks. When discussing new ideas, they displayed a full range of circumstantial reasoning with which these risks could be evaluated. Involved with an idea's "interest" were the chances of convincing the research leader of its value, being able to recruit laboratory assistants, finding the necessary equipment, being the first to publish, having time to do the work, etc. As René, a chemist, told me in regard to his own innovative ideas:

> "You try to discriminate. You can get one idea a day, or . . . (in) two days, or one a week, and you discriminate (in terms of) your time and your ability to use it. You know, we have idea files, either in our minds or on paper, but you can't spend a lot of your time on things you don't have the opportunity to perform, or to prove, or to verify. *So you try to limit your interest to the idea you know is going to be most productive as quickly as possible within the frame of facilities at hand*" (9-27/9, emphasis added).

The biochemist Holzman's version of this was that he said he usually knew what he should drop and what he should pick up on. A lot of unsuccessful scientists, he said, "are not dumb, they just work on the wrong things". He felt that "if you are up against terrific competition, there is no sense in struggling. By now, I can gauge these success factors, and my own secret of success is that I work on things that aren't too unlikely to work out" (9-29/4). The scientists I listened to were not only aware of the risks associated with their analogy-based "ideas", but were also concerned with keeping these risks at a *low* level.

When scientists follow the lead of an unrealised solution, they do not foolishly commit themselves to a journey of unknown destination and uncertain arrival time, in which the chances of getting anywhere at all are poor. Instead, they choose a known destination at which it seems likely they will arrive not only on time, but ahead of everyone else. There seems no reason to believe that scientists are, by nature or by necessity, devoted to risk taking. Research as a high-risk enterprise may reflect the feelings of those who finance it in hope of obtaining a specific result. It does not reflect the reasoning of scientists in the laboratory.

Scientists can build their *own* success on almost any "solution", provided they can follow its lead and make it work. Consequently, many of their arguments focus on securing such opportunities, and on sorting out the circumstances which will allow them "to be most productive as quickly as possible within the frame of facilities at hand". Analogical transfers provide a firm ground for controlled risks, since they mobilise a solution which has already been proven to work, albeit in another context.

The scientists' analogy-based innovations imply a conservative strategy in more than one sense: first, that one starts from an unrealised solution rather than an open problem; and second, that one follows the lead of ideas which hold the greatest promise of success, rather than expose oneself to risks and uncertainties. Generally speaking, the interest of an "innovation idea" is not that it is new, but that it is *old*—in the sense that it draws upon available knowledge as a source for producing knowledge. In this process, previous selections are circulated to new areas rather than being invented, and thereby reproduced and transformed. Thus, in so far as analogy-based "discovery" represents the spatial expansion of previous selections into new territories, it is part of "consensus formation" and the solidification of knowledge. If the respective recontextualisation leads to a transformation of scientific objects, it is part of scientific change. In both cases, the circulated objects enter a process of conversion in a new research context, and thereby generate new scientific objects. To the scientist, they constitute a resource mobilised in a process of production.

If this process is characterised by practical reproduction, then the hallmark of an analogical extension of knowledge is not mere "conceptual" interaction, but the mobilisation of resources for making things work in the ongoing process of laboratory production, and the transformation of the selections transferred through this process. Resources are not only "ideas", but available instruments, source materials available from colleagues, effective lines of laboratory action, scientists who might be consulted, timings, quantifications, successful composition formulae—in short, whatever contributes to the mobilisation and instantiation of a means of production.

In the case of the slime mould, the idea that the hormones involved might be steroids suggested an array of isolation methods and a laboratory equipped with the necessary instruments, as well as a group of scientists "interested" in the work and a journal in which to publish the results. It triggered the idea of using purified hormones and led, through laboratory work, to the discovery that the steroids involved differed from those found in the urine of pregnant women. Subsequent research led to the discovery of steroids in all kinds of moulds, and to the identification and exploration of their various characteristics.

Just as the analogies relevant here are not simply "ideas", so "conceptual interaction" is not merely "conceptual". The new results initiated by the creation of an analogy are not just derived from the associations invoked by a striking and unexpected similarity (as in the literary use of analogical reasoning), but are grounded in the transformations of knowledge which result from laboratory reproduction. The process is material, and has material consequences.

3.5 Ethnotheories of Innovation, or the Assumptions Behind Accounts of Innovation

"You asked me where the origin is—I remember the origin of everything because it isn't something you simply drift into! (In research) you have a concept based on somebody else's work, you are standing on somebody else's shoulders, you are putting two pieces of something else together. But when an idea comes, it comes. It's not something that develops from a series of routine investigations!

There are maybe half a dozen developments that we have been involved in, and I think each one has its own origin. *There is no pattern to the origin of ideas!*" (emphasis added).

Thus far we have looked at the metaphor theory of innovation advanced by the logic of science and found that it needs to be extended to include a more general form of reasoning by analogy. We have heard scientific accounts of the origin of various research efforts, and discovered that analogy-based "ideas" are indeed pervasive in what is considered innovative work. We have been confronted with the social scientist's interpretation of the role of metaphor and analogical transfer in research production. And we have qualified this analogical reasoning as "conservative", since it implies a reproduction and solidification of previous selections, and the controlled risk of transformations associated with the circulation of scientific objects. We can now return to metaphor and analogy as the basis for a theory of innovation. To begin, let us examine some ethnotheories of innovation held by scientists themselves.

The quotation which heads this section is from a chemist, René, who had made his reputation by developing a microbiological assay of proteins using the microorganism *Tetrahymena pyriformis* W. In a nutshell, the theory of innovation contained in his statement is a version of the "lightning bolt" theory of creativity, which holds that ideas come out of the blue, rather than emerge as the (logical) result of previous investigations. But before the conversation was completed, he suggested two other theories of innovation. For example:

"... as far as the innovations are concerned, I think it means ... perceiving what the state (of affairs) is and taking what, in your mind, is the next logical step. ... Maybe that's what creativity is—summing everything up, putting it together, and getting a new answer. ... *It's a logical, a logical sequence of events* which may not (look) so logical to someone else, and it ends up being 'creative'. But I think most of it is going down the path, exploring and prospecting the road as you go along" (emphasis added).

Later, while discussing the group's "fortuitous" observation, during an experiment on a physical effect of humidity, that there was an optimum where they had expected a linear decreasing relationship, René said:

"... so this was an anomaly, right? *The trick in all this, in what you might call innovations, is observing the anomaly*—what is different about *this* set of characteristics? And I think if you characterise any of the accomplishments (of science) it says: you tried something, you did something, you found an anomaly, and (you investigated) the reason for the anomaly. Investigate the anomaly!" (8-5/1, emphasis added).

In addition to the lightning bolt theory of innovation, we are exposed to a "logical" theory in which discovery is nothing more than one step in a logical series of events, and an "anomaly" theory in which innovation is bred by the occurrence of unexpected events and relationships. These ethnotheories of innovation appear to contradict one another, especially since they were promoted by a single scientist in regard to a single context. Yet there is no necessary contradiction. "Ideas" can indeed be triggered by anomalies which require explanation. And while the occurrence of an "innovative idea" may seem pure chance in terms of prediction, it can also be a step in a logical sequence of events when one reconstructs a research problem after the fact. What actually happened, then, is that the scientist looked at a single process from three points-of-view, and his theories reflect different aspects of this process. He also answered somewhat different questions in each of his theories.

Let us now consider the social scientist's theory of innovation by means of metaphor or analogy. It adds to the picture painted by the above ethnotheories in that it tells us something about *how* an "idea" leads to a creative extension of knowledge by mobilising knowledge from a different context. Yet like the ethnotheories of innovation, it proceeds selectively. For example, it does not address the question of *when* an innovative idea tends to occur (as does the anomaly theory). Nor does it consider the question of *how* an innovative idea relates to *preceding* research (as does the logical theory).

More important, the metaphor/analogy account of innovation is based on a series of assumptions which tend to obscure, rather than illuminate, the process of practical research. A theory of innovation which draws upon metaphor and analogical transfer is streamlined in terms of a clearly identified, successful end-product of investigation. It begins by assuming the existence of an innovation with a name and an author, located in time through publication or participants' accounts. In other words, it assumes that the "who", "when" and "what" of an "innovation" or "discovery" have been settled (or can be settled by means of further enquiry), and answers the question "how" by reference to conceptual interaction and the extension of knowledge induced by establishing a similarity relationship.

However, "innovations" are embedded in a past and future of constructive (and destructive) work. When we look at this process in sufficient detail, we see that questions of date and authorship are not settled by the mere existence of a phenomenon called innovation, nor do they seem to get settled through close empirical studies of the phenomenon. Instead, clearcut answers to such questions require that decisions be made about what is and what is not significant with a view to the end product of innovation.

For example, we cannot assume that the person who invokes an analogy, the one who works out the experiments and the one who gains credit for the work are one and the same. The comparison cited earlier between protein and sand was made by a scientist who had nothing to do with the research in question, and arose from a simple chat between colleagues. Needless to say, the question of an "idea's" authorship is by no means settled by the scientists themselves, and one need not cite disputes over priority in the published literature to see this point illustrated. In accounts of "their own" innovations, the scientists often blurred what they had to say about the origins. For example, the biochemist who told me about the discovery of cholesterol in plants began by saying that "they (his colleagues) pooled their resources—and, uh, of course, mine too—and *together* we came up with the conclusion that this was in fact cholesterol", only to end up, some 15 minutes later, talking about "*my* idea that cholesterol is present in all plants. . . ."

Questions of authorship and the timing of innovation are the established battlefield for historians of science, and as such need not bother the theorist interested in the logic of conceptual interaction. But to a degree they *will* bother the social scientist who observes a process of research. Does one credit the scientist who jokingly points to a similarity, or the one who links the idea to a workable procedure? The post-doctoral researcher who performed the experiment, or the technicians and research leaders? And what does one count as the "origin", apart from the question of who was the originator? Why not the observation that the urine of pregnant women stimulates the transformation of the slime mould, rather than the "idea" that steroids may be involved in that transformation?

Of course, these questions are of an analytic rather than practical nature. In practice, the necessary decisions are routinely made in an *ad hoc* fashion, and vary among different purposes and observers. The metaphor or analogy theory of innovation does not specify which decision criteria should be preferred in such cases. And the observer of laboratory research cannot as yet dispose of the integrating principle of an acknowledged and identified "innovation" for which a history can be reconstructed.

This brings us to a second point about the assumptions implicit in the metaphor or analogy theory, and one which is relevant as long as this theory claims to be one of innovation. As indicated earlier, this theory tries to explain the (conceptual) origin of innovation by starting from the successful end products of research—those which qualify as "innovations". Having presupposed that innovation is a given, unproblematic phenomenon, the theory then jumps to an "origin" located in the conceptual sphere. We can also say that it *identifies* innovation with the conceptual occurrence of an analogy or metaphor, since it virtually ignores the process of research production which ties these two end-points together.[15]

Questions of timing and authorship refer us to this process, yet they are only part of the more general question of how a research result becomes an "innovation". It is hard to see how this question could be approached without due consideration of the process of production and reproduction of research, for it is here that the ideas of the laboratory are turned into "innovations". In consequence, any theory of innovation will have to be grounded in this process.

3.6 A Metaphor- or Analogy-Theory of Failure and Mistake

To expound the thesis, let us suppose for a moment that we are not interested in a theory of scientific innovation, but in one of scientific failure and mistake. The laboratory provides ample evidence of such failures. Indeed, all we have to do is to take one of the accounts of "innovation" presented earlier and place it into an ever larger context of ongoing research which surrounds it. What we end up with is a genealogy of *failures* which at one point seemed to be (or actually were) successful innovations. For example, the use of ferric chloride to precipitate protein (see Chapter 2) was embedded in a whole chain of similar "ideas", each involving an analogical transfer, and most leading to specific research efforts.

To choose an arbitrary starting point, the first such transfer involved phosphoric acid. The method had just been published and documented in a biochemical context. It seemed particularly attractive since the major author also worked at the research centre. Having access to the method's author meant a quick transfer of know-how resulting in an easier process of adaptation. It could also mean collaboration, and consequently, access to equipment, material and laboratory-assistance pretrained for the purpose.

But after further exploration, interest in the method faded away, since the previous context did "not really match" the new situation. For example, the experiments had to be conducted under nitrogen, which was difficult in the large-scale laboratory needed to generate large quantities of protein. Moreover, another paper suggested that phosphoric acid would generate toxic side-effects. And finally, the method could prove very expensive on a large scale. Nevertheless, the method was pursued until one scientist happened to read about ferric chloride, which immediately struck him as a "better idea".

The "discovery" of ferric chloride not only sealed the fate of phosphoric acid as a non-solution, but also marked a change in the research focus. As we have heard in Chapter 2, the generation of protein from plants became a research topic in its own right, replacing the original interest in doing biological assay tests with rats (for which large amounts of protein were needed). Ferric chloride was made to work in subsequent experiments, and the resulting proteins were highly soluble—a property considered highly desirable.

So ferric chloride proved to be a success and remained so throughout the period of observation, as indicated by a quickly published paper dedicated to the promotion of the method. More specifically, it was a success from the point of view of protein generation. This success was threatened, however, so long as the protein could not be adequately purified. As a result, much effort went into an attempt to solidify the success by finding a means of purification.

One idea was suggested in a somewhat *ad hoc* fashion when, on the eve of a large-scale experiment, it was discovered that the laboratory had run out of the necessary adsorbing agent. Since the date of the experiments could not be changed, there was no time to order the chemicals. In the somewhat nervous discussions which followed, a colleague suggested an adsorbent which had worked in his previous research on proteins. The other scientists did not seem intrigued with the idea, expecting that it would be difficult to remove the adsorbent from the proteins. Yet once they got started, attempts to purify the protein with this adsorbent agent went on for several months.

At one point, the results were enthusiastically described as "better than anything achieved so far", the implicit reference being to another group at the institute which had failed "for 25 years" to isolate and purify a similar protein. However, this success was short-lived; after they looked at the results of chemical composition tests, the scientists qualified it as an artifact. Shortly thereafter, the attempt to work with this adsorbent was abandoned altogether.

While these efforts to use the adsorbent were still under way, the "idea" of using citric acid was picked up from the research leader's travel report, as mentioned before. As it turned out, citric acid could not only be used in place of the adsorbent to alter the disturbing properties of the proteins, but could also substitute for ferric chloride as a method of protein generation. The experiments were begun in the autumn of 1976, toward the end of my observations, and mark the beginning of the deconstruction of the success of ferric chloride. This deconstruction was not completed until 18 months later, when some of the data on citric acid were finally analysed and reported in a paper demonstrating its advantages over ferric chloride.

Some such demonstration had been anticipated when the scientists turned to using aluminium sulphate instead of ferric chloride, an "idea" which came up in a discussion with a visitor from Israel who suggested that it had been used in the context of environmental research in his country. Since the resulting proteins had a lower nitrogen solubility and other less desirable properties than those obtained with ferric chloride, the method had been qualified as a failure. However, this did not prevent the scientists from publishing the results in a paper which compared several methods. At the time, this failure had strengthened, rather than threatened, the potential of ferric chloride.

In the meantime, two other research lines have been actively pursued. One involves the chemical modification of the protein molecule, a procedure which allows for engineering the properties of the proteins. As a consequence, all of the previously "successful" methods may be deconstructed, since protein properties are no longer a decisive criterion for their success or failure. Note, however, that this potential deconstruction did not hinder the scientists from promoting citric acid as a successful coagulant in a paper which has been submitted for publication. The second effort involves an enzymatic weakening and subsequent mechanical destruction of the cell walls of certain microbes in order to obtain the protein found in the cell juice. Since these microbes are available in immense quantities, the potential of this procedure also bodes ill for the use of ferric chloride, or its present substitute, citric acid.

The last two procedures are too new to predict their eventual fate (although there are indications that the chemical engineering of proteins will be abandoned because of the associated hazards).[16] But the fragments of the process presented above demonstrate that one need not go outside the laboratory to observe the demolition and replacement of previously successful innovations: the scientists themselves constantly engage in such deconstructions and transformations.

Moreover, many ideas which seem "innovative" and "promising" in the laboratory do not work out under practical circumstances, or are abandoned before being tested experimentally. Our genealogy of methods used in protein generation, beginning with the projected use of phosphoric acid and continuing through ferric chloride (and its ramifications) to aluminium sulphate and citric acid, includes both kinds of failure. Since the origin of each method is marked by the circulation or a "displacement" of knowledge from one context to another, why not propose a theory which traces the origin of scientific failure back to the occurrence of analogical reasoning?

The point here is simple but consequential: analogical transfers of "ideas", as well as metaphors, are routine features of both scientific and everyday reasoning. They occur as often in the case of "blind alleys", "degenerative problem-shifts", or simple failures to make something work as they do in "innovative" successes. Thus, a theory of innovation which limits itself to an account in terms of conceptual interaction induced by analogical relations must recognise that it is at the same time a *theory of failure and mistake*. It does not discriminate between the differing degrees of success that analogy-based "ideas" encounter in the process of research. Without a due consideration of this process, the fate of "ideas" remains uncertain. I have said that "ideas" based on metaphor or analogical transfer orient research in terms of the resources they mobilise and the investment opportunities they open up. Closure of this process is achieved through the *active constructions* of the laboratory; that is, through negotiation and instrumental fabrication. Innovations, then, are not the beginning, but the *transient and temporary end-product* of this process.

3.7 Conclusion

What conclusions can we draw with respect to the metaphor theory of innovation? We have heard that invoking a metaphor or an analogy mobilises a source-model (Harré) which serves to illuminate a new situation. This is undoubtedly why ancient rhetoric, demagogy and the more general art of persuasion make such systematic use of analogical relations.[17] Yet the invocation of a metaphor or an analogy is not in itself a piece of "scientific innovation". Research products classified as scientific innovations must include a crucial element of construction and success: success in the laboratory, success in its adoption by other scientists, success in convincing others that the product is in fact an "innovation".

The metaphor theory of innovation does not look at the fabrication and negotiation, or the construction and deconstruction which either establishes or demolishes a "scientific innovation". We have said that the metaphor account of innovation must be extended to include analogy in general, but it must also be *restricted* in its claim that it accounts for scientific innovation. Reference to metaphor and analogy tells us something about the sources and consequences of problem shifts, and about the *circulation* and *transformation* of selections in scientific—as well as everyday—practical reasoning. It suggests how scientists come to be intrigued by analogy-based "ideas", qualified as "solutions", and why their research is orientated by the "opportunities" they provide.

But reference to metaphor or analogy tells us nothing about whether the problem shifts will be, in Lakatos' terms,[18] progressive or degenerative; that is, whether they will be viewed as failures, or as innovations. Studies of metaphor and analogy in science are only concerned with those similes and conceptual shifts that have made their way into the literature. But the process of research production and reproduction is more complex than the equation of metaphor and innovation suggests.

Notes

1. See the English translation of Nietzsche's *Über Wahrheit und Lüge im aussermoralischen Sinne* (1973, Vol. 3, Part 2: 374 f.), in Oscar Levy's edition of his works (1964, Vol. 2: 179 f.). See also Walter Kaufmann's 1968 translation of Nietzsche's *Will to Power*.

2. For a summary of the metaphor theory of innovation, see Black (1962) and Schon (1963). For the distinction between metaphor and analogy, see Hesse (1970). See Harré (1978). An overview of recent discussions on the philosophical, cognitive and semantic aspects of metaphor can be found in the "Special Issue on Metaphor", *Critical Inquiry*, 5, (1978). For an implicit critique, see Restivo (1978).

3. The example is cited in Hesse (1970, e.g. 167).

4. In spite of numerous calls for definition, the notion of similarity has been notoriously resistant to precise explication. Defining resemblance between two objects in terms of the number of properties held in common leads to a sorry state in which nearly any two objects could be seen as common members of some broader class. Set theory definitions which hold that all members of a set are more similar to one another than to things outside the set fall prey to Goodman's problem of imperfect community. For example, while all red round things, red wooden things, and round wooden things would meet the definition, we would not want to admit round dinner tables and red rubber balls as members of the same set. For a more extensive discussion of this problem, see Quine (1969, Chapter 5) or Goodman (1966: 163 ff.). According to Quine, similarity classifications are pervasive: the notions of induction, causality, and disposition to react can all be defined in terms of similarity classes. See Quine (1969: 125 ff. and 144 ff.).

5. cf. Hesse (1974, Chapter 1). Hesse approaches the relationship between theory and observation from the

perspective of a logic of resemblance which does not require an ultimate definition of what the primitive resemblance between the properties of two objects is.

6. For a summary of what cognitive psychology has to say in regard to the interaction between theory and data in science, see de Mey (1980).

7. For a general discussion of shifts of meaning, and particularly shifts in the degree of "entrenchment" of terms used in primary recognition in our natural language, see Hesse (1974: 14 ff.). In Hesse's view, similarity is "primitive but at the same time complex since it comes in varying degrees and relates pairs of objects in respect of different property dimensions". See page 67.

8. See Koestler (1969) for a fuller explanation of these ideas.

9. For a discussion of what is involved in seeing something as something, and the need to presuppose an institution of seeing, see Gombrich (1960). In regard to pictorial representation and resemblance, see N. Goodman (1968).

10. The notion of "displacement of concepts" was introduced by Schon and used by Mulkay to refer to the transfer of ideas which comes about when scientists alter their research network. Both Schon and Mulkay identify the notion of displacement of concepts with a metaphoric extension of ideas, although Mulkay's examples, if I understand them correctly, involve literal rather than figurative similarities. This is probably due to Schon's tendency to identify metaphor with analogy in general. See Schon (1963) and Mulkay's work on "Conceptual Displacement and Migration in Science" (1974). For a different example of a conceptual shift, see Krohn (1977).

11. See Cooper (1966: 229).

12. In this sense, Small's classical definition of an interest as an "unsatisfied capacity" seems appropriate (1905: 433).

13. See Callon, Courtial and Turner (1979).

14. cf. Cooper (1966: 230). Albert Wood finds himself in the uneasy situation of having to create an "innovation" he has already announced in public, but not yet worked out. In the book it says: "Albert had two things against him; the first, that he could not lay himself open for something to strike a spark on him—he had got to strike a spark on it; the second, that his obsession could not take its natural course—completion and perfection had got to be reached in a couple of months if not earlier."

15. Disregarding the question of whether any result of scientific research is ever unanimously acknowledged as an "innovation".

16. According to personal communication with members of a group currently (1979) at work in the area who have had second thoughts about the use of the toxic compound mentioned in Chapter 2 in the paragraph about the oscillation of decision criteria. Note that the method of obtaining cell juice mentioned here with respect to the generation of microbial proteins is *not* the same as the one reported in the above paragraph, but a new development dating from 1978/79.

17. I have not considered other elements which add to the popularity of analogy and metaphor in persuasive discourse, e.g. the pictorial element in referring to those things of which one has a concrete mental picture.

18. See I. Lakatos (1970).

Chapter 4

The Scientist as a Socially Situated Reasoner: From Scientific Communities to Transscientific Fields

<table>
<tr><td>Gina:</td><td>Look at the tiny star out there. . . .
For all we know that star disappeared millions of
years ago and it's taken that light, travelling
186,000 miles a second, millions of years to
reach us.</td></tr>
<tr><td>Kleinman:</td><td>You're saying that star may not still be out there?</td></tr>
<tr><td>Gina:</td><td>That's right.</td></tr>
<tr><td>Kleinman:</td><td>Even though I see it with my own eyes?</td></tr>
<tr><td>Gina:</td><td>That's right.</td></tr>
<tr><td>Kleinman:</td><td>That's very scary, because if I see something with my
own eyes, I like to think it's there.
. . .</td></tr>
<tr><td>Gina:</td><td>Kleinman, who knows what's real?</td></tr>
<tr><td>Kleinman:</td><td>What's real is what you can touch with your hands.</td></tr>
<tr><td>Gina:</td><td>Oh? (He kisses her; she responds passionately)
That'll be six dollars, please.</td></tr>
</table>

(Woody Allen, *Death* (A Play))

4.1 The Scientific Community as a Unit of Contextual Organisation

In the Introduction, we said that the selections which mark the constructive operations of the laboratory are contextual ones. In Chapter 2, we illustrated this contextuality by looking at the opportunistic logic of research. And in the previous chapter, we saw how the opportunism of the laboratory ties into analogical reasoning and how it orients the process of construction (along with a corresponding interest-structure on the part of the scientists). The question to occupy us here is how these interests display themselves as socially organised; or, more generally speaking, how the contextual contingency of laboratory selections emerges simultaneously as a social contingency.

Laboratory selections situated in a locally circumscribed space where closure can be reached display themselves simultaneously as situated in a field of social relations. The contextuality observed in the laboratory is constantly traversed and sustained by social relationships which transcend the site of research. What can we say about these relationships from observing scientists at work? To be sure, the contextual organisation of science has attracted much attention in the literature. While the actual site of research has been notoriously neglected in empirical investigations of science, the same cannot be said of more global contextual structures. We have already discussed the idea that organisations function as one of these structures. More relevant here is a conception which has penetrated into virtually every social study of science: the notion that professional membership groups (called scientific communities) are the relevant units of social and cognitive organisation in science.

Most recent perspectives on science operate in terms of some notion of scientific community, even when they dispute other theoretical and methodological orientations and pursue different goals. Thus, studies of citation and communication (emerging in the wake of questions raised by Kuhn), investigations of the "social system" of science, and analyses of the social and cognitive institutionalisation of scientific disciplines all invoke the notion of a scientific community. A key concern of such studies is the identification of scientific communities and their integrating mechanisms.

Citation studies seek to identify scientific communities through patterns of selective referencing found in the scientific literature. Although this assumption has met with scepticism, references are taken to represent relations of intellectual indebtedness.[1] Clusters of such relations form scientific "specialities", "problem domains", "research areas" or "research networks" with which cognitive communities are equated.[2] A similar conception of scientific communities is found in Kuhn (1962), who defines them in terms of shared paradigms, and identifies paradigms with the technical knowledge and traditions a community of scientists holds in common. This circularity has reinforced efforts to identify scientific communities without resorting to the notion of a paradigm, such as through patterns of communication and argumentation, or through problem networks with which social properties are associated.[3]

A different focus is found in those studies which are primarily interested in the social mechanisms that characterise a specialised community. With Hagstrom (1965), for example, this mechanism consists in the non-contractual exchange of information for community-specific rewards, above all for recognition. With Storer (1966), creative products are exchanged, and once again for recognition. A third line of research takes the notion of scientific community to refer to groups of scientists within which patterns of mobility, career, and informal communication can be analysed.[4]

It appears, then, that science is generally held to be organised by means of scientific communities, which can be seen as small social systems with inherent boundaries and internal mechanisms of integration, and which are most frequently circumscribed by a speciality area represented in the scientific literature.[5] Of course, the original merit in Merton's structural-functional sociology of science was to point out the social organisation of science, and it seems that "scientific communities" have remained the locus of this organisation ever since. Certainly, much can be learned from investigating the clusters of scientists which, by whatever means, come to be associated with a speciality area, provided that one asks the proper questions. But are these communities also the units within which scientific action as observed in the laboratory is contextually organised?

Based on a study of communication patterns in a number of research laboratories, Whitley has recently argued that such relatively broad organisational units as specialist communities are largely irrelevant and often unknown to many scientists who work in research institutes.[6] To be sure, some studies of science have replaced the notion of scientific community with other, less "cooperative" conceptions. The sociological notion of community connotes both normative and, more broadly speaking, cultural integration, as well as some form of cooperation and interdependency. The idea of consensus as a mechanism for decision-making among scientists fits well into the image of community life. Even if this image is replaced by a more antagonistic conception (such as Bourdieu's idea of a field), it is still assumed that the respective collectivities consist of scientists in one or more specialities, and that they exist as relevant units of contextual scientific organisation.[7] However, this assumption is not borne out by a venture into the laboratory, and may need to be replaced by an alternative concept.

4.2 Quasi-Economic Models: From Community Gift-Giving to Community Capitalism

Strictly speaking, the problem of the contextual organisation of scientific action has been posed in terms of two distinct questions: the first refers to *units* of organisation, and has generally been answered by the search for scientific communities; the second refers to the *mechanism* of integration which characterises the respective collectivities. Answers to this second question have been dominated by economic analogies ever since the earliest sociological conceptions of science. The movement of these analogies is interesting in itself: the early postulation of relatively isolated economic mechanisms (such as competition) was replaced by the assumption of a pre-capitalist economy, which was then succeeded by strictly capitalist versions of an economy of scientific production.

One of the first to use the idea of quasi-economic competition was Merton himself, whose work is commonly associated with the beginning of a sociology of science. The idea was developed in his study of struggles over the priority of scientific discoveries, and later refined in his work on the Matthew Effect to mean imperfect competition, i.e. that recognition accrues to those who have already established a reputation.[8]

Explicit use of a pre-capitalist economic model is found in Hagstrom (1965), who grounds the normative-functional behaviour of scientists in a mechanism by which creative, scientific achievements are exchanged for a variety of rewards specific to the system. This mechanism of exchange is linked to the idea of gift-giving in a normatively integrated community, rather than to maximising profits in an antagonistic market. The existence of competition does not interfere with the notion of such community life, for it is competition among achievers for the most highly valued achievements. It has nothing to do with the capitalist appropriation of surplus value or scarce resources. Reiterations of the basic ideas of this model can be found in a variety of other authors, the most noted of which is Storer (1966), who turns science into a form of *l'art pour l'art*. Storer combines an archaic economy of exchange with the notion that science is a response to the desire to create, which he grounds in the basic nature of man.

The transition from pre-market exchange to a capitalist market economy of science came ten years later at the hands of Bourdieu (1975a). The scientific field was no longer seen as a community of specialists competing for creative achievement, but as the locus of a competitive struggle for a monopoly on scientific credit. The concept of "credit" must not be confused with the "recognition" advanced in earlier studies. Recognition was defined as a specific form of reward, and referred to the operation of a system which resembled a psychological stimulus-response situation. Rewards like recognition operate as selective mechanisms to reinforce the kind of behaviour by which they are won. Thus, recognition presumably reinforced the truth-seeking, achievement-oriented behaviour considered most essential to the scientific system.

In contrast, credit is defined as a symbolic capital acquired by scientific agents through the imposition of technical definitions and legitimate representations of scientific objects on the field. Such capital is composed at once of scientific competence and social authority, and like monetary capital, can be converted in all kinds of resources necessary for the continuation of scientific production. Most important, it is actively pursued by scientific agents through strategies of domination and monopolisation directed against other relevant producers in the markets formed by scientific fields and disciplines. While recognition operates as a functional sorter to select norm-fulfilling scientific behaviour in an essentially cooperative universe, thus helping the system to maintain itself, Bourdieu's credit or symbolic capital governs the market in an essentially antagonistic universe. And yet it also advances "the progress of reason", at least in the natural sciences. The scientific producers and clients "cross-control" each other and thus promote truth—a suggestion first made by Polanyi and adopted by Bourdieu.

No such assumptions are made by Latour and Woolgar (1979), who propose the notion of *credibility,* rather than credit, to refer to the reproduction of capital. Scientists invest in the fields and topics which promise the greatest return. The credit they gain from producing a surplus of information (the new information) is intended solely for reinvestment, which means that scientists are not interested in truth, nor their subject matter, nor in surplus information *per se.* Nor are they interested in recognition *per se.* What *is* of interest is the acceleration and expansion of the reproductive cycle which produces new and credible information; that is, information for which the costs of raising an objection are as high as possible. Reproduction for the sake of reproduction is the mark of pure, scientific capitalism.[9] Few other versions of a scientific market economy linked to the model proposed by Bourdieu have as yet been developed.[10]

Such economic models of scientific agents have not as yet been pushed to their limits. For example, analyses of the increased role of the state, the partial redistribution of economic surplus, or problems of legitimation and motivation in theories of late capitalism have yet to be incorporated into any model. The inflation of scientific authority, the movement towards a native, "appropriate" technology (as opposed to that associated with basic science), and the expansion of scientific policy suggest that such analyses are by no means irrelevant to a theory of science. But the economic model poses questions which are more general than those regarding the sophistication and elaboration of the analogy.[11]

The first such question is what to make of the analogy itself, crude as it may be. As the theory outlined in the previous chapter suggests, the advantage of a metaphor is that we bring to bear upon a little-known phenomenon the knowledge derived from a better understood yet similar phenomenon. Clearly there is no such advantage in replacing single terms (for example, calling scientific prestige "symbolic capital").

Recent economic models of science have gone to some length to incorporate the mechanisms specified by capitalist interpretations of industrial economies into their picture of science. I have already said that Bourdieu's notion of credit or symbolic capital is not merely a substitute for the notion of recognition found in earlier writings. The idea of a monopolistic market structure found in these models differs substantially from the previously proposed mechanisms for gift-giving or exchange. And the analogies drawn between the accumulation of information and the accumulation of economic capital in their respective market economies do not seem to have much in common with earlier conceptions of scientific progress.

Yet there are essential elements of economic capitalism which seem to be ignored in the market models of science. Most conspicuously neglected, perhaps, is the idea of exploitation and individual appropriation of surplus value, together with its correlates of class structure and alienation. Without an adequate conception of these phenomena, the capitalist model loses its most constitutive mechanisms, and the analogy with science is deprived of its plausibility.

To expound upon this critique, let us consider the question of exploitation in science. We can define exploitation in science as the appropriation of the products created by staff scientists by scientists in superior positions, who then accumulate the symbolic benefits from this work. Clearly, such an interpretation requires us to introduce class distinctions among scientists. More concretely, we would have to distinguish between scientific capitalists and scientific workers in terms of the possession of (symbolic) capital and control over the means of production.

The obvious difficulty here is that the possession of symbolic capital (as operationally defined by some notion of recognition, credit or credibility through publications, citations, educational record, institutional affiliation, or control over relevant social relations) is a common—albeit graded—characteristic of everyone to whom the term "scientist" is usually applied. In order to make a class distinction, we would have to define some *level* of symbolic capital and classify scientists as workers or capitalists in terms of whether their share of symbolic capital fell above or below this level. It is hard to see how such a distinction could be anything less than arbitrary.

A second difficulty is that those who would become symbolic capitalists according to such an arbitrary criterion are not necessarily those who control the means of scientific production, such as equipment or research facilities. In most cases, the means of production are owned not by the scientists, but by non-profit organisations, foundations or associations, which usually means that there is some rule of public or generalised access to them. As we saw in Chapter 2, scientists tend to restrict this access, and try to appropriate control by being in a position to decide when these means of production can be used, and by whom.

The point here is that this sort of hierarchical control over scientific means of production is not necessarily identical to the hierarchy of prestige and recognition, nor any other component of symbolic capital. Among the scientists of the laboratory, excessive attempts to control the means of production were considered to be the last resort of those who had little scientific authority. The same problem exists with respect to the notion of appropriation, since those with scientific authority are not necessarily the ones who appropriate other people's research (for example, by claiming authorship or co-authorship).

Part of the difficulty arises from the fact that "symbolic capital" is a conceptual composite for which we lack not only a clear definition of components, but also the aggregation procedure which specifies their relative weight and substitutability. But a greater difficulty is due to the restricted reference of the capitalist model of science, which raises a second major point of criticism: the capitalist model continues to promote an *internalistic* view of science, despite the more or less explicit rejection of such a view in all its recent uses.

This internalism is no longer due to the once dominant distinction between the social and cognitive elements of scientific undertaking, but to a continuing limitation of the perspective to *scientists* themselves. Scientific communities have turned into markets in which producers and clients alike are colleagues in a speciality or related areas. Normative and functional integration has been replaced by a competitive struggle in the scientific fields with which these markets are identified. Scientists have indeed become capitalists, but they are still treated as though they were isolated in a self-contained, quasi-independent system.

If we fail to define the class differences which distinguish the scientific capitalist from the scientific worker, we end up with communities of petty capitalists who sustain themselves by somehow exploiting—or not exploiting?—each other. In terms of classic economic theories, the existence of such community capitalism would certainly be a curiosity; and even more so in regard to the absence of those who provide the actual resources in which symbolic capital must be converted before it can renew itself. In the capitalist model of science these institutions act like an invisible hand, related to nothing and with no official role in the ongoing community business. Since this invisible hand appears to have a rather decisive influence not only on the distribution of research money, but also in regard to what is researched (i.e., the very business of our capitalists), its hidden nature is all the more surprising.

My last point of criticism refers more specifically to the model of man implied by the economic metaphor. In the crudest version of the economic construct of man, *homo economicus* is a conscious maximiser of profit. He is either assumed to have an insatiable appetite for property, or is thought to accumulate for the sake of accumulation. The two things are not quite the same. In the first case, we seem to be confronted with an implicit assumption about human nature which results in conflict, competition and exploitation. In the second, individual economic behaviour is a consequence of market requirements which are in turn a consequence of well-known historical developments.

More sophisticated versions of economic man not only tend toward the latter interpretation, but also drop the assumption of conscious maximisation. The problems surrounding the idea of maximisation run deeper than those of incomplete information. Decision theory demonstrated long ago that, even within the range of available information, actors do not seem to maximise, but *"satisfice"*; that is, they make do with the first satisfactory solution they come across.[12] The assumption of a *conscious* calculation of returns is also questionable, and has been replaced by the idea of *habitual* selection of a strategy which meets one's general interest. Rationality is no longer a matter of purposeful calculation, but one of habitus formation and socialisation.[13]

Economic models in social studies of science tend to fall short of those amendments which might lead to a more plausible picture of the agents they are talking about.[14] Their strength is in demonstrating the basic identity between science and other parts of social life; between the scientific domain, which has often been exempted from the mechanisms held to rule elsewhere, and the economic domain, which produces and exemplifies some of the most conspicuous of those mechanisms. Their strength is not that they increase the complexity of these mechanisms, nor that of the respective theories. Consequently, economic models in social studies of science tend to promote an understanding of scientific agents which returns to the classical *homo economicus,* and thus provokes the same kind of debates which have characterised economic theory for some time.[15]

To be sure, economic models of science have consistently defined their goals in terms of explaining the (social) system of science rather than accounting for the behaviour of individual scientists. Yet to describe a system in terms of accumulation of capital or competition and monopolisation requires that we assume a corresponding individual behaviour, or specify some mechanism to explain why the description of the system does not hold similar implications in regard to the units (the scientists) which constitute it. Lacking such a specification, we must assume that scientific community capitalism comes about through the petty but pertinent entrepreneurship of individual scientists; that is through their conscious or habitual interest in the accumulation of symbolic profit, or in the renewal and acceleration of the cycle of capital. And we would have to assume that practical scientific decisions reflect this interest in the sense that relevant choices are actually made in terms of the accumulation and utilisation of capital.

4.3 The Scientist as an Economic Reasoner, or "Who are the Entrepreneurs?"

When we look at the laboratory, we find that at least part of the reasoning which relates to the scientists' practical decisions does incorporate economic notions, and this sort of scientific discourse has undoubtedly lent plausibility to the model of the scientist as (yet another) economic man. Thus, any criticism of a model which implies a petty community capitalism must decide what to make of the economic reasoning found in the everday discourses of scientists.

Scientists talk about their "investments" in an area of research, or an experiment. They are aware of the "risks", "costs" and "returns" connected with their efforts, and talk about "selling" their results to particular journals and foundations. They seem to know which products are in high "demand", and the areas in which there is nothing to "gain". They want to put hot "products" on the "market" as quickly as possible and "earn credit" for them. Does this language reflect an intrusion of economic—more specifically, capitalist—mechanisms into a previously non-economic domain? Did these mechanisms develop from a pre-capitalist exchange of gifts into capitalist competition and monopolisation between 1965 and 1975; that is, between Hagstrom's proposal and those of Bourdieu and his followers some ten years later? Or do we have here a phenomenon for which alternative and equally plausible interpretations are available?

It seems to me that there are at least two distinctive forms of economic reasoning used in the context of laboratory work. Economic notions are frequently employed when scientists talk *about* their research strategies, when they *reflect upon* the way research decisions are made. Let us recall the biochemist who talked about his discovery that cholesterol is present in plants as well as animals. In the course of his story, I had asked how he had decided to pursue this "idea". He responded with a series of reflections about how successful scientists make such decisions. I repeat two of his points:

> "*We always calculate our risks, even though we don't know how to calculate.* It's just a feel, you know, and I am very good at this by now. Through many years of experience, I can more or less tell what I should drop and what I should pick up on. I think this is a problem with a lot of unsuccessful scientists—they are not dumb, they just work on the wrong things. . . .
>
> Another thing is that, if you are up against terrific competition, there is no sense in struggling. *So by now I can gauge these success factors,* and my own secret of success is that *I work on things that aren't too unlikely to work out . . .*" (9-29/4, emphasis added).

We heard a similar line of argument from a chemist who recalled the development of paper-chromatography as an "obviously good thing". When I asked him what he thought a successful idea was, and how he selected them, he said:

> "You try to discriminate. You can get one idea a day, or . . . (in) two days, or one
> a week, and you discriminate (in terms of) your time and your ability to use it.
> You know, we have idea files, either in our minds or on paper, but you can't
> spend a lot of your time on things you don't have the opportunity to perform, or
> to prove, or to verify. *So you try to limit your interest to the idea you know is go-*
> *ing to be most productive as quickly as possible within the frame of facilities at*
> *hand*" (9-27/9, emphasis added).

When I asked one of the chemist's colleagues if he kept his ideas in stock too, I received
a similar reply:

> Question: "You have always more ideas than you have time to work on?"
> Answer: "Yes, yes, and I try to select those things which are feasible
>   under the circumstances. In other words, I have to gauge how
>   much time I have, what sort of facilities are available, what the
>   competition is doing. All this is not done by mathematical
>   calculation, but just *(by) weighing, you know, the probabilities*
>   *of success*" (8-29/5, emphasis added).

The important element in these quotes is not that scientists claim to calculate the
risks and returns of their work, or to discriminate between ideas according to some
criterion of productivity, but that they *describe* their ways of *decision-making* in such
terms, thereby displaying themselves as rational according to common sense standards.
To calculate outcomes, weigh alternatives, and make selections according to some
prior calculation of consequences is part of reasoned choice—the sort of rationality
that characterises decision-making in general. Given the frequent blend of rational and
economic discourse, notions commonly associated with economics frequently appear
when questions of selectivity are at stake. Note that scientists refer to the concrete
circumstances under which decisions are made (in accord with an opportunistic logic of
research), and that they refer to them in terms of success rather than truth.

There is, however, a more implicit form of economic reasoning, examples of which
are found in the following quotations. One scientist, after discussing an experiment
required by the effort to eliminate a toxic compound from proteins, summed up the
conclusion he and his colleague had reached:

> "I am interested in the problem, but the experiments are too simple. . . . It's work
> for a technician or a laboratory assistant. It does not challenge me, nor for that
> reason Holzman" (3-20/3).

A second piece of talk refers to publication strategies. A scientist became embroiled
in an argument with his superior over the choice of a rather general journal in which to
publish a paper they had written together. The junior partner defended his choice by
saying that the paper itself was too broadly focused. When I asked why he had taken
such a general approach in the first place, he said:

> "The reason is . . . if I don't do it now and Alix publishes the stuff later, after
> I've left the laboratory she will be senior author, because her laboratory assistant
> has done part of the work. If I select the material on this protein and publish a
> paper on its functional properties now, *I* will be (named) first, because I did most

of this work myself. So I will do this and put the rest (of the material on other proteins on which the technican had worked) in another article'' (8-24/4).

A third example comes from a scientist's comments following a lecture on the use of a new electron microscope the institute had purchased. The scientist felt that the new microscope was "much more expensive and interesting" than the one available to his own group; but he said he had to use the less desirable instrument because it, too, had just been acquired, and the expenditure had to be justified. Still, the new one "really interested" him, and he went on to explain the laser mechanism on which it was based and how he could perhaps use it to examine the particle structure of the proteins he was investigating. The microscope, he said, was "very expensive and interesting in its applications"—so much so that he later attempted to arrange for a cooperative effort with the scientist in charge of it (2-2/1).

Finally, let us look at the following entries in my notes. In describing an experiment on the stability of a particular functional property of proteins, one entry runs:

"There is a new aspect. Koenig has worked a lot on functional properties, and this (*the property on which the experiments were done*) is one. R. says he always wanted to get into functional properties to a larger degree. Koenig has this position opening at C. for which R. applied."

Shortly afterwards, we read:

"R. mentions that he looks forward to writing the functional property paper. He wants to start next week. The reason is that he could give it to Koenig when he meets him at the June congress" (4-18, 28/2).

A final example illustrates a similar point. Walter too had applied for a position at a university department, and had been invited to present a lecture to the department. He said he would emphasise his competence and "professional quality" in the two areas of interest, and make clear the significance of the problems he was working on. In particular he said he would

"focus on my future interests. . . . There is a famous MIT study on protein resources and needs. Two million dollars are projected until 1985 . . . (I) want to show that of the 14 research needs I work on 5 . . . in order to make clear to them that I work on the hot issues and that not only do I know something, but I might be able to get them money . . ." (7-25/3).

In the most general sense, the economy implicit in these bits of conversation lies in their concern with value. Whether the subject is experiments too simple to warrant a scientist's work, or publishing a paper as senior rather than junior author, or using a highly expensive (and hence scarce) instrument in place of a more usual one, or the application for a position, the concern is with maintaining, increasing or displaying value. Needless to say, there are many more examples which could be cited here.

A concern with *names* figures prominently in this respect, and debates about the best names with which to associate oneself pervade the laboratory. The name of a famous co-author, a prestigious journal or a well-received publishing company weighs heavily in scientific calculations of value, as does the name of a respected university or department head. In fact, the question of who a scientist *is* seems literally answered in the curriculum vitae by a string of names: universities attended (and degrees received), institutions in which positions were held, association memberships, fellowships awarded, etc. Of course, names are associated with reputation, or origin, descendance, and the value which accrues through inheritance.

It is important to note that what is at stake in such scientific calculations is not the value of some product, but the value of the scientist themselves. The string of names we find in *curricula vitae* provides an updated balance sheet for a scientist, not a product. The quality at issue in choosing an experiment, a piece of apparatus or a lecture topic is the quality of the scientist. And the success to which scientists most often refer is their own. If we want to use the economic metaphor, we can say that scientists' concern with their own investments and returns, with the risks and productivity of a line of research, with opportunities, or the interest of results, does indeed refer us to a market. But it is a market of positions where the commodity is scientists, and not a market for the products of free—or semi-free—entrepreneurs.

Scientists say of themselves:[16]

> "I went into *this business* with the idea of disproving hidden variables once and for all" (emphasis added).

and turn out to mean

> "*I was looking for a postdoc position, or someplace to go* when I finished my (Ph.D.) thesis in astrophysics, and I wanted to do something in the foundations of quantum mechanics, although I really did not have anything in mind until I read about . . ." (emphasis added).

In more traditional terms, we would say that the scientists' economic reasoning displays a concern with *career*. To be sure, there is no shortage of comments in which scientists directly address this issue:

> "We were good friends, he's much older than I, but *we had both more or less staked our careers on this.* I had staked my career on my ability to predict the response of the instrument, that the instrument would work and be sensitive in the way I said it, and he in spending his major, almost his entire efforts in building the equipment" (emphasis added).

But the point here is not to advocate a return to the concept of career, although it may well account for the very same aspects of scientific behaviour as the metaphor of symbolic capitalism. What does matter is to exchange the picture of the scientist-entrepreneur in a capitalist community of specialists for one which recognises the basic dependencies of scientific work that lead us beyond these communities. If we do not take these dependencies into account, we will find it difficult to interpret such well-known phenomena as the structural unemployment of scientists in the United States and other countries, or the increasing unionisation of scientists. Who are the entrepreneurs in a system in which a scientist's ability to work, including the ability to raise money, may depend on decisions made at top organisational levels?

Consider the following example of a biochemist (Holzman) who told me about his shifting position in moving from one organisation to another:

> "At the National Institute of Health, I was under a guy who is in the same position I am today. In other words, I was at the lowest level and he was between me

and the top echelons. So he trusted me, and he appreciated my work and he fur-
thered it, and that's what is important. But people above him hardly knew what I
was doing. The second one in Cal-Tech. There, the person who was directly
above me, the professor, had confidence in me, and a certain amount of admira-
tion. He gave me a completely free hand. When I came here, it was just the opposite. I was dumbfounded. You know, I was regarded with suspicion, and, uh,
they cut off my funds, my equipment, *I was all by myself. It was just like being in
gaol . . .*'' (9-29/5, emphasis added).

Or the following example, which concerns Holzman's move from the California Institute of Technology to the institute in Berkeley at which the observations were conducted:

''. . . the money gave out, and maybe (the director's) predecessor was hostile, or
developed a hostility, and they just said, 'That's it.' *One day they came into the
lab and said 'You are ready to pack up, aren't you?* Come up to Berkeley.' I said,
'Why, what happened?', and they just decided one day they couldn't afford my
staying at Cal-Tech. So it was an organisational decision. Maybe they actually
were strapped for money'' (9-29/6, emphasis added).

Incidentally, a change for the better in a scientist's life does not change the underlying
dependency of scientific work. For example, Holzman described the effects of his
''sudden recognition'':

''I was greatly surprised yesterday. I had a meeting with M. (the director) and the
man has completely changed his ideas. I told him yesterday more or less what I
told him when I first started here, and whereas at our first meeting he was full of
contempt for all the stuff that I proposed, yesterday he was willing to listen. He
encouraged me; he even suggested that I drop some stuff that I am doing that is
more or less applied and that, in my opinion, is not worth doing.''

He offered the following explanation for the change:

''Well, he (the director) underwent a personality change (*laughing*). Maybe the
ARS and the government in general have undergone a character change, the
government is shaken up'' (9-29/6).

What the change actually reflects is an increase in the interest of his work for those who
support it, and consequently control his ability to work.

4.4. The Labour Interpretation

One interpretation which begins with the assumption of a direct dependency of scientists on institutions other than science takes as its basic analytic premise the notion that
scientific work is wage-dependent labour, like any other kind. Despite the emphasis on
this basic equivalence, the special problems linked to specifically scientific labour have
not gone unnoticed within the respective approaches.[17] These problems relate to the
relatively privileged position held by scientists, compared to factory workers, with
regard to the amount of money earned, the relative autonomy at work, or the degree of
social authority conceded to them. They also relate to the fact that scientists in non-
industrial organisations do, as a rule, ''own'' the products of their work, in the sense

that their names are associated with them, and they may collect substantial benefits from their authorship. Such benefits are not only symbolic, but financial as well, as in the case of royalties for books and patents, or outside consulting contracts. Undoubtedly it is these aspects of scientific work which lend a certain plausibility to the model of the scientist-entrepreneur.

In approaches which consider the wage-dependent character of scientific work as essential to the analysis, these variant aspects of scientific work have been related to the difference between *manual and intellectual labour,*[18] and to general discussions of the role and socio-economic function of intellectuals in industrial society.[19] At least three distinctive positions can be distinguished in such discussions.

According to the first position, the socio-economic function of research is to promote the interests of capital-utilisation through improving the efficiency of the technical and organisational means of production, and through product development.[20] Thus, the affiliation of science is with the owners of capital, and not with the other members of society. As a result of this affiliation, scientists enjoy certain privileges, including high income and prestige. Since scientists may profit only from the difference between manual and intellectual labour, the disjunction between the two becomes an absolute quality reflected in scientistic "ideologies", according to which scientific progress—rather than the interests of capital utilisation—determine scientific production. Note that with this position, a scientist's "symbolic profits" are associated with a specific function of science in economic production, and the affiliation of scientists with industry.

A second position leads to a less pessimistic prognosis in regard to the "social" character of science by reversing the previous interpretation given to the wage-dependent character of scientific work. The instrumentalisation of science by industry is taken to indicate the *limited* influence of all wage-dependent labour (scientists included) on what is produced and how it is produced. If scientific innovations can be used to produce surplus value and accumulate profit, so can all other kinds of labour. All labour produces not only use values for production and consumption, but also the means of continued capital utilisation. Scientists may have privileged working conditions, but they share the unpleasant consequences of technical development with other workers, and contribute through their own work to the increasing social organisation of scientific work. Progressive division of labour, collective or institutional authorship, and devaluation of scientific labour through increasing numbers of university graduates are held to indicate that the gap between the working conditions of scientists and those of skilled or unskilled workers is closing. Scientists in privileged positions may not be conscious of the basic identity of all wage-dependent labour but their attitude may shift as conditions change. Moreover, in light of their special qualifications, scientists are often expected to take a leading role in the articulation and organisation of labour interests.[21]

A third opinion links scientists with neither workers in general nor the owners of capital, but with a new middle class whose social position is as ambivalent as that of the old middle class made up from small shop owners or tradesmen. Note that the position of scientists is not equated with that of trades or crafts, as in the models of pre-capitalist exchange proposed by social studies of science. The wage-dependent character of scientific work remains central to the nature of this new middle class, as with the two previous conceptions. The literature on scientific professionals in organisations, and most of the work on the question of the status and function of intellectuals in relation to power and the modern state, fall in this category.[22]

In sum, we might say that the three conceptions presented here associate scientists with the working class, a new middle class, or the owners of capital, depending on the significance they attribute to the various privileges scientists enjoy, and their evaluation of the consequences of those privileges. If these privileges are seen as the reward for selling one's soul to capital, then scientists will be associated with the owners of the means of production. If privileges are seen as diminishing and limited to a minority of scientists in academic research, then scientists are classified with other wage-dependent labour. If privileges are held to constitute a specific consciousness and class behaviour, then scientists are most likely to be associated with a new middle class, or in non-Marxist terms, with "intellectuals" or "professionals".

What social studies of science add to this picture is the *organisation* of privileges in terms of the exchange of scientific products for recognition, or in terms of markets for symbolic capital, credit or credibility. Yet they have done so at the expense of having to equate scientists with pre-capitalist or capitalist entrepreneurs operating in entrepreneurial peer communities; that is, they have neglected the basic dependencies of scientific work. The capitalistic or pre-capitalistic markets for the exchange of scientific products constituted by peers are not independent of the markets for scientific labour or of financing research, as seems to be suggested by the respective studies of speciality communities. Nor is this market for symbolic capital unequivocally dependent, in the sense that being able to sell one's products successfully to community peers is the one and only criterion for getting a position, advancing a career, or gaining financial support.

The assumption that a career in science is made by accumulating credits for one's scientific achievements and then converting those credits into positions and resources could lead us back to Kingsley Davis' famous theory of social stratification, in which those who achieve best earn the better positions in a society. Present economistic models of science tend to be more subtle than this functionalist interpretation of social stratification by pointing to the mechanisms of power and dominance inherent in scientific undertakings.

Yet, by limiting their perspective to scientific communities, the operation of such mechanisms remains isolated from the areas in which the dependencies of scientific work and of its products are negotiated and reproduced, for example from the areas in which the labour is funded and its results utilised. To be sure, the labour interpretation of scientific work has taken this dependency as a starting point of its own analysis of science. But given its restricted definition of this dependency, and its predominant interest in scientific class affiliations, the labour interpretation adds little to an analysis of concrete scientific work.

More important, by distinguishing between manual and intellectual labour, this interpretation of science has built into its approach the same kind of decontextualisation found in the naturalistic cast of science. Intellectual labour has become equated with abstract, quantitative thinking whose historical origin lies in the abstractness of economic commodity exchange. For Sohn-Rethel, commodity exchange is abstract because it excludes use during the time of the transaction. This abstractness imposes itself upon a people's mode of thinking when exchange relations are mediated by coined money. The commodities exchanged "describe a pure linear movement through abstract—that is empty, continuous, and homogeneous—space and time as abstract substances which thereby suffer no material change and which are capable of none but quantitative differentiation''.

The affinity between this description and the Galilean concept of inertial motion is taken as proof of the thesis that the basic concepts of natural science (such as time and space, matter, movement and quantity) derive from physical activities of exchange which preceded science. Science emerges from such an analysis as social by origin and descent, and as abstract and theoretical through the postulated character of intellectual labour. The hallmark of intellectual labour is abstract, quantitative thinking and, its origin aside, is once more exempted from situated social production.[23]

4.5 Variable Transscientific Fields

In contrast to an approach which seeks the social constitution of scientific work in its historical descent, I wish to locate it in the ongoing presence of scientific production. In contrast to any interpretation which identifies scientific production with a theoretical (abstract) activity oriented toward describing a world, I have proposed that we consider scientific products as, first and foremost, the result of a process of construction. In Chapter 1, this process was characterised as one which involves a series of necessary selections; or, phrased differently, as a process marked by the selectivity it incorporates. Scientific work was said to consist of the continued thematisation of this selectivity, which means that the selections realised in previous scientific work become both topic and resource for further scientific investigation. We have also seen that selections can only be made on the basis of other selections; that is, they require translation into further selections.

The question of the contextuality of scientific reason involves the way in which the selectivity of scientific construction is contextually organised. It asks where we should locate the constraints into which the laboratory selections translate, and how we should specify the relationships which nourish those constraints. It wants to know who has a part in the ongoing play of laboratory construction, even if the part is not played at the predominant site of scientific action. In a sense, it wants to determine the locus of scientific production beyond the concrete site of production.

From the point of view of radical situationalism, the question itself may appear absurd. What, it might ask, is there to observe beyond a series of concrete, interconnected situations monitored as such by the actors themselves? The answer is that, while there may not be anythng else to observe, there is something else to take into account. The scientists' laboratory selections constantly refer us to a contextuality beyond the immediate site of action.

How does this contextuality manifest itself to the observer? We hear a scientist pleading to the director over the phone, asking that a certain instrument be bought immediately. We watch a group writing a grant proposal, and hear that the research leader will meet with ''the relevant person in Washington''. We listen to the report of that meeting, and see the proposal modified. We watch a scientist sending samples to an industry-sponsored laboratory which has contracted certain experiments, and read the correspondence within which this contract is realised. We see a scientist write to the head of a search committee in regard to a position, and see him invited to give a lecture on his research. Above all, we hear the scientists reason about matters at stake for them, and about the people involved in those stakes, and notice that it refers us not only beyond the immediate site of action, but beyond the speciality area and the community of scientists identified with it.

I assume that it will be considered obvious that laboratory reasoning constantly refers us beyond the site of laboratory action. It will probably be conceded as well that this reasoning takes us beyond the specialty under which a scientist—or a piece of research—come to be classified. Suppose, then, that we draw the conclusion that the relevant contextual organisation of laboratory production is not the scientific community, but variable, transscientific fields which in principle transcend the speciality networks of social studies of science? Presumably, we have now trespassed the bounds of accord. But if we do not draw this conclusion, we have to introduce a partition into the scientists' reasoning, lumping certain references to scientists who are community colleagues on one side, and putting everyone else on the other. The problem is how to justify such a distinction in the laboratory, given the mix of persons and arguments which do not fall naturally into such classes.

When the group's research leader returned from Washington, the scientists not only changed the title of the grant proposal that had occasioned her visit, but also rewrote a substantial part of its content. When a scientist applied for a university position, he realigned his research (including the use of certain methods), to match the orientation of the appropriate department head. When a representative of industry did not respond enthusiastically to a scientist's results, he began to pursue alternative procedures. In each of these cases, an external contact—a negotiation about money or a career strategy—had immediate technical repercussions.

Just as there is no reason to believe that the interactions between members of a speciality group are purely "cognitive", there is no reason to believe that the interaction between these community members and other scientists (*or* non-scientists, as defined by institutional role) are limited to money-transfers, credit-negotiations and other exchanges called "social" by scientists or sociologists. If we cannot assume that the "technical" selections of the laboratory are exclusively determined by a scientist's speciality membership group, it makes no sense to postulate the respective communities as the relevant contextures of knowledge production. And it makes no sense to exclude without further consideration anybody who does not qualify as a member of the community in question.

If a partition between references made to the speciality group and those made to others cannot be reconciled with the scientific reasoning relevant to laboratory selections, then what does this reasoning refer us to? The argument here is that the discourse into which the selections of the laboratory are fitted points to *variable transscientific fields*; that is, it refers us to networks of symbolic relationships which in principle go beyond the boundaries of a scientific community or scientific field, however broadly defined.[24]

The crucial point is that a variable transscientific field is not primarily determined by characteristics held in common by its members, as in the case of a logical class. In addition to the scientist in the laboratory, it may include the provost of the university, the research institute's administrative staff, functionaries of the National Science Foundation, government officials, members or representatives of industry, and the managing editor of a publishing house.[25] For the most part, it will include other scientists, from areas different from and identical to the one in which the laboratory production proceeds.

The argument here is not that a transscientific field is non-scientific, in the sense that it excludes colleagues in the same speciality area. Instead, the claim is that if we are interested in the concrete reasoning of scientists as it relates to laboratory selections, we cannot start by making shared membership-characteristics the criterion for the contextual organisation we admit. The networks I encountered in the laboratory were hybrids in respect to membership characteristics, at once smaller and larger than the speciality groups determined from citation clusters. For the most part, they seemed to comprise no more than a few agents with or against whom the scientists proceeded in the laboratory.

But when a certain expansiveness prompted them to pursue an issue beyond its usual limits, the scientists could weave a more extended fabric of relationships from their references to these agents. By piecing many of these interchanges together, the social scientist can arrive at an impression of what I have called variable transscientific fields. These fields not only criss-cross the borders of a speciality group, but also shrink and expand in response to the issues at stake.[26] Let us now look at the symbolic relationships which characterise these fields.

4.6 Resource-Relationships

What are these symbolic relationships that we have said characterise a transscientific field? On the most general level, transscientific fields appear to be the locus of a perceived struggle for the imposition, expansion and monopolisation of what are best called *resource-relationships*. Resource-relationships are at stake, for example, when a position is to be filled by a scientist, when money is to be distributed among scientists or groups of researchers, when a speaker is to be chosen for a scientific lecture, or when a result produced by a scientist is incorporated into the research of others. The respective decisions usually relate to the value of the prospective resource (whether a candidate or a candidate's work) in the ongoing games of those who make the selection.

When an academic position is filled, for example, consideration will be given to the candidate's potential for teaching and grant-raising, to affiliation with relevant groups or institutes, to interest in local activities (including sports and committee work), or, I have been told, to the standing and position of the candidate's spouse. As we know, curricula summarise a candidate's value in regard to some of the dimensions involved in these decisions. In terms of the economic model referred to earlier in this chapter, it is the value of the commodity scientist which is at stake in such decisions.

For the academic institution, this value may depend on the degree to which a candidate attracts student- and research money, or contributes to the reputation of a department. In the terms chosen here, it depends on the degree to which a scientist promises to be and proves to be a *resource* which can be converted into other resources relevant to the institution. For the foundation which awards a research grant, this resource-value of a scientist or research group may depend on the degree to which they can be trusted to engage in warrantable and publicly displayable research; that is, the degree to which they can be trusted to produce, within an acceptable period of time, credible results that can be published and publicised as relevant and important.

The crucial point about resource-relationships is that they do not presuppose an *a priori* delimitation of the universe to which they apply. To speak of *trans*scientific fields constituted by *resource-relationships* is to say that these relationships are basically the same, whether they establish a link between scientists of the same speciality group, or between scientists and non-scientists, according to role and institutional affiliation. According to most conceptions, what is at stake in a speciality field is that others accept and recognise a scientist's work through citation and subsequent incorporation of the results proposed. This is the context of acceptance referred to as consensus-formation, and variously described as a form of rational evaluation or the more social process of public opinion formation.

But what is at stake in the present formulation is the establishment and expansion of resource-relationships as manifest, for example (but not exclusively), in the imposition of one's own work as a resource to be used in the subsequent work of others. Consequently, the subsequent use of a result in the literature should depend on the degree to which it is perceived—or has succeeded in becoming perceived—as a resource in the ongoing research of other scientists. What we are dealing with, I argued, is not a detached process of opinion formation, but the involved perception and mobilisation of resources in a process of research production and reproduction.

Case studies in progress on the recent acceptance of the "charm model" in place of the "colour" explanation of certain elementary particles in high energy physics demonstrate that the charm model succeeded by proving to respective scientists that its use could "enrich" their approach and generate "new soluble puzzles". The opposing colour explanation could not offer this potential.[27] The charm model proved to be "of interest" to other scientists because of its perceived *unrealised capacities,* or because it inserted itself as a new *resource* in the fabric of research production in the field.

In the previous chapter, I argued that what characterised an "idea" as "interesting" to a scientist was its value as an unrealised capacity and solution, or as an opportunity for success. In other words, it was their character as a *resource* to which the scientists responded, and which prompted them to take over, adopt and adapt in their own research the results which had been proposed or exemplified by others. In the genealogy of different approaches to protein generation previously outlined, each development, from the response to phosphoric acid to microbial proteins to engineering the properties of the protein molecule, can be seen in this light.

The emphasis placed on resource-relationships does not contradict the long-standing thesis, found it citation-studies and other areas of the sociology of science, that what leads a scientist to use a result in the literature is its "usefulness". However, it does link this "usefulness" to the resource-character of a work *for* particular agents *in* the process of laboratory production, rather than to some sort of abstract, independent evaluation. The laboratory process of production exposes such distinctions as that between discovery and validation or justification as not only practically irrelevant, but analytically false, as implied before.

But let us now look at another kind of resource-relationship which links scientists from overlapping speciality areas. The story of a post-doctoral researcher from India serves as an example. Roy felt that he was being "used" by the head of the laboratory. The continuation of his visa and his one-year contracts depended on this man. In 1977 and 1978, he was paid less that $10,000 a year, on which he had to support a family. He actually wrote the journal reviews which the head of the laboratory signed, and he said it was his "ideas" and information that resulted in "innovative" research. Needless to say, he conducted all the research in a project and supervised the students and technicians in the lab, occasionally informing the head of the laboratory of his progress. While he was a co-author of papers published from his research, the decisions about what was published when and where were made by the head of the laboratory. His name did not appear on the patents to which the research gave rise, and presentations of his work were made by the head of the laboratory.

Within the capitalist model of the scientific community introduced earlier, he would represent the class of the scientist-worker exploited by the scientist-capitalist who controlled the laboratory research enterprise, monopolised access to resources, and disposed of the means of production. But while this model fits the first part of the story perfectly, it is hard to see how it would incorporate the other side of the coin. For Roy said that while the head of the laboratory was using him, he was using the head of the laboratory. Roy had decided to come to the United States after finishing his education because it would enable him to get a high-paying, high-prestige position at a university or research institute in his own country. He had chosen a highly regarded laboratory because this would enhance his own qualifications, as would a letter of recommendation from an esteemed head of a laboratory. He used the head of the laboratory to get access to journals, research money and "hot" topics of research which he felt would otherwise be denied to him. If, on the other hand, he decided to stay in the United States, he could use all of this accrued credit to fully establish himself in the networks which controlled the area. In sum, he suggested that he used the head of the laboratory (and the resources he controlled) in a carefully orchestrated career strategy, just as the head of the laboratory used him as a resource for intelligent and innovative research.

We cannot discredit our post-doc's interpretation of the situation as part of the false consciousness of members of a working class which is exploited without realising it. Unlike factory workers, American post-docs (and their equivalents in other countries) regularly advance to higher positions in the hierarchy, even if they don't win the Nobel prize. Roy, for example, stood a good chance of heading a large scientific institute in India if he succeeded in the power game he played. His sense of the situation could hardly be described as out of touch with reality, and certainly it was not out of touch with what he saw as the normal career pattern among his older colleagues.

He described his relationship with the head of the laboratory as a perfectly symmetrical, albeit unbalanced, "contract" for a limited period of time in which what mattered was to "strike a balance" between the personal interests of the two parties involved. He knew that he needed the head of the laboratory and was "kept dependent"; but he also knew that the head of the laboratory depended on his "cleverness" at work, his willingness to come up with "ideas" and "solutions", and his ability "to run" the research-work.

In the terms used to characterise the more general case of scientists working in the same area, the post-doc had already *imposed* himself as a resource needed by the head of the laboratory. What was at stake for the post-doc now was to *monitor* this resource-relationship so that the balance would be favourable, or at least not negative. If we ignore the sense of symmetry in this resource-relationship, we also ignore the *microphysics* (Foucault) of power found in the production of knowledge, and may well find ourselves out of touch with the reality of this production.

4.7 Resource-Relationships: Ultrafragile and Grounded in Conflict

As suggested by the variety of examples in the previous section, resource-relationships can be mediated by a variety of "resources", of which control over laboratory production is but one. Obviously, more than one kind of resource is involved in nearly every case. Moreover, it is clear that in practice these resources are not perceived or responded to as independent entities.

Unlike a relationship in which discrete products are exchanged at a specified value at a given time, resource-relationships are dominated by what could happen in the future and by what has not happened in the past, by resources which are hidden or hold implications for others, by promises and expectancies rather than a concrete flow of goods. More specifically, the resource-character of the symbolic relations relevant here is a *continuous and generally reciprocal accomplishment* in at least three senses.

First, the respective symbolic relations are a continuous accomplishment in the sense that what *counts* as a resource is itself at stake. A reciprocal definition of something as a "resource" is not stable, but a *stabilisation*. It can become more permanently stabilised through processes of institutionalisation and routinisation, but it must continually be sustained by practices which endorse this definition. For example, the institutionalisation of formal criteria (such as citation rates) to gauge a scientist's value as a resource do not prevent negotiations in regard to meaning and relevance when an academic position is at stake. Resources assume a specific meaning only in terms of the personal games played by those involved in the relationships. Like rules (see Chapter 2), what counts as a resource can be reinterpreted, ignored or transformed, depending on the particular game.

The issue of stabilisation leads to the second sense of continuous accomplishment, which is that resource-relationships must be *renewed* in order to survive. In its most vulgar version, this phenomenon can be seen in the disproportionate amount of effort which some research groups put into getting their grants and research projects renewed. Or when the main concern of researchers employed under one-year contracts is to fulfil or surpass the requirements for renewal of that contract. Subtler versions involve the renewal of a scientist's reputation in terms of the degree to which their work is perceived as a resource.

A third sense of continuous accomplishment refers to the scientists' active engagement in *building, solidifying* and *expanding* resource-relationships. Scientists in the laboratory are interested in establishing their own resource-value within the concrete network of relationships in which their research is embedded, but they are also interested in the network itself. This interest is displayed by cultivating relationships with persons deemed important, by transforming one's position in the network, or by associating in various ways with those people found to be "of interest".

Finally, let me point out again that resource-relationships seem to be *reciprocal* accomplishments, even though they may appear to be unbalanced (as when one party feels heavily dependent on the resources provided by another). Take, for example, the biochemist who had transferred from the California Institute of Technology to the research centre, where he complained that he and his work were "regarded with suspicion" for several years before finally being recognised by the director. The institute had cut off his funds, left him "all by himself" and made him feel as though he were "in gaol". Unlike the post-doc, the biochemist did not succeed in establishing himself as a resource. Recognition arrived only when the director became "interested" in the potential of his work as a result of more general changes in the centre's research policy.

It may be tempting—but incorrect—to view resource-relationships as marked by a lack of conflict and a state of cooperation. To be sure, they involve cooperation, but not the sort from which conflict is excluded. The resource-relationships which emerge from scientific reasoning are not related to some *shared* interests on the part of the agents, but come about as the result of a negotiated *fusion*[28] of interests from which conflict is not excluded. In the case of the relationship between the post-doc and the head of his laboratory, conflict lurked behind the fragile balance achieved by interest-fusion, and surfaced whenever this balance broke down temporarily. Oscillations between conflict and cooperation, between the fission and fusion of interests, are routine correlates of the moves agents make in the hidden process[29] of negotiation which characterises resource-relationships.

Indeed, there would be no need for negotiation were it not for the agents' perception of discrepant and conflicting interests. For example, resource-relationships often link competitors in an area, thus creating a major source of latent conflict in any necessary cooperation. Less complex cases of competition are those in which a resource relationship is up for grabs among agents with competing interests, as when a position or research grant is to be allocated. Well-known strategies in such a case are the devaluation or appropriation of the competitor's resources and the promotion of one's own.

The most striking example of this is perhaps found in what the scientists called "the art of writing a grant proposal", which requires the ability to manoeuvre between two contradicting requirements—that of being as concrete, substantial and precise as possible, and that of saying as little as possible about the proposed investigations. According to the scientists, the need for the first arises from a surplus of proposals in relation to a diminishing supply of grants, and the second from the need to protect one's ideas from peer reviewers, who could well be the most dangerous competitors in the area. Holding back a grant proposal for several months before accepting or rejecting it gives a competitor a significant advance in time, particularly if the proposal provides a significant hint about the direction of the research in question. Since there are often only two or three "strong" groups working on a given topic, such fears are by no means unwarranted (especially since the competitors are the ones most likely to conduct the review).

It might be noted that legitimation can also be associated with the need to renew and reinforce resource-relationships. For example, current allegations of a crisis in the legitimation of science[30] suggest that it is no longer taken for granted as a social resource, and may even be held accountable for alleged contributions to world problems. Needless to say, thematisations of the legitimacy and the resource-character of resource-relationships are not only a sign of their inherent instability, but also a source of conflict within and around such relationships. To speak of a correspondence between resource-relationships and a temporary, negotiated *fusion* of efforts in need of stabilisation underlines the potentially "explosive" character of a cooperation we *cannot* assume to be based on shared values, interests or thematisations. It *emphasises* rather than neglects or denies, conflict, and locates it within, as well as around, the relationships we have been talking about.

4.8 The Transscientific Connection of Research

My thesis is that the contextures we have characterised in terms of resource-relationships are important because they relate to the process of research production. Therefore, we must ask *how* they relate to this process of production, or *how* we might conceive of this relation in somewhat more precise terms. Note that what we have here is a reformulation of the traditional question concerning the relationship between "internal" and "external" factors in science, this time based on the observation that the contextures invoked in the scientists' practical laboratory reasoning are in principle neither exclusively "scientific" or "cognitive", nor exclusively "external" or "social".

The most frequent answer to the question of how the context of science relates to scientific production refers to problem-input. According to this model, science-external problems defined by practice are translated into research problems defined by scientists who seek science-internal solutions.[31] As pointed out before, this model assumes that there is a core of exclusively "scientific" decision-making exempt from external influence. But we need merely to look at a project proposal for which external financing is sought to realise that negotiations in such proposals involves more than the overall research goal. The proposals I looked at included whole sets of carefully elaborated problem-circumscriptions, and chains of ever more concrete problem translations which found a natural end in the methodical steps proposed for the investigation.

It is precisely through these *elaborations* that financing agencies and scientists negotiate *what* the problem is and *how* it is to be conceived, and they do so not only in grant proposals, but in direct interaction. To refer to research problems as an "external" input ignores the fact that the process of defining a problem penetrates into the very core of research production through the negotiations of its implications and operationalisations.

We can perhaps say that problem definitions are either implicit or explicit (project proposals!) anticipations of research products and productions negotiated in contextures which generally criss-cross the borders of various scientific and non-scientific idiolects and groups. As such, problem definitions have at least a guiding and orientating function in the process of research production. This function may provide one answer to the question of how the contextures invoked in practical laboratory reasoning become relevant to the process of research. More specifically, we can say that a specific definition of a problem activates a set of presuppositions which determine a set of subsequent questions asked in the laboratory and at least partly elaborated in project proposals. In so far as research results are "answers" to these questions, they bear the mark of the presuppositions which led to the questions.[32]

But the definition of research problems is not the only issue negotiated in the transscientific contextures within which scientists situate their work. A second answer to the question as to how these contextures bear on laboratory production relates more directly to the constructivist interpretation of research production; that is, that transscientific fields are relevant in so far as they bear on the decisions which mark the production of a scientific result. In other words, they must bear on the *selections* incorporated into scientific constructions. Since at least some of these selections are anticipated when the definition of a research problem is negotiated, our first answer can be seen as a special case of the one proposed here. On the other hand, we know that problems tend to become redefined in the process of research, and that anticipated selections may be overthrown and replaced.

It is clear that, to a large degree, scientific work consists of actually *making* (as well as foreseeing, planning, or reconstructing) the respective selections. In fact, an undeniable aspect of scientific competence and authority is the control of decisions made in the laboratory. But does this mean that the respective decisions—and consequently, the laboratory constructions as well—are independent of the transscientific contextures we have been talking about? The answer is no, for the simple reason that control over a decision is not the same as control over the necessary translations involved.

We saw in Chapter 1 that making a selection requires a translation into further selections. Transscientific fields can be associated with the orders of selectivity in these translations, or phrased differently, with recurring problem-translations, the so-called decision criteria. It is clear that only thematised selections of topical interest lead to translations in which the choices are explicit. Many (perhaps even most) laboratory selections are made without their ever becoming a topic of discussion or reflection. Scientists speak of such selections as the "normal", "natural" or "logical" thing to do. The selectivity incorporated into the "normal" course of scientific action is rarely noticed unless something interferes with the "natural" sequence of events, or an "anomaly" creates problems in the procedure.

Only when a scientist noticed that one of two samples subjected to a standardised, calibrated dilution procedure felt soft and soggy, while the other seemed dry, was the standardised procedure called into question. In another case, the amount of water added to protein samples was standardised at 500 units, as measured by the device which determined the consistency of the samples. As the result of a subsequent thematisation, the measurement units varied for each sample, depending on optimal volumetric results after exposure to heat. This became the criterion for a new standardisation.

In the above case, the selection seems to have been translated into a question of which amount of water would yield optimum volumetric results—a decision criterion linked to the eventual use of the proteins as a food additive. Other translations would clearly have led to different selections. For example, an interest in stability over time, or physical texture rather than volume, would have required different degrees of dilution from those chosen in regard to volume.

The point here is that the translations which connect laboratory selections and the transscientific contextures of research are made by the scientists.[33] It is here that the commitments and interests negotiated in transscientific fields are invoked and taken into consideration, and that consistency with the requirements of a network of resource-relationships is built into a scientific result. Through these translations, the transscientific connections of research penetrate into the core of research production and shape the products of research into a resource.

4.9 Indeterminacy and the Transscientific Connection of Research

When the scientists translated the choice between different measurement units into the question of which would produce the best volumetric results, they reverted to a decision criterion related to the practical use of the proteins as a food additive. In other words, they chose a criterion which appealed to the food industry by reflecting current practice in the area. On the other hand, at a crucial point in the research, the same scientists had opted for a criterion which made the results irrelevant for practical use. Not only did their formulation contradict current practice, it also contradicted what was considered feasible, with no other practical appeal to offset the loss.

Thus we find in the same experimental series an amazing inconsistency in the kind of translations chosen to ground scientific decisions. Moreover, we must realise that the interests and commitments negotiated in contextual involvements do not unequivocally determine decision-translations in the laboratory. Just as the elaborations of research problems anticipated in grant proposals tend to be renegotiated in actual laboratory investigations, so these pre-set decision criteria tend to be revised, ignored, or overthrown in the process of research.[34]

Furthermore, respective interests and commitments often remain implicit rather than explicit, and are at times deliberately left unclear. For example, one scientist I observed was worried about what sort of results would most interest a cooperative research institute with which he had a contract to explore the properties of plant proteins. He "figured", "felt" and "hoped" to "sell" them certain results which he deemed "important". But clearly he did not *know* exactly what they wanted or expected from him. When he sent them an intermediate report of some results he "thought" would be immediately turned into a patent, he was surprised by several weeks of silence. Finally, he "gathered" from a short note acknowledging receipt of the report that his results had not met with the expected interest, and therefore redirected his guesswork.

The frequent inconsistencies between laboratory selections, the change of criteria, and the often unclear or implicit basis of decisions remind us of the indeterminacy of scientific action discussed in Chapter 1. To postulate a connection between the scientists' contextual involvements and the selections of the laboratory mediated by decision criteria is not to suggest that we can *read off* these criteria from specific contextual involvements. To talk about the fusion of interests brought about by resource-relationships is not to suggest that these interests correspond to lists of specific preferences and priorities which we can identify once and for all as guidelines for laboratory decisions. If the selections of the laboratory could be predetermined by a set of specific criteria effective under specified conditions, research would be reduced to a preprogrammed execution of the respective decisions, and nothing new would be learned. As we have seen in earlier chapters, the issue is not to deplore the existence of indeterminacy, but to see it as *constitutive* for the increase of knowledge, as defined by an increase in contextually relevant complexity and variety. Thus a certain indeterminacy of laboratory selections seems to be a *sine qua non* for the emergence of new information.

But there is another relevant point, if we reconsider the notion of resource-relationships in the light of this indeterminacy. We have already said that resource-relationships are not constituted by a particular kind of exchange (such as the exchange of scientific information for recognition, or by particular flows of goods and services) but are dominated by what could happen in the future and what has happened in the past—by promises, expectancies and anticipations. In informational terms, one could say what is at stake in resource-relationships is more the *channel* than the message, as described by its permeability (for messages or exchanges) and the built-in resistances by connections to other channels or the kind of applicable decoding.[35]

More generally, it is the structure and borders of the system or field which emerge from these properties of resource-relationships. The degree of indeterminacy manifest in one relationship or channel corresponds to the degree of independence of the two units linked. The significance of this indeterminacy depends on the properties of the field. In the extreme case of a field restricted to one relationship, complete indeterminacy or full independence is equivalent to a breakdown. In a complex network, complete indeterminacy of one relation can be adjusted for through other relations and eventually result in an increase of resources for the system as a whole.

More concretely, if the interests of one party in a transscientific field do not rigidly rule over laboratory selections, the results may not be fully to that party's advantage because of the indeterminacy involved. But the results may still add to the resources of others in a complex network, if we take complexity to refer to the variety of interests interwoven in a field.

Thus, to say that scientific constructions display themselves as situated in transscientific fields is not to claim that the interests of either party involved do simply determine—via resource-relationships—the laboratory selections. To achieve consistency of scientific results with the context from which they emerge but from which they are at the same time partially independent is a problem for the field itself. Luhmann has consistently argued that the reduction of complexity is the result of constant effort in social systems.[36] In our reinterpretation, this means that the degree of indeterminacy—and with it, the degree of consistency between laboratory selections and the transscientific connections of research—results from the active efforts of those involved in the matter.

Such effort is manifest in attempts to "figure" the sort of results that would interest a financing agency, or efforts to work on "relevant" and "timely" (i.e., easily published) subjects. It crops up in the effort to keep abreast of new developments in order to stay on top of changing contextual conditions of research. It can be found in social control and the enforcement strategies (such as review procedures) used to assure consistency. And it appears, especially in recent years, in scientific policy or government regulations concerning science and scientific priorities. Just as the degree of indeterminacy in particular relations appears as the result of the active policy of agents, so does the degree of contextual adequacy of a scientific result, its success, and its survival, appear as the product of active work.

Notes

1. For representative statements in regard to this assumption, see de Solla Price (1970) or Cole and Cole (1973). For a very recent example, see de Solla Price (1979), which reviews the interlocking complex of bibliometric parameters. Scepticism with regard to citation studies can be found in Chubin and Moitra (1975) and Edge (1979).

2. For example, see Small and Griffith (1974), Mullins et al. (1977) or Sullivan, White and Barboni (1977).

3. For the conception of such networks, see Mulkay, Gilbert and Woolgar (1975). For the study of patterns of argumentation, see Böhme (1975). And for the attempt to identify scientific communities by means of patterns of communication, see the citation studies mentioned above.

4. See Crane (1972), Gaston (1973, 1978), or Studer and Chubin (1980).

5. Citation studies usually start with the social scientist's somewhat arbitrary circumscription of a subject and selection of a literature to represent it, an arbitrariness which has been repeatedly criticised. For example, see Woolgar (1976b). On the other hand, it is hard to imagine how some such arbitrariness (which can be remedied through the iterative hermeneutics of progressive analyses) can ever be avoided in sociological methodology.

6. cf. Whitley (1978: 427).

7. Bourdieu sees the scientific field as the locus of a struggle for a monopoly of scientific credit (1975a). We will return to his conception in the next section. For a non-economic model in which scientific credit (reputation) acts as a steering mechanism, see Luhmann (1968), also reprinted in Luhmann (1971).

8. See Merton (1957) and (1968). For a more extensive review of the use of the idea of competition in recent sociology of science, see Callon (1975: 105 ff.).

9. The most coherent and pertinent presentation of this model is found in an unpublished paper by Latour (1979). See also Williams and Law's use of the credibility model (1980).

10. I know only my own adaptation (1977), in which I attempted to combine a constructivist interpretation of science, the notion of success (rather than truth) as a guiding principle of laboratory action, and Bourdieu's concept of scientific field as the locus of an antagonistic struggle into a first sketch of the path which led to the theory of scientific practice outlined here.

11. Greater sophistication can be found, for example, in Rossi-Landi's attempt (1975) to apply the capitalist metaphor to the production of speech.

12. Following the work of Simon (1945), rational models of decision-making have become more and more replaced by alternative models. See for example March and Simon (1958), and more recently, March and Olsen (1976).

13. The concept of a habitus is expounded in Bourdieu's theory of practice (1972). See particularly Chapter 2 of the English translation (1977), which has been revised in important respects.

14. Except for those of Bourdieu, whose interest is less in science than social practice in general. Consequently, he has paid much more attention to a concept of social agents. See his theory of practice (1972, 1977).

15. Compare also Williams and Law's interpretation of the limits of the market analogy in science 1980, particularly pp. 311 ff.). Short of an adequate conception of the crucial mechanisms of capitalist economy, the analogy indeed boils down to replacing the formulation that scientists compete for recognition with the idea that they maximise symbolic capital (credit, or credibility). The advantage of substituting the classical *homo economicus* for the archaic gift-giving man is not obvious, particularly since Marcel Mauss' original conception was filled with subtleties not found in the crude analogy with *homo economicus*.

16. These statements are taken from Harvey's interviews with physicists (1980: 145, 147), and from the physicist Bahcall's description of his cooperation with Davis (Pinch, 1980: 92).

17. For a detailed discussion of these special problems, see Engelhardt and Hoffmann (1974).

18. The distinction between manual and intellectual labour is central to the work of Sohn-Rethel, which was briefly introduced in Chapter 1. See Sohn-Rethel (1972; 1973; 1975).

19. The literature which bears on the subject is vast and varied, since virtually all analyses of industrial society refer to the role of science and technology. Recent discussions have been stimulated by the work of the Frankfurt school (Marcuse, Habermas) and that surrounding Althusser in Paris. For the English-speaking reader more interested in sociology than philosophy, Gouldner (1976) summarises some important aspects of the discussion.

20. This seems to be Sohn-Rethel's position (1973). See also Engelhardt and Hoffmann's summary of positions on the topic (1979), or the recent discussion of technology and power in Ullrich (1979) and the contributions in Böhme and Engelhardt (1979). I am principally aware of German discussions of the topic.

21. See the comprehensive discussion in Lange (1972). For the English-speaking reader, articles referring to either position 1 or 2 can be found in nearly every issue of the *Radical Science Journal*. See also Young (1977) for a summary of relevant questions and problems, and particularly the papers collected in Rose and Rose (1976).

22. For example, see Gouldner's position on modern intellectuals (1979), or a sample of recent French positions on the topic found in a special issue of *L'Arc* (1978) devoted to *"La crise dans la tête"*, particularly the contributions by Foucault and Touraine.

23. See Sohn-Rethel (1975), particularly pp. 85 ff. and p. 93. In the Editorial Introduction to this summary of the theory of manual and intellectual labour, Sohn-Rethel is criticised for demonstrating the formal congruence between commodity formations and scientific conceptions, rather than providing a causal, genetic amount of the origin of scientific conceptions. Part of the problem, as I see it, is that notions like those found in scientific textbooks are once again equated with scientific action, here referred to as "intellectual labour". While a physicist's notion of time and motion may well warrant the predicates "quantitative" and "abstract", the actual work in the laboratory is no less a form of situated social production than other kinds of work.

24. For an earlier argument which points toward a breakdown of organisational borderlines between government bureaucracy, private industry and science, see Hirsch (1971), particularly pp. 247 ff. For a recent historical study which makes a similar point but chooses a systems approach, see Hughes (1979). The notion of a "hybrid community" to which Weingart has alerted me is usually used more restrictively to refer to the interaction of scientists and policy makers in their institutional roles outside the laboratory, as when science policy issues are decided with the help of appointed scientists who act as government consultants.

25. Note that variable transscientific fields are not taken to be relevant only in the "applied sciences". For the purpose of this study, no distinction between "applied" and "basic" research is made. For an attempt to specify particular characteristics of technology and the applied sciences, see Bunge's work (e.g. 1967).

26. For a contrasting conception, see the "social frameworks of knowledge" proposed by Gurvitch (1971), who distinguishes between masses, communities and particular groups (such as families, churches or states), which he correlates with specific types of knowledge.

27. Pickering talks about a massive intersection of "cognitive interests", a notion developed in analogy to Barnes (1977). For other uses of the conception, see Barnes and MacKenzie (1979) and Shapin (1979a,b). Part of Pickering's case study is published under the title "The Role of Interests in High-Energy Physics: the Choice Between Charm and Colour" in Knorr, Krohn and Whitley (1980).

28. I borrow the notions of *fusion* and *fission* from Callon, Courtial and Turner (1979).

29. As implied earlier, negotiation refers to all the moves that agents make, and not simply to open disputes or episodes of bargaining, which represent no more than the tip of the iceberg.

30. For recent formulations of this crisis of legitimation in science, see Weingart (1979). See also the literature on the role of experts in public policy (e.g. Nelkin 1975, 1978; Ravetz 1977), on countermovements in the sciences (Nowotny and Rose, 1979), and the example of the dispute over nuclear energy (e.g. Nowotny 1979). See also the special issue of *Daedalus* on the "Limits of Scientific Inquiry" (Spring, 1978), as well as Restivo and Zenzen (1978).

31. One of the more recent versions of this answer is found in the thesis of finalisation, which claims that, at their most developed, post-paradigmatic stage scientific theories need—and profit from—"external" problem-input to stimulate further development in a situation where all major science-internal puzzles have been solved. Cf. Böhme, van den Daele and Krohn (1973) or the English version by Böhme, van den Daele and Weingart (1976).

32. For an interesting attempt to found a formal description of the process of scientific enquiry on an interrogative model in which the kind of questions answered by a theory and the kind of questions posed through scientific observation are integrated into a logic of (scientific) question-answer sequences, see Hintikka (1979). See also Hintikka's monograph on "The Semantics of Questions and the Questions of Semantics" (1976).

33. As mentioned in Chapter 1, the idea that making a selection requires a translation into further selections implies an infinite regress of translations, for it is not clear why one would be able to make a further selection without a further translation. Thus, if a choice between two instruments is translated into a problem of the costs, the selection of the criterion of costs should require further translations, and so on. In practice, the regress ends whenever a selection between different decision criteria is no longer thematised as a selection; conversely, it is pushed one step further when decision criteria become problematic or have to be legitimised. I prefer to talk about translations of selections, rather than decision criteria, to give credit to the character of criteria as secondary selections which presuppose or imply further translations.

34. The whole issue of decision-making is of course quite complicated. Not only is there a vast amount of non-decision in the sense of Bachrach and Baratz (e.g. 1963), there is also the issue of "decisions" for which nobody feels responsible and which nobody wanted to be taken, and the general problem of an adequate model of human decision-making. For a recent discussion of the complexities involved, see for example March and Olsen (1976). The preference here is to talk about the selectivity—rather than the decision-making—of the laboratory.

35. In this sense the concept of transscientific fields advocated here invokes, literally speaking, a network model. At the same time it invokes the idea of a social field in analogy to field-theory in physics. For an overview of field-theory and its application in the social sciences, see Mey (1972).

36. See Luhmann's collection of papers (1981).

Chapter 5

The Scientist as a Literary Reasoner, Or the Transformation of Laboratory Reason

5.1 The "Products" of Research

We have illustrated the contextual contingency of laboratory selections and linked the opportunism of research to those unrealised capacities which attract scientists in the laboratory. We can now assume that scientists conceive of these capacities in relation to the transscientific connections in which they are engaged. In the laboratory, the contextuality of science is traversed and sustained by resource-relationships which constantly criss-cross the borders of speciality areas. In the reasoning which circumscribes the opportunity presented by an "idea", scientists orchestrate the fusion of interests which marks these resource-relationships. Such reasoning is found not only in and around the process of research fabrication, but also in the scientific paper.

For in the main, it is the scientific paper (or its equivalents) which confronts us as the removable and removed "end-product" of research. It is the declared relevant result of a process beyond which we cannot generally penetrate. In a study of the manufacture of knowledge, the manufacture of the scientific paper must be of special interest; in particular, we will have to pursue the conversion of reasoning as we move from the laboratory to the paper. It will be clear that neither the selectivity of constructive operations nor the contextual reasoning in which this selectivity is inscribed stop short of the scientific paper. In this sense, the paper is a construction of the laboratory, perfectly similar to other laboratory constructions. Yet at the same time, the written products of science contain an argument of their own, which contrasts with that of the laboratory.

This contrast is not only one between the piecemeal and *ad hoc* projections of laboratory utterance and the edited, polished coherence of written discourse. In the laboratory, scientific reasoning displays its concerns in savage purity. But in their papers, the savage reasoners of the laboratory seem to change their faith. The reasoning of the paper, one imagines, is faithful to the scriptures (the authoritative writings) of an area, rather than to the concerns from which it originates. Yet at the same time, this reasoning contains a conspiracy to appropriate or overthrow part of the scriptures. The scientific paper hides more than it tells on its tame and civilised surface. For one thing, it deliberately forgets much of what happened in the laboratory, although it purports to present a "report" of that research. Second, the written products of research employ a good deal of literary strategy largely unnoticed by the readers.

What does it mean to say that the research paper displays a good deal of literary competence in the art of writing? Are not most scientific papers tediously technical, if not outright boring? Literary and linguistic investigations of philosophical and social scientific writings (of which several are available) suggest that the language in these disciplines cannot be regarded as a neutral medium through which technical results are reported.[1] At present, there are not many analyses of writing in the natural and technological sciences. Those which do exist demonstrate that papers in the natural and technological sciences tend to be rhetorically standardised with regard to paragraph organisation, choice of vocabulary and grammatical means of expression.[2] Hence literary skills, as defined by individual variation or stylistic excellence, are poorly developed, in contrast to much philosophical and some social scientific writing.

On the other hand, if we define literary skills in terms of a repertoire of techniques for persuasion, there is no shortage of such devices in natural and technological science writing; their results can be seen at work in every scientific text. It is by now almost a commonplace to say that scientists write in a language which is ostentatiously neutral. Studies of scientific texts reveal such common strategies as the use of a simplistic language, separation of "information" and "interpretation", use of the passive voice and of the regal we, redoubling (in the sense of offering both sides of an argument), and avoidance of explicit value statements.[3]

Manuals devoted to teaching the scientist how to write a scientific paper invariably censure the sorry results of some of these habits, like passivity, while reinforcing others, like brevity and "straightforwardness".[4] These, and more subtle devices in scientific writing, are rhetorical strategies of objectification, which says less about the intentions of scientific writers than about their conventions.[5]

However, the persuasive effects of the scientific paper do not rest upon linguistic manipulation alone. The institutionalised definition of a scientific paper is that it constitutes a *report* of (laboratory) work, and it is this definition which accounts for part of its persuasive credibility. With Cicourel, I believe that understanding the formal properties of a text classified as a report requires that we understand the relationship between the text and the reality from which it originates.[6] As argued by Bourdieu, the formal properties of a work are at the same time social strategies, and cannot be grasped by a science of discourse considered in and for itself.[7]

In the next chapter, we will be interested in the written products of science *per se*, as that part of scientific reasoning which most obviously leaves the laboratory to be circulated and integrated in subsequent scientific work. At the same time, we will look at the transformation of scientific reasoning as we move from the selections of the laboratory to those presented in the paper. In other words, we will reconsider the authenticity of the scientific paper's claim to be a research report.

That there are discrepancies between what we find in the laboratory and what is written in a scientific paper has long been noted—Merton traces the questions raised by these discrepancies back to Bacon and Leibniz,[8] and Medawar is famous for his observation that the conventions of the research paper not only "conceal, but actively misrepresent" what happens in the laboratory (1969: 169). The problem is that we do not have any close empirical investigations which would illuminate those differences.[9] The issue, then, is not to reiterate the puzzle created by the discrepancies, but to begin to document and analyse the transformations which take place. The scientific paper I have chosen to examine presumes a conversion of resources which serves to illustrate a more general mechanism of connection in the networks we have called transscientific fields. Characteristically, this conversion is found in the first part of the scientific product (its Introduction). In the following paragraphs, we will attempt to recover the laboratory reasoning in which the selection of a research effort was embedded, and contrast it with the conversion of this reasoning in the written products which followed.[10]

The reader should note that the research under analysis was chosen only because my records of it were complete,[11] and because the scientists made available to me the complete set of drafts, as well as the final manuscript, of the paper based upon this work. The number of drafts (including comments by co-authors, colleagues or reviewers) is 16; for the present purpose, it is enough to draw on the first and final versions of the paper. The laboratory work to which the paper refers was largely conducted between November 1976 and April 1977; the first draft of the paper which was circulated is dated 13 May 1977. The final version was finished on 14 September, submitted on 4 October, and accepted for publication (with the condition that a reference be completed) on 28 October 1977.

Since the paper only appeared in 1978, we cannot turn to citations as an indication of its reception. But the fact that it was quickly accepted without corrections gives some clue to peer response. Of its three authors, two were highly ranked with regard to journals and professional societies.[12] The oldest author has published more than 250 papers, and acts as a government consultant. The youngest (and the one principally responsible for the work) was 33, with 40 publications. The paper refers to the technological part of the work observed, which was to propose an alternative method of protein precipitation to be used in protein recovery.

5.2 The Grounding of a Research Effort in the Laboratory

Among others, the story of the research under analysis (which was briefly introduced in Chapter 3) features Walter, a chemist/technologist we have met before, scientists at the institute such as Fuller, a chemist from another group, a university department, a cooperative research institute connected with the agricultural industry, journal editors, and the generalised "anyone" to whom the research is addressed—many of them not present at the scene of laboratory action. The story is told in response to my questions, and through my notes on various comments and remarks. It is the only equivalent we can find in the laboratory to the grounding of a research effort in the scientific paper. The story weaves the intended results of the research as a *presumptive resource* into the web of concerns in which the scientists at the same time insert themselves. We will first recall the reasoning which surrounded Walter's launching of the effort:

> Question: "Did you originally intend to work on these recovery methods?"
> Walter: "No, originally I did not want to do any recovery research. Rather, it turned out that I would have to generate the protein I needed for the assay work and texture measurements and these (sorts of) things myself because I did not get it from the agricultural industry. But originally I did not want to make a separate paper out of this work. . . . I wanted to finish it as quickly as possible, and thought about simply working together with Fuller (14-1).

Walter had decided to rely on Fuller's know-how but go to the large-scale lab, when he learned about a series of problems Fuller's method caused (see Section 3.6). Then Walter happened to read that

> "they use ferric chloride for protein precipitation of s.w. . . . . It must be cheap,

otherwise they would not use it. And I read that it can be done at low temperature without heat treatment.''

This came about at a time when Walter had been reading about the exploding energy needs in agriculture, and was fascinated by the notion of energy savings. When asked why he thought ferric chloride was such an excellent idea, he said:

"In Europe (where this sort of protein recovery is done extensively), everybody who recovers this protein uses heat coagulation. Since the protein concentration is only 0.5%, one has to use enormous quantities of solution to get 1,000 grammes of protein. . . . They realise that this is a problem and attempt to concentrate the liquid *before* heat coagulation—but this is expensive, too. And the result is an insoluble protein causing all kinds of problems!'' (4-4/4).

The idea was simple: "If one does not have to use high temperatures on the protein, the solubility must be higher and the whole process must be more interesting in terms of energy''. The appeal of a protein recovery method which used less energy and resulted in proteins with a high nitrogen solubility was immediately apparent. It was not difficult for Walter to convince the other members of his research group to try his plan. But there were other reasons at play in regard to the four scientists who subsequently became involved with the research. Walter himself can provide a sample of these reasons.

Since Walter wanted eventually to return to the university he had come from, the value of his work in regard to career requirements remained, as he said, constantly in the back of his mind. In particular, he was concerned about a lack of purely technological work in his profile. This, he believed, would cause problems in the advancement of his career. At the time he came across the idea of ferric chloride, he said later:

"I was also already concerned about the fact that I had not covered any technological topics in my protein work up to then. I thought that, if I have to go into the large-scale laboratory anyway and generate the protein myself, I might as well make some comparisons and see whether the ferric chloride works. This would fill the gap . . .'' (14-13/1).

At another point, it became clear that Walter had a contract with a cooperative research institute financed by the agricultural industry to work on some of the problems concerning their proteins. He said:

"I know that their (recovery) procedure is bad, and I know from pretests I did that the solubility of their protein is very low. They should be interested in this work . . .'' (6-3/2).

He knew that he had "to offer them something at some time in return for the contract'', and thought that the new method would be exactly what they were looking for. However, he did want to publish the method, but was afraid the industry would not go along with this. (His solution was to write to them about the method and insist that he *had* to publish because of all the other people at the institute who were involved with the research).

But there was another reason for Walter's attraction to the new recovery method, one which I have cited before. Like others, Walter considered the expensive equipment and well-trained staff at the large-scale laboratory highly appealing—and even more attractive because access to it was not easily obtained, as we have seen in Chapter 2. On several occasions, I heard that any project which allowed this opportunity to be "exploited" for one's own work would be welcome. The new method of protein precipitation provided such a reason (27-1/1).

It doesn't really matter that reasons such as these often seem to be *post hoc* rationalisations of a decision that more likely "happened" than was "made". When the "occurrence" of ferric chloride was caught in a web of reasons, it generated a context of action circumscribed by that web. Laboratory action proceeds in the space of possible selections carved out by this context, until the context is redefined again. The reasons which appear *post hoc* in a logic of decisions are simultaneously presumptions of the future in a logic of action.

But there is another aspect which should be emphasised here. When the scientist cast the new method as a resource with respect to various demands (for covering a technological topic in one's curriculum, for the protein needed in other research, for fulfilling a contract, for using opportunities of success) in which they found themselves entangled, those demands called forth a series of actors whose hidden participation in laboratory work became suddenly apparent. For example, the university professor whom Walter frequently mentioned in connection with his worries about covering a technological topic in his work, or the research director at the institute with which he had a contract. Moreover, there were leading scientists at the institute who were interested in the experiments for which the protein was needed, including the group's research leader. There were also the colleagues whom Walter called upon to interpret potential journal interest. And there were two well-known senior scientists with whom Walter felt he might profitably publish a paper.

With respect to these and other agents, the scientists plotted the fusion of interests which marks resource-relationships and which sustains (in their reasoning) the construction of a piece of research. To be sure, the respective agents would have to be convinced of the projected fusion of interests. (From a previous reference, we know that, judging from his reaction, the director of the institute with which a contract existed was *not* convinced.) The fusion of interests rests upon the *convertibility* of the scientist's "resource" into the currency with which the respective agents make their transactions. In other words, it rests upon its capacity to insert itself as a resource into the context of concerns which *they* have woven for themselves.

But the point to be noted is that the mechanism of connection in the networks to which we have referred as transscientific fields must be linked to this convertibility of the respective resources, and not to some characteristics which the members of the network share. To paraphrase an expression used elsewhere,[13] resources which cannot be converted remain *socially ad hoc*, in the sense that they do not lend themselves to the reasoned continuation and integration of practical action (an issue to which we shall return later on). We shall see that scientists presume a form of this conversion when they write a scientific paper. Let us begin by looking at the first version of the relevant scientific paper.

5.3 The Grounding of a Research Effort in the Scientific Paper

In contrast to the flux of reasoning which constantly springs from the activities of the laboratory, the scientific paper presents a tame, tightly regulated flow of reason within a structure provided by page and paragraph. This structure is well-known. A title page first locates the paper at the intersection of particular author with particular (scientific) connections, a particular journal, and a topic doubly determined by title and running head. A following page repeats all but the name of the organisation, and includes the *Abstract,* followed in turn by the *Introduction.* Sections on *Materials and Methods* and *Results and Discussion* appear in due course, followed by *References, Acknowledgements,* and a set of *Tables* and *Figures.*

With slight variations, this is the standard form of a scientific paper, which in the present case, remained the same between the first and final versions of the paper. The sections on methods and results are usually further subdivided by paragraph headings which for the first time touch upon the substantial content of the work. The only special characteristic in the paper analysed here is that it included, on page 2, an "Interpretative Summary" for "internal use" at the institute.

In contrast to the mix of reasoning we find in the laboratory, the scientific paper sets the different issues neatly apart in the subdivisions provided by the paragraphs. Rather than collect scattered remarks throughout a period of observation in order to learn a scientist's reason for the research, we need merely identify the correct subdivision of the paper. Rather than mould one's notes into a readable account of scientific rationale, all we have to do is to listen to the story presented by the relevant part of the paper. To be sure, we will not find any part of the scientific paper which directly reflects the scientists' accounts of the grounds and origins of their work. However, we do find a section of text which corresponds to the role played by these accounts: the *Introduction.* It is in the *Introduction* that a work which has been purged of personal interests and situational contingencies is inserted into a new framework of reason; in which, quite literally, the work is recontextualised.

When we read the *Introduction* to the first version of the paper analysed here (see Appendix 1 at the end of the book), two characteristics are striking. First, there is a clear structure consisting of paragraphs ordered in terms of decreasing generality. The paragraph-topics begin on the most general level (protein from potato plants) and proceed to the most specific (an alternative method of coagulation), followed by a mandate to act (to find the method). Second, there is an almost exclusive reliance on categories of quantity and quality in terms of the topics presented.[14]

The argument suggests in a rather straightforward manner that there are enormous quantities of high-quality protein available in the world (11. 2-11), and that there is a "tremendous" waste of these resources (11. 12 ff.). Recovery of protein pays off in terms of the amount of available raw material, total costs, and yield compared to other plant proteins, as confirmed by its commercial recovery "in different European countries" (11. 38-53). However, the current method of recovery has serious disadvantages, such as low nitrogen solubility and limited applicability of the protein, energy-costs, and possibly carcinogenic results (11. 54-69). There could be a major alternative coagulant (11. 70 ff.) which would turn the disadvantages of the current method into advantages. Moreover, the "nutritional significance" of the iron used in the new method greatly offsets the possible "carcinogenic" effect of heat treatment (11. 65-67 and 74-76).

The predominant tense in which this state of the world is described is the present. Only one direct recommendation (11. 28-29) and a rare conditional phrase point to a possible world:

> "If the remaining 70 - 80% of the material could be converted into nutritients, total nutritional resources could be vastly increased . . ." (11. 18-20).
> "Ferric chloride . . . could be another major coagulant for the recovery of PPC" (11. 70-71).

The final sentence (11. 79 ff.) represents the work as the result of the authors' attempt to bring about such a possible world—finding a method which yields comparable quantities and better qualities. The use of the imperfect tense suggests that the method has actually been found, although it is not identified here.

The transition from predominantly quantitative propositions to explicitly qualitative evaluations comes about in paragraphs 5 and 6, marking the dramatic climax of the tension and its subsequent resolution—the use of ferric chloride. As befits a discourse in which sections called *Materials and Methods* and *Results and Discussion* are to follow, this resolution is not elaborated upon here. Nevertheless, the *Introduction* is complete with respect to such conventional elements of literary structure as tension and resolution, identification of good and bad, and organised development of action. Subsequent sections function more as appendices to this structure than as the unfolding of a dramatic structure.[15]

Let us stop here at this global characterisation of the argument of the *Introduction* (a more detailed investigation will follow in Section 5) and highlight some of the main areas in which it differs from the reasoning of the laboratory as exemplified before. In the laboratory, the scientists invoke a series of parallel, if not independent, needs or mandates ("have to do-s") to which the potential of some new method to eliminate the need or to accomplish the task was related: the need to find a method for generating large amounts of protein demanded by bioassay work, the mandate to come up with some relevant results in return for contract money received, the perceived need to research a technological topic in order to qualify for a position, the demand for a method resulting in high nitrogen solubility and low energy costs. Or they referred to a potential from which, with the help of a principle of rationality, a requirement of action could be derived, as when the "resource" of the large-scale laboratory was cited as a ground for doing research which required its use.

The point is that in the laboratory we encountered a multiplicity of reasons and projected uses for research which cannot all be subsumed by an interest in publication, and may even run counter to it—as when the need to generate large amounts of protein quickly conflicted with the need to investigate the method more thoroughly for a publication, or when the projected interest of industry in patenting a method raised problems for the would-be author of a paper. Furthermore, these reasons were tied to the personal interest structures which establish the link between agents in a network of resource-relationships in which the scientists inserted themselves.

In the story of the *Introduction*, this multiplicity of laboratory reason is reduced to a single line of argument. Of the demands invoked by the scientists, all but the need for an improved recovery method are absent. In contrast to the laboratory reasons (which are usually not elaborated in depth or detail), the demand for a new method of protein coagulation is grounded in an extended chain of reason. Except for the authors themselves, none of the agents through whose concerns and interrelationships the laboratory research was sustained appear in the text.

I am not suggesting that scientists *intentionally* misrepresent or "cover up" the reality of the laboratory. The impressions created by the text often follow the pattern: "Why are you trying to make me believe you're going to Lemberg by telling me you're going to Krakow, when in fact you're going to Krakow?" which has been described, among others, by Lacan.[16] The best example of this, perhaps, is the *Introduction*'s reversal of the dynamics of research we find in the laboratory. In the laboratory, the scientists responded to the chance occurrence of an opportunity of success by instituting a new line of research. In the paper, it is the demand for an alternative protein recovery method that moves them.

The scientists in the lab did not begin with the problem of wasted resources or the health hazard associated with heat coagulation, and then search for a solution. When I asked Walter if he had specifically searched for a method which would work at low temperature and thus meet the energy-reduction and nitrogen-solubility requirements outlined in the text, he said:

> "No. I think I was not clever enough originally to see that it would be better to recover protein without applying heat treatment. I probably first read about the ferric chloride. One needs stimulation to see . . ." (14-13/1).

The impression of a problem-pushed solution which has been researched, rather than encountered by chance, is created in the text through the hierarchical organisation of arguments through which the solution appears *derived* rather than original. And it is created through formulations like the final mandate of the *Introduction*, which says that "The aim of this work was *to find* an alternative precipitation method . . ." (1.79), thus suggesting that the solution was a result of the authors' search. In sum, we can say that the potential instantiated in the laboratory by the discovery of $FeCl_3$ coagulation leads to the mandate of realising the potential through experimentation; whereas in the *Introduction*, it is the scientists' mission that established the potential of an alternative protein recovery method (see Exhibit 1). However, this reversal is not the effect of misrepresentation, but part of the literary strategy of the text, of which we will hear more when we compare the first and final versions of the paper.

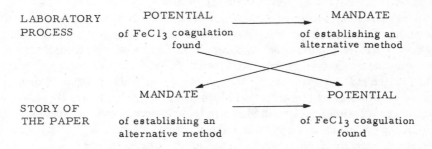

Exhibit 1: The Origin of the Research Effort According to the Introduction and the
Observer's Story

5.4 First and Final Versions: The Dissimulation of Literary Intention

I now invite the reader to look at the final version of the *Introduction* (see Appendix

2 at the end of the book) and compare it with the version we have been discussing thus far. The impression we get from the final version is that it dissimulates the dramatic emphasis and straightforwardness found in version 1. If we look more closely, we will see that this dissimulation results from a series of modifications which run counter to the rhetoric of the original presentation. Three major strategies of modification appear to operate: *deleting* particular statements made in the original version, *changing the modality* of certain assertions, and *reshuffling* the original statements.

Characteristically, the statements deleted in the final version are of two different kinds: either arguments which essentially reinforced a certain point, or assertions considered "weak" or "dangerous" (some arguments, of course, are both reinforcing *and* dangerous). For example, four of the fourteen statements eliminated from the first-version text accentuated the negative value of the prevailing protein recovery method by commenting on its "disadvantages" or the "advantages" of $FeCl_3$ as a "major" alternative (11. 61 ff.). Another group of eliminated statements reinforced a previous point, such as the phrase, "if the remaining 70—80% could be converted into nutritients . . ." which immediately followed the phrase "According to Kramer and Krull (1977) only 20—30% of the vegetable plants are utilized directly for human consumption . . ." (11. 16 ff.). The former statement was deleted because it was "obvious". Yet the latter statement did not meet with approval either. It was later deleted as a "dangerous" claim which was expected to generate opposition and disbelief. Two-stage processes of this sort are not rare. Note that eliminating "dangerous" claims and arguments which reinforce the problems of the ruling method effectively weakens the character of the *Introduction* as a dramatic production.

A similar effect results from the strategy of modification, which consists of changing the modality of certain statements from the necessary to the possible, and generally from the strongly asserted to the more weakly asserted. Instead of saying that something "is" the case, we find that "it has been suggested as possible"; instead of "should", we find "could" (11. 6 and 29 of version 1). Expressions like "mainly" are watered down to "usually" or "commonly", and the "good" solubility of PPC becomes merely "enhanced". The scientists either hold back their claims, or couch them in terms which denote hesitation and doubt.

The final softening of dramatic impact comes about through a *reshuffling* of the remaining original statements over subsequent revisions, resulting in a loss of clarity and straightforwardness. For example, paragraph 1 of the final version contains statements from three paragraphs of version 1. As a result, the introductory paragraph no longer remains on the most general level of the worldwide quantity and quality of proteins, but shows a pronounced tree structure which proceeds from the world production of protein to production in the United States, to that portion of U.S. production available as processing effluents, and the percentage of protein which can be recovered from these effluents. In other paragraphs, reshuffling results in similar changes[17] (see Exhibit 2).

Both the reshuffling and the deletion of statements lead to a new overall paragraph structure which no longer moves from the general to the specific. Instead, the new paragraph organisation is *nested*, in the sense that previous topics are resumed at a later stage. As a consequence, the final *Introduction* proceeds by a spiral-like *hedging in* on the purpose it gives to the study. This hedging in is accentuated by the softened surface of propositions produced by strategy 2, with the result that any dramatic

First Version:

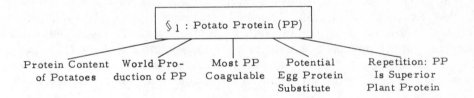

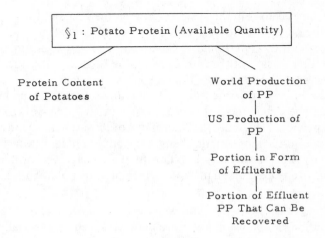

Final Version:

Exhibit 2: Organisation of the First Paragraph of the Introduction Before (1st Version) and After (Final Version) Reshuffling (See App. 1 and 2)

climax is diffused and difficult to identify.

In paragraphs 1 and 2 of the final version, the situation is not explicitly defined, as it was in the first, in terms of the enormous waste of tremendous resources. Paragraph 3 foreshadows a preference for $FeCl_3$ when the latter is said to "compare favourably" with HCl (11. 30 ff.), but the message is obscured by the subsequent references to other, irrelevant methods. In the following paragraph, energy costs and insolubility are cited as disadvantages of heat coagulation, and ferric chloride is credited with potentially adding to the value of the proteins. Yet the relevance of this is once more obscured, this time by its distance from the study's statement of purpose, which is found only in the last paragraph. In between them is paragraph 5, which discusses the general quality of potato protein, mentioned at the beginning of the first *Introduction*. Paragraph 6 continues with an outdated economic analysis of different methods of precipitation. By its focus on comparison and the dating it proposes, paragraph 6 prepares for the purpose of the study which is, according to paragraph 7, "to compare the effectiveness" of different coagulation methods and "to evaluate" the characteristics of their results on different scales.

With the climax of the next to last paragraph of the first *Introduction*, its resolution, via the discovery of an "alternative" method of coagulation as a step toward a possible world of adequate resource-utilisation, has also disappeared: the mission of the published paper is no more than a comparative analysis and evaluation. Note that this evaluation is not simply the text's original proposal in disguise. The paper concludes, as we shall see later, by disavowing any explicit recommendation of an "alternative":

> "The ultimate selection of a precipitation method for potato protein will depend upon an analysis of the nutritional and antinutritional, economic, engineering, compositional and functional parameters, within the constraints of the end product use of the PPC" (11. 97 ff., App. 2).

It is noteworthy that changes in the abstract between the first and final versions of the paper replicate the kinds of changes made in the *Introduction*. The result is most conspicuous in the case of the *Interpretative Summary*. The first such summary is a condensation of the first version of the *Introduction*; the final summary, according to the authors themselves, is "nothing more than a somewhat extended title" for the paper (see Exhibit 3). In this case, deletion ruled over all other strategies of modification. The first such steps can be seen in the first version, which (as in the case of the *Introduction* reproduced in Appendix 1) includes the corrections of the last named and senior author of the paper. See also the more subtle changes introduced here, as when the sentence "The present study shows a way to precipitate all of the coagulable protein . . . "turns into "The present study describes a method of precipitating potato protein . . ." (1. 15 of version 1).

Given such changes as these, the final version of the *Introduction* (and analogous parts of the paper) is emphatically *not* a dramatic elaboration, especially when compared with the first version. In terms of literary strategy, the final version is a consistent understatement of the first, and the interesting point here is that it is *not* a *deliberate* understatement. We cannot assume a *coup de la modestie* by which the agents amass symbolic benefits from displaying a possibly fitting humility and sincerity.[18]

The final version of the paper is not only the product of its authors, but of several other scientists as well, whose critical comments have been taken into account. The process of rewriting the first version is one of negotiation among authors and critics. The dynamics of this process is interesting in itself, since there is no smooth transition from one version to the next via the incorporation of comments and criticisms. Comments may be solicited, but not received, or unsolicited but received, or received one way or another and not taken into account, or received several times in different versions and resented, etc.

For example, version 4 of our paper (the first official draft[19] passed on to the two co-authors) came back with "minor" corrections by one co-author to which the original author responded by saying that "he accepted it without corrections, very much against his habit". A later copy given to the head of the group includes an author's handwritten note " . . . please check the manu.". It came back without corrections, apparently unread. A second copy, including the note, "sorry, but you should and must read it", was passed on; this time the scientists apparently paid no attention to the sug-

76 words mat.
made to be cut further

1   Interpretive Summary

13,000   *13 × 10⁶*

2   About ~~12,750 × 10³~~ metric tons of potatoes (containing 26~~8~~,000

3   metric tons *of* crude protein) are ~~utilized in the USA for food processing~~ *processed annually in order to*

4   ~~every year.~~ (Only ~~20-30% of the vegetable plants in the USA is~~

5   ~~utilized directly for human consumption.~~) √ *For this reason* the potato processing

effluents *resulting from the manufacture of*

6   ~~plant~~ (potato chips, flakes, granules, french fries, starch, ~~etc.~~) *and represent a potential*

7   ~~effluents are a major~~ protein source as well as a major waste

8   disposal problem.

is

9   ~~The~~ commonly used *for the* recovery ~~process for~~ *of* potato proteins, ~~is~~

is an energy intensive

10   (Acid/heat precipitation.) ~~This~~ *the* heat treatment ~~leads to~~ protein *process and*

N-solubility.

11   concentrates with ~~low~~ solubility, ~~which is a limiting factor~~ *low*

12   ~~for their use in food systems. Another disadvantage of the~~

to

13   ~~heat treatment are the energy costs~~ √ : ~~heat the protein~~

14   ~~water up to the precipitation temperature.~~

describes a method of precipitating potato

15   The present study ~~shows a way to precipitate all of the~~ *protein*

16   ~~coagulable protein of the waste effluents~~ at room temperature.

N-solubility of the

17   The resulting potato protein concentrate ~~has a nitrogen solubility~~

concentrates precipitated by

18   7.5 times higher than the ~~solubility of the~~ acid/heat

19   ~~precipitated concentrates.~~

Interpretive Summary

simulated

Protein in waste effluent resulting from potato processing were recovered by three methods, i.e., hydrochloric acid and ferric chloride,
both at room temperature, and hydrochloric acid at 98-99°C. Protein
recovery, compositional, and functional characteristics were studied.

Exhibit 3: The Interpretative Summary in the First and Final Version of the Scientific
          Paper

gested corrections, for they do not appear in the updated and retyped version.

Versions 9 and 10 were accepted with minor corrections by two official reviewers and supplemented by version 11 which, apparently without request, had been reread by the head of the group, who recommended more "serious" modifications. Comments such as "is this speculation or fact?" and the question as to whether the "excellent" nitrogen solubility advocated in the paper was "necessarily an advantage" provoked considerable annoyance. Nevertheless, two co-authors introduced some rewordings (version 12), which were then retyped and corrected by one author (version 13) and slightly modified by the other (version 14). This version was passed on by the senior author to the head of the group, prompting further criticism and the comment "better, but still not satisfactory" (version 15). Needless to say, the critique was greatly resented.

It is important to see that those who act as reviewers and critics in this process of modification are not only friends of the author who want to help anticipate and fence off negative response. They are also *opponents,* often working on similar topics within an overlapping network, with stakes of their own (or of those to whom they are related) to defend. The antagonism which developed between the first author and the head of his group (acting as a critic, but not a co-author) illustrates this ambivalence. The author became hostile because he felt he was being forced to "weaken" his case by reducing the claims made in the first version.

Version 15 of the paper amply documents this antagonism, since it includes not only the comments made by the head of the group, but also the author's biting reactions to the criticism. For example, a request to delete a sentence is generally annotated with an underlined "Why?". A new wording proposed by the head of the group is met with a "Thanks!". To the question "What happens when you wash the other ppts?", the author responded "What one expects!", followed by an explanation without addressee (the annotated paper did not go back to the head), and when the question "how much less" was added to the paper's assertion that "less protein is recovered . . .", the author wrote an angry "see figure 2" and underlined it three times. The paper contains a whole battle of annotations.

The battle (but not the hostility) ended in a compromise which favoured the group head—who, after all, had a say in what left the institute by way of publication and what did not. The existence of this battle (and in general, the process of negotiation which precedes publication) illustrates the fact that the content of a published paper is not merely the result of an author adhering to the conventions of scientific writing. As I pointed out before, even the youngest of the three authors had forty publications, and was well aware of those conventions.

Given the amount of expertise involved, we can safely assume that the first version was written in accord with the relevant conventions. The features of the published paper, then, must be taken as the result of a process of negotiation between authors and critics in which *technical critique* and *social control* are inseparably intertwined. This implies that the published paper is a multilayered hybrid *co-produced* by the authors *and* by members of the audience to which it is directed. Furthermore, the published paper is not a *final* product in any reasonable sense of the word. A published paper is stabilised in print, but not in the discourse into which it is inserted and by which writing is sustained.

The negotiations which follow the author's version but precede the publication of a paper document the reconstructive work done by a social field *long before* the paper appears in print. This reconstructive work is interrupted, but not halted, by publication. The readers of the published paper dissect and contest the text much as the reviewers do; they believe some arguments, disbelieve others, qualify some claims as warranted and others not, and cast a web of interpretations and relevances upon the bare words.

5.5 The Construction of a Web of Reason

We have contrasted the reasoning found in the first version of the *Introduction* with the reasoning heard in the laboratory, and examined some of the most conspicuous modifications by which the first version was transformed into the final draft. We shall now consider the *final Introduction* in somewhat more detail. In the laboratory, the web of reasoning surrounding a research effort (and the relationships instantiated in this reasoning) provided its decision-translations and selections. In the paper, these selections are ushered in and encircled by the web of reason spun in the *Introduction*.

The *Introduction* is the locus of the paper (and the *only* locus, if we disregard those parts, such as abstracts and summaries, which act upon the core of the paper), which frames it in a context of relevances,[20] and provides a key to what follows. The authors do this by naming those agents to whom their work matters, and by specifying the circumstances of their mandate. They construct a real world which requires them to depart for a possible world. Let us pursue the thread of reason which leads to this departure.

The *Introduction* begins by specifying a resource: protein from the potato plant. The first sentence specifies how much protein the plant contains; the second states the amount of protein produced from the plant world-wide; and the third indicates U.S. production. That we are correct in reading this as the specification of a *resource* is made clear by the first sentence of the *Abstract* which precedes the *Introduction* and talks about potato processing effluents as a "potential source of valuable protein . . ." Remember, too, that the beginning of the first version of the *Introduction* stated that:

> "potato tuber(s) . . . *provide* the world with 6 million metric tons of protein per year" (emphasis added).

Resources exist only in relation to an interest, need or demand. The *Introduction* specifies a chain of resources, or a series of potentials, related to a series of interests and needs which remain *implicit*. (The one exception is the explicit reference to the "interest in the recovery of potato protein during the past 60 years . . ."[1. 21 f.].) The *Introduction* connects the resources it specifies by an equally implicit mechanism of *sequential contingency*.

Let me clarify this. The potato tuber is introduced as a source of protein and related to an implied protein need. However, it becomes a resource for fulfilling this need only in so far as it has not been used already for this or another inevitable purpose. In other words, it is a resource only if some portion of it is still available for generating protein. The available portion, in this case, is the processing of waste effluent, whose resource character in turn depends on the possibility of recovering the unused protein. The text's next move is to state that such recovery methods are available, most commonly by heat coagulation (paragraph 3).

Continuing the chain, a recovery method becomes a resource only if its own qualities (such as low cost) are desirable, and lead in turn to certain favored qualities in the protein (such as high nitrogen solubility). Heat coagulation is pictured as a negative resource, since the text states (in paragraph 4) that it fails to meet these requirements. At the same time, it promotes $FeCl_3$ as a method which meets these demands.

The next two paragraphs reiterate the resource value of potato protein in relation to the implied need for a favourable amino acid balance, and the negative resource value of heat coagulation in regard to energy costs. Ferric chloride, on the other hand, can only be considered as an alternative to heat coagulation if it can be shown that it compares favourably with other methods. It is this comparison which the text takes to be its mandated task.

The implication of this final contingency is clear: if $FeCl_3$ can be shown to fulfil the specified requirements, then all other resources may be instantiated for their respective purposes. Given the sequential contingency between the respective objects of (positive or negative) resource-value, the instantiation of $FeCl_3$ as a proven alternative transmits itself from the bottom of the *Introduction* to the top: the heat coagulation method is deinstituted, a recovery method which fulfils the authors' requirements is established, protein can be regained from waste, waste can be reduced, potato protein can be made fully available for human consumption, and the need for more protein in the world can be met. Exhibit 4 illustrates this logic of the *Introduction*.

Note that the authors prefer to talk about available resources, rather than needs. This is an effective *literary strategy* which, unlike the strategy implied by the above sequential contingency, must remain hidden to textual analysis alone. Unlike the claim that there are large quantities of unused protein in waste effluents, the assertion of a significant need for more protein suitable for human consumption might not have gone uncontested. At the time the paper was written, the controversy in regard to the world food problem as largely a question of protein had already begun.[21] Thus, to avoid the question of *what* is needed in favour of emphasising what is available, to speak of potential rather than necessity, represents not merely a reliance on the reader to fill in the obvious, but serves to counteract expected criticism which might otherwise threaten the paper's value from the start.

If the scientists had begun by referring to a world-wide need for protein which could be alleviated through their work, they would have been forced to confront the controversy, either by addressing it directly in the paper, or via the response of their critics. But to propose the use of "wasted" resources requires no further legitimation, since both the reduction of waste—a potential environmental hazard[22]—and the more effective utilisation of plants for human consumption are values in and of themselves.

Note, too, that the emphasis on "waste" redoubles the emphasis on what is available and on what can be done, rather than on what might be needed. The heavy use of numbers has the same effect. This double emphasis on available resources and their waste brings into play an element of irrationality which is linked to the agents with which the authors populate the *Introduction*: the irrationality of a world which wastes part of the protein it produces and needs, and that of a manufacturing industry which has thus far remained insensitive to the need for change brought on by increasing energy costs. The implication—although not the explicit proposal—is that this irrationality can be remedied through the authors' work. By playing upon the issues of waste and available, but unused resources (which it associates with practical agents),

SEQUENTIAL CONTINGENCY   NEEDS IMPLIED BY
OF RESOURCES IN THE TEXT   THE ARGUMENT

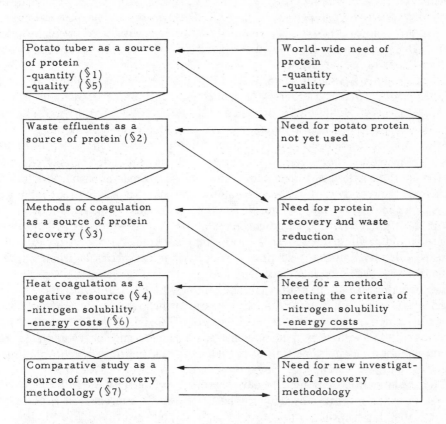

Exhibit 4: The Sequential Contingency of Resources and the Transformation of Implied
          Needs in the Final Version of the Introduction.

the text recalls the outworn image of science as the standard-bearer of rationality.

Practical situations linked to practical agents and ordered by sequential contingency constitute the (contextual) weave of reasons into which the work of the paper is inserted in the *Introduction*. Yet the part which science plays in the argument also follows a certain logic, although one which seems to be independent of paragraph structure and the general pattern of textual organisation. The *Introduction* lists several methods of protein recovery which have been "reported", "propagated", "studied" or "demonstrated" by science (paragraph 3). Among these, three are qualified in particular at several points in the *Introduction*: heat coagulation, trichloroacetic acid (alone and combined with heat coagulation), and ferric chloride precipitation. The first two are qualified as those used in practice, and resulting in disadvantages.

The third—ferric chloride—has been "demonstrated" to compare favourably with trichloroacetic acid in laboratory experiments and "could add" to the nutritional value of the protein. The paper will demonstrate that it works at low energy costs in large scale production and results in a protein of "excellent" nitrogen solubility. The two-step transition from heat coagulation/HC1 to $FeCi_3$ can be extended by yet another step—one not addressed in the paper, but of key concern in the laboratory: the purification of the resulting proteins. In Chapter 3 we saw briefly that this issue led to the preference of yet another coagulant, as well as to work on the chemical modification of proteins. But the subject is avoided in the paper because of the relatively "unsatisfactory" results available when the paper was written, and because it was to be "spared" for future publication.

The paper specifies the first two steps of this progressive transformation of methods in the *Introduction*. The progress of sequential transitions is assured by means of (out)dating and disqualifying earlier methods, and by solidifying the new alternative through the extension of its advantages. In accord with the subject of the paper, what is implied is a *progress of technology*. Exhibit 5 illustrates the respective transitions.

Thus, the *Introduction* inserts the author's work into a double frame of technology and practice, the latter being much more elaborate. The mandate for the work is derived exclusively from a string of practical demands. The paper refuses to even hint at a progress of technology which does not depend on the frame of a better use of practical resources, even though the paradigm in Exhibit 5 (which is present *in parvo* in the paper) would easily lend itself to a more dominant role. As one might expect, the recessive role played by the "scientific"—as opposed to the practical—frame is reversed in papers classified as basic science.[23]

The point here is that the double-threaded framework of the *Introduction,* no matter which way it leans, is a construction of contexture which replaces the circumstances of practical action encountered in the laboratory. If the scientific paper is a de-contextualisation with respect to practical circumstances and local idiosyncrasies of scientific action, at the same time it provides the reader with a *recontextualisation,* found in the *Introduction*.

Like the laboratory reasoning we have heard, the argument of the *Introduction* launches a resource and carefully delimits the space and time in which it is placed. The space is that of practical circumstances which, whether "world-wide", "in the U.S." or "in various European countries", surround the production and recovery of protein. The time is that of a present marked by increased energy costs, and a possible future (in the U.S.) in which wasted protein is recovered, and done so more effectively than at present (in Europe). The resource, however, is no longer a resource *for* the scientists, variously convertible within the network of relationships in which they deem themselves entangled. In the context created by the *Introduction,* one of these conversions has already been accomplished: the resource has been transformed into a resource for the generalised practical agents with which the *Introduction* is populated.

5.6 The Management of Relevance

In any conversation, a speaker's contribution at a given point in time is generally intended—and heard—as *relevant* to the preceding exchange, or the agreed direction of the talk. To sum up what happens in the introductory section of a scientific product like the published paper, we might say that it serves to *manage relevance* by (re-)constructing the *prior stage* and *direction* of an exchange in which it inserts itself. First, the

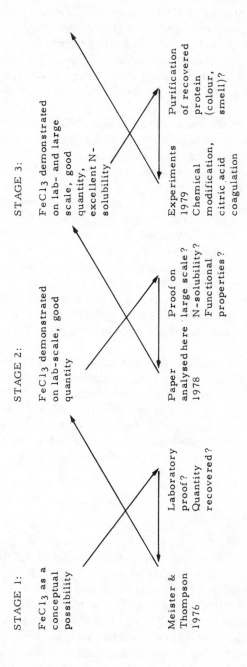

STAGE 1:

FeCl3 as a
conceptual
possibility

Meister &
Thompson
1976

Laboratory
proof?
Quantity
recovered?

STAGE 2:

FeCl3 demonstrated
on lab-scale, good
quantity

Paper
analysed here
1978

Proof on
large scale?
N-solubility?
Functional
properties?

STAGE 3:

FeCl3 demonstrated
on lab- and large
scale, good
quantity,
excellent N-
solubility

Experiments
1979
Chemical
modification,
citric acid
coagulation

Purification
of recovered
protein
(colour,
smell)?

Exhibit 5: The Progress of Technology of Which Two Stages Are Present in the Scientific
Frame of the Paper

authors have established *that* they have something relevant to say, given their description of the state of affairs existing *prior* to their contribution. Thus, their right to insert their statement into the scriptures of a field through publication is legitimate. Second, the authors try to indicate *how* their statement is relevant. For example, they have drawn upon the device of sequential contingency in the practical frame to suggest to the reader, step by step, how $FeCl_3$ could be converted into assets for a variety of agents whose interests they invoke—the U.S. which could use its plants and protect its environment more effectively, or the potato processing industry which could profit from a better, more cheaply recovered protein. Third, by arguing in terms of energy costs, nitrogen solubility and nutritional value the authors invite the reader to favour ferric chloride which fares best on these dimensions, implying that other variables discussed in the section on *Results* such as the absorption capacity of the precipitates which is higher with traditional methods, are less relevant. Thus, the *Introduction* provides criteria of relevance according to which some results presented can be seen as more important than others despite the refusal to make an explicit recommendation.

Note that we are talking about the *management* of relevance. The practical relevance elaborated in the *Introduction* is, first of all, a phenomenon of the discourse *about* practice, not a phenomenon of practice itself. By this I mean that the generalised resource-relationships which integrate scientists, the potato processing industry, a population which profits from more and better protein, or the U.S. which profits from less waste, have no correlate in the scientists' practical interaction. Nor do the scientists' actual transscientific connections have a correlate in the *Introduction*. The resource reasoning which is part of a scientific paper is a *move* in these fields, not a representation of them.

To be accepted for publication, this resource reasoning must provide a *plausible script* for (in this case) practical action, and not a scenario which has been or will be realised. While the same kind of reasoning has been found in the laboratory, the conversion which has taken place has moved to a level devoid of social corroboration through the enactment and negotiation of respective relationships. More precisely, the relevance managed in the *Introduction* has no correlate in social action which does not depend on further conversions through the practical response of those the paper manages to interest.

5.7 The Story of the Laboratory Continued

"R. had used OIA protein for a try to filter out the Fe (for the rat-testing) on lab scale, but the attempt did not work since the vacuum in the filtration process was not strong enough. Originally he said he would freeze the stuff, then stopped because it was such a mess. The attempt to get out the Fe worked (but not too well) in the P- lab on Friday, and since he was so angry with the terrible gel-like protein, he decided to centrifuge in analogy to P- lab(?) on smaller scale and to see what happens, come what may. R. did, however, not really believe it would work, since he had tried it already on a very small scale and without citric acid and it had not worked. Furthermore, R. thinks centrifuging not an ideal solution since on a technical scale, it involves too high . . . (etc.)"

The above quote is an unedited entry from my laboratory notes dated 18 April 1977, and refers to research following the decision to work with ferric chloride. It is part of the summation of a day's work, a hurried jotting rather than a verbatim account of what R. actually did and said. But if we turn to the scientific paper (and specifically, to the sections which follow the *Introduction*), we will search in vain for anything which even remotely approximates this summary. Indeed, we will find nothing in the publish-ed paper that corresponds to the series of experiments on removing the iron from the protein concentrates to which the above note (and many others) refers.[24]

Our goal is to extend the analysis of the scientist as a literary reasoner from the paper's *Introduction* to the sections on *Methods* and *Results,* and to pursue further the transformations between laboratory-reasoning and its written presentation. However, given the lack of correspondence I have indicated, this task becomes an almost preposterous undertaking. How can we compare the incomparable in terms of se-quence, spacing, reference, or even content? In the case of the *Introduction,* this task was made easier because the scientists grounded their choice of a new research focus in a multiplicity of reasons, to which the *Introduction* offered an equivalent. It is precise-ly the lack of such an equivalent in the subsequent sections of the paper that creates the difficulty.

We have seen that the *Introduction* of the scientific paper is a co-produced, double-threaded recontextualisation whose function as discourse is to manage the relevance of the text. A recontextualisation presupposes some form of *decontextualisation*. In the paper, we find no trace of the agents, the relationships and the concerns which permeated the scientist's laboratory reasoning. The *Methods* and *Results* continue this strategy of decontextualisation, but do not provide any further recontextualisation. In-stead, they are marked by a conspicuous *avoidance* of arguments which might ground their assertions.

Let me illustrate this decontextualisation by first considering more closely the laboratory operations referred to in the section called *Methods and Materials.* Notes taken in the laboratory provide us with a full-blown "action description";[25] that is, with a presentation of the scientific tasks and doings which dominated the laboratory scene. That these tasks are rarely specified in full is apparent from the constant inter-pretations and (re-)negotiations: the space created by the indeterminacy of laboratory action is filled with reasoning about "what is the case" and "what is to be done". More precisely, the scene is dominated by what *could* be the case, and what *should* or *might* be done. Let us look at an example from the work to which the paper refers.

The date is 9 February 1977, one day before the second run of the large-scale recovery experiments. Dietrich learns, through a phone call from Jackie, his senior in the laboratory, that Watkins has finally agreed to let them have the large-scale laboratory, "after making lots of difficulties". The experiments are set for the next day, which puts them, by their own account, under considerable pressure. Only ex-treme circumstances could alter the date set by Watkins. Moreover, they feel grateful for *any* opportunity to use the laboratory. My notes continue the story:

"According to Dietrich the first thing to do is to get the Bentonite (an adsorbent agent) needed for the tests. He goes to search for it. . . . When he returns only after about two hours, he says he did not find any of it in the storage room nor in some of the labs which usually use it. He also says he realises that the Bentonite might be bound with the protein. They could risk it in this case, since the effect is pH depen-dent, but he does not like taking the risk.

The problem is discussed among those present. Anderson suggests that they try calcium carbonate, one of the most important adsorbents in general use. He says he used it once to separate protein from other ingredients, and it worked perfectly. Dietrich says they will have to try it tomorrow, since there is no other alternative. The major problem is that the calcium carbonate will probably contaminate the protein. They decide to see what the results look like first, and then try to get rid of the calcium carbonate.

The second problem is to decide at what point in the process to add the calcium carbonate. If it is added before they make the split into HC1 and $FeC1_3$ treatments, they can compare the new HC1-precipitated protein with the old one (for which no adsorbent agent had been used) and see what they've gained, if anything. If the calcium carbonate is added at the beginning, it will bind with the starch and be removed with it during centrifugation. To add it later in the process would better correspond to conditions as they hold in practice, but this raises fears concerning colour.

Furthermore, it is questionable whether the calcium carbonate can be removed. In any case, it implies using the Sharpless (large-scale, high-speed centrifuge) a second time, and Kelly (the technician heading the large-scale laboratory) must be persuaded to agree to this. If Kelly says it can't be done, they will not be able to change his mind.

A third possibility would be to add the calcium carbonate after the split into different treatments, and go into the Sharpless with only half the product. Dietrich says he wouldn't dare to do this with Bentonite. Since he had read that fractions of the protein are responsible for the volume decrease effect (obtained in another series of experiments under way), he thinks that Bentonite might bind with precisely those inhibiting protein fractions, in which case they would obtain artifacts . . .'' (2-9/1).

The example need not be extended to illustrate the sort of reasoned choices within which laboratory doings are temporarily stabilised, and the ways in which what is selected is contextually contingent on a local situation and the dynamics of local interaction. Note that, in principle, there is *no difference* between the reasoned selectivity of laboratory doings in regard to an experiment and the reasoned selection of a new research focus illustrated earlier. The reasoned doings involved with the process of scientific production are no more than an extension of the reasoned selections which scientists qualify as a beginning; they may be more finely grained, but are often no less consequential than the making of an initial choice. Making such a difference is the work of the scientific *paper,* which strictly distinguishes between the management of relevance and warranty through the resource-reasoning of the *Introduction* and the process of production (the section on *Methods*) of what has been warranted and declared as relevant.

5.8 The Paper-Version of Method

If we now turn from the laboratory to the scientific paper, we find ourselves in a different world. The world of *Methods and Materials* is a place full of brand-names of instruments, lists of materials, and descriptions of procedures tied together by nothing but sequence. In the paper, method has no dynamic structure of its own: no problems, no resources to transform problems, no fusion or fission of interests to carry out the operations.

Despite being couched in the past tense, method resembles, more than anything else, the recitation of a formula. We find, not laboratory tasks, but a laconic checklist of steps taken. Rather than reasoned selections in which the doings of the laboratory are inserted and stabilised, we find a catalogue of sequential manipulations stripped of both context and rationale. In place of an account of the social negotiations of particular agents through which the laboratory choices were derived, we find a selective recording of the transient results of those negotiations permeated by technical particularisation. In sum, method is presented as a flow-chart of selections disguised as *non-selections,* for lack of relevant contextualisation.

Let us be more specific as to what we mean by this lack of relevant contextualisation. Clearly, we would not expect a scientific paper to detail the personal interests and interpersonal negotiations which sustain the manufacture of knowledge.[26] We have seen that the scientific paper is, in a sense, an exercise in depersonalisation. However, it is not clear why the paper should rigidly refuse to include any technical justifications or problematisations in its "report" on laboratory procedure. In other words, it is not obvious why the selection of a particular technical instrument, composition of chemical ingredients, temperature, duration of an experimental process, or interval of measurement should not be justified in technical terms, or why relevant problems should not find their place in a research "report".

Every reference to a device or chemical substance in the *Materials and Methods* section, as well as every figure cited, represents the outcome of a technically justifiable choice. Only a few of these choices are standard preferences, such as the methods issued by the Association of Official Analytical Chemists used to determine chemical composition. Some of these choices involved several months of testing and modification, as when several adsorbent agents were examined between 29 January (first reference to "the problem") and 11 April (final decision), and finally rejected in favour of an alternative procedure.

Most of the procedures which lead up to the naked doing which appears in the paper left traces in official laboratory protocols, where technical rationales are often minutely documented. Exhibit 6 reproduces an example taken from the official protocol book of the technician who performed those chemical analyses not provided by service laboratories. The example refers to an HCl-hydrolysis method of lipid extraction which had to be modified because of the problems encountered. Needless to say, no rationale for the modification is given in the paper.

Clearly it is not feasible to include in a scientific publication the full story of the reasoning, or the doings and undoings which lead to a selection which, in terms of the product launched by the paper, is a final one. The point here is not that the *whole* story is missing,[27] but that *any* (technical) argument which accounts for a (final) choice, as well as any problematisation of alternative possibilities, is rigidly avoided in the section of the paper which purports to report on laboratory procedure. Compared with the relevant work in the laboratory, where the *making* of selections dominates the scene, the paper offers a curiously purged *residual* description, constituted more by what is *not* at stake in the research (such as the brand-names of devices, or the origins of a technique) than by what is.

Moreover, this residual description is highly *typified*. As implied by previous examples, the protein recovery experiments referred to in the *Methods* section were per-

Amended Procedure for Extraction of Hydrolyzed Fat*:

Transfer the mixture to a 125 ml separatory funnel.
Using 25 ml ether in 3 portions, rinse the tube into the funnel. Stopper
and shake vigorously, venting often initially, for 1'. Add 25 ml petroleum ether [PE]
b.p. 30-60°C (Skelly F), cap, and shake vigorously 1'. Centrifuge, cd 500rpm GSA [in clear Nalgene bottle]
(40×G), 10' ⇒ upper layer: clear ether extract; lower layer: H₂O/alcohol fraction.
With a pasteur pipet, draw off the upper layer into a funnel with stem packed
with cotton to permit only the passage of clear extract into the tared boiling flask.
Re-extract the slurry twice as above, but use only 15ml portions of each
ether. Collect extracts into the same flask.
Finally, rinse the funnel with a few mls of ether-PE mixture (1:1) into flask.
Evaporate the ethers as described.

* Rationale:
A dry run using reagents only and the sep funnel, proceeded smoothly.
However, problems were encountered when the first material, d846-6A (rice) [also 6B,C]
was attempted. A murky, possibly imaginary interface appeared only after
~1½ hrs, separating an opaque, purplish upper layer which did not clear,
from a blackish lower layer. Further, the "interface" could not be even moving
when the outlet was opened to drain off the lower fraction. Lastly, filtration of
the extract (drawn from the top of the sep funnel) proved impractical:
the cotto plug was overloaded with particulate matter almost immediately.
The same occurred with potato products, though not with soy. In the latter case, [or occasion]
the clear ether fraction which separated did so incompletely, for the volume
recovered appeared far less than the 50 or 30 mls added ∴ Centrifugation
seemed appropriate to recover maximally the ether fraction in all three materials.

Reference: AOAC Official Methods of Analysis, 1975. Procedure 14.019 (Wheat Flour)

SIGNATURE: _____   DATE: _____

Read, Understood, and Witnessed by: _____   Date: _____

Transcript
----

*Rationale:

A dry run using reagents only and the sep funnel, proceeded

smoothly. However, problems were encountered when the first

material, 286-6A (rice), also 6B,C was attempted. A murky,

possibly imaginary interface appeared only after about 1 1/2

hrs., separating an opaque purplish upper layer which did not

clear, from a blackish lower layer. Further, the "interface"

could not be seen moving when the outlet was opened to drain

off the lower fraction. Lastly, filtration of the extract

(drawn from the top of the sep funnel) proved impractical: the

cotton plug was overloaded with particulate matter almost

immediately. The same occured with potato products on occasion

though not with soy. In the latter case, the clear ether

fraction which separated did so incompletely, for the volume

recovered appeared far less than the 50 or 30 mls added.∴

Centrifugation seemed appropriate to recover maximally the

ether fraction in all three materials.

Exhibit 6: Rationale for Modifying a Procedure in the Laboratory Protocol

formed three times within five months, each time under different environmental conditions and in response to different demands, rather than as straightforward repetitions. Accordingly, different issues and relevances structured the work, and different problems were encountered and attended to.

For example, the first series of experiments was dominated by the question of whether the procedure would "work" and provide enough of the desired protein. The series included two other plant protein sources which were compared with the potato protein, but are not mentioned in the paper. The second series centred around efforts to purify the protein, for which recovery constituted a necessary, but uninteresting prerequisite. The third series used real, rather than simulated, waste water, and focused on a different method of purification.

The problems tended to reflect these various issues. In the first case, the main problems seemed to be those of keeping the process under control, which meant, among other things, making sure that the desired temperature was indeed obtained, or that the instrumental manipulation of the different proteins remained "comparable". The scientists spent most of their time trying to prevent things from going wrong, or fixing things that had gone wrong (such as the sudden development of foam, for which the technicians were unprepared and which created problems with their instruments). Standardising procedures among the different technicians involved proved to be another major concern.

In the second case, all of the visible problems were concerned with purification, and the shift in focus left the scientists seemingly unconcerned about any of the previous "problems". The third set of experiments was marked by a general deproblematisation. The issue was still purification, but the procedure being tested was not expected to create difficulties or to work effectively.

To be sure, all three experimental series included "comparable" designs with respect to recovery, and hence resulted in the "same" protein, with variations attributed to measurement error. The argument is not that the residual description of the paper is a fraud, but that it is based on typification. The sequence of steps outlined in the paper is a normalised, average depiction in which many of the particularities and exactitudes of the laboratory have been omitted or transformed.

We can illustrate this transformation by comparing two more pages from the laboratory protocols with the final description of the recovery process included in the paper. The first page is an example of a scientist's handwritten notes taken during a run of the experiments. The second is one of the many charts prepared and modified before, during and after the tests. The third part of the picture is Fig. 1 of the *Methods* section of the paper, introduced by the scientists as a "simplified" flow diagram. The comparison between the three affords us a glimpse of the kind and amount of "simplification" (see Exhibit 7).

In sum, we can say that the avoidance of reason and the typification of the paper's version of *Method* converts the painfully constructed "way" (or method) of the laboratory into a *natural consequence* of the work's overall purpose and the reasoning contained in the *Introduction*. The double-threaded reasoning of the *Introduction* is the only place we can turn for an answer to the question "why" in respect to a methodical selection. Yet clearly the reasoning of the *Introduction* does not contain the answers to such questions. While the choice of a research focus argued in the *Introduction* impregnates the decisions made in subsequent laboratory work, it also implies that the scene of action is reset, with renewed indeterminacies requiring new selections.

Thus, the reasoned selections of the laboratory cannot be deduced from the choice of a research focus, and the absence of any grounds for decision in the *Methods* section is not remedied by the grounding of the research found in the *Introduction*. Such non-thematisation of selectivity with regard to the process of research production may well play a role in our tendency to believe that the research topic alone, and not its "internal" execution, is a matter of social choice and negotiation. This rejection of thematising selectivity not only hinders the outsider from perceiving and analysing the constructive operations of the laboratory, but also makes it more difficult for other scientists to evaluate the work.

PROTEX SAMPLE CODE: C280-47 nach pH

Achtung beim Einrühren | Einstellen mit NaOH

START: ca. 7.30 alt; PH Einstellen 7.50 (gegen Ende mit Wasser nochgewaschen)

TEMPERATURE during stirring: 18°C

PH - 9.01 bei start → 8.71 gegen Ende | 3500 ml top pH 11

SAMPLES: Ashes | 1700 ml 2N HCl
Dann 8.05 - 8.50 | dann Protex
| dann 2000 ml

SAMPLE RESIDUE

SAMPLE EXTRACT: C286-441 | PH Korr mit
SAMPLE RESIDUE wird genommen | Puffer um
der nicht wieder | 0.35 db von 9.65 auf 10.0

PH TITRATION:

PH + 1000 ml — 4500 ml 5.72 MHE | +700 5.12 | 7700 ml 2N HCl
+ 200 — 5.48 | +700 4.89
5.20

Temp: 19°C | 34 minutes

COOL: Temp. after cooling: 26°C | Steam cold WATT

[diagram] ← Product

to cooler

DE J+14 : Danw, SHOOT TIME: 45"
Prod. fluss rate 40 lbs/min —1— PRESS: 16 lbs

PH - 1. Supernant: 4.86
Temp. —1— 26°C
Produkt austragung alle 45 sekunden
SAMPLE CONCENTRATE CODE: C256 - 45

DH - Waschstep: 4.93
Stir 10 minutes than start
Temp. 2 supernant 22°C
pH 5.00 | 4800 ml 1N NaOH

211 pounds wet concentrate, Adjust to pH: 6.95
storage of concentrate at +34°C | finished 1.00

SIGNATURE: _____ DATE: 22/11/76
Read, Understood, and Witnessed by: _____ Date: _____

PRODUCTION OF POTATO PROTEIN PRODUCTS

D.
11/20/76

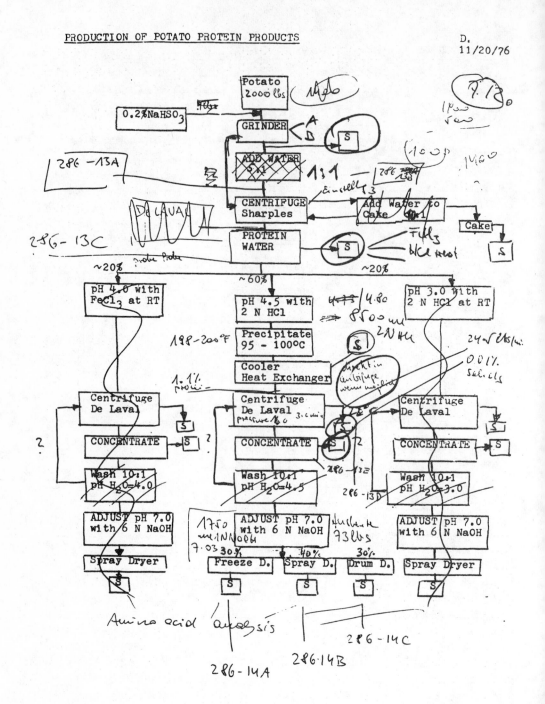

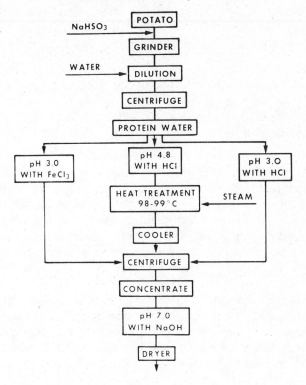

Example of Flow Chart Used and Notes Taken During Experimentation, and Flow Diagram Published in the Scientific Paper

5.9 The Results and Discussion of the Paper

It should come as no surprise that the section called *Results and Discussion* continues the trend set by the section on *Methods* by refusing to propose any other grounds for decision than those specified in the *Introduction*. And it, too, creates a separate reality which is at best residual to the reality of the laboratory. The reality of the section on *Results* (see Appendix 2) is not invoked by a formulaic recitation of procedural steps, but by statements of similarity and difference, mingled with occasional comparative evaluations. This distinctiveness, however, is not matched by any similarly distinctive pocket of laboratory work.

While we can track down those momentary crystallisations of determinacy in the laboratory by which scientists mark the beginning of a new line of research (and which are recontextualised in the *Introduction*), such distinctions as "methods", "results" and "discussions" are hopelessly intermingled. The scientists observed did not first perform experiments, then obtain results and finally interpret the outcome. The methodical constructions of the laboratory are reasoned doings, which means interpreted, discussed (and thereby negotiated), and decision-impregnated actions. Furthermore, this reasoning proceeds with respect to, and in terms of, the results of methodical construction.

Methods and results are dependent upon each other in a very simple way. For example, when I asked a scientist if some values he had obtained in a previous experiment weren't proven wrong in the light of results from a new method he had tried, I was told:

> "You have to stop thinking in absolute terms. The water content of a substance depends on the method chosen, on the time, the temperature, and so on. In general, you dry for 3 to 5 hours at 105°; if drying is done for 30 hours at 150°, then you get a higher water content. . . ."

The lesson here was that results are always the results of specific methodical selections (which says nothing more than that they are constructed). What is obtained is not independent of *how* it is obtained, although it can be detached and removed from its construction to take on a reality of its own. For the scientists, the relationship between methods and results was a vital part of their reasoning. Methods were chosen with a view to the anticipated or intended results, just as results were rejected because of the methods used to obtain them. The divorce between methods and results is the work of the paper, just like the exorcism of selectivity and reason from the actions recited in the *Methods* section.

This work is achieved by a specific form of argument by similarity and juxtaposition, which is—and this is the interesting point—heavily restricted with regard to the phenomena admitted for comparison. For the most part, the results are merely related to each other, in partial agreement with the declared goal of the paper which was "to compare" and to "evaluate":

> "Compositional differences among the PPC precipitated by various methods included higher crude protein in the HC1/heat precipitate, higher vitamin C and ash in those precipitated at ambient temperature (HC1, $FeCl_3$), and higher Fe values in the $FeCl_3$ precipitate . . ." (11. 89 ff.).

Or they are related to results published in earlier work:

> "Although laboratory experiments by the authors indicated that slightly less protein would be recovered at pH 4.0 (Fig. 2), Meister and Thompson (1976) showed that $FeCl_3$ precipitation produced maximum recovery at PH 4.0" (11. 32 ff.).
> "The increased ash content associated with HCl precipitation at room temperature was also observed by Meister and Thompson (1976), who noted . . ." (11. 42 ff.).

Note that no conclusions are drawn from these comparisons. The evaluative component is present in only a few statements which evince characteristically mild support for the *Introduction*'s preference for ferric chloride:

> "Laboratory experiments showed that $FeCl_3$ compared favourably with HCl/heat treatment at pH 2-4 with respect to the amount of coagulable protein recovered from the protein water (Fig. 2)" (11. 3 ff.).

Yet in a later comment, even this preference is qualified:

> "The PPC precipitated at ambient temperature with HCl and $FeCl_3$ would be more appropriate for human consumption if ash values were reduced" (11. 45 ff.).

Explanations, like evaluations, are rare. Among the 101 lines of the *Results and Discussion,* only one sentence offers a tentative explanation, and only one refers to a pattern of influence. In the final, summarising paragraph, each sentence contains a notion of similarity and difference, but draws no conclusions. As mentioned before, the last sentence relegates the "ultimate selection of a precipitation method" to a future comparative analysis of a series of parameters, including those not investigated in the paper.

In sum, we might say that the section on *Results and Discussion* effectively *denies* the interdependence of methods and results which ruled laboratory reasoning by relating the results *not* to their process of production, but to other results. Furthermore, the reasoning in terms of similarities and differences found throughout the *Results and Discussion* sets the scene for eventual conclusions. Yet curiously enough, these conclusions are not drawn. In fact, they are explicitly disavowed. Finally, the *Results and Discussion* utilises some earlier studies in its comparisons of individual results, but again without drawing conclusions or searching for explanations in those cases in which a dissimilarity is noted. The pattern is well suited to the stereotyped image of science as presenting the "facts" which others may use in making decisions. Yet this pattern cannot be attributed entirely to the authors' strategy. While "factualising" results by refusing to relate them to the process of production is present even in the first version of the paper, the avoidance of conclusions is not.

5.10 From the First to the Final Version Once Again

Now that we have looked at the final version of what the paper presents as the *Methods* and *Results* of laboratory work, let us ask again just how this final version (Appendix 2) differs from the authors' first official draft (Appendix 1). In both sections of the paper discussed here, the differences are less conspicuous than those found in the *Introduction*. And, unlike what we saw in the *Introduction,* the changes in the final version do not run counter to the original rhetoric of presentation. The final version of the sections on *Methods* and *Results* reinforces rather than dissimulates the original strategies.

To begin with, the section on *Materials and Methods* is almost identical in both versions. Changes are limited to splitting some longer sentences in half, inserting two statements originally included in the section on *Results,* and changing a few references and measurement details. The most interesting aspect of these changes is that two statements of reason and purpose present in the first version were wholly eliminated from the second. Thus, where the first version had said:

> "*Because* of the inconvenience of transporting a dilute solution and because of possible compositional changes, it was *decided to simulate processing water in the pilot plant in order to* compare different precipitation methods" (11. 3 ff., emphasis added).

The final version reads:

> "*Potato processing water was simulated in the pilot plant*" (1. 3, emphasis added).

Similarly, this statement in the first version:

> "The slurry was diluted with water (about 1:1) and centrifuged . . . *to remove* the starch" (11. 13 ff., emphasis added).

is deprived of purpose in the final version:

> "The slurry was diluted with water ($\approx$1:1 v/v) and insoluble solids were removed by centrifugation . . ." (11. 11 ff.).

The avoidance of any grounds for decision, and more generally, of any thematisation of the reasoned selectivity related to the methodical doings of the laboratory had been the most striking feature of the section on *Methods*. This avoidance is made complete in the final version.

The final version of the *Results and Discussion* continues this tendency to reinforce a previous mode of presentation, in this case, the relational, comparative argument. The first version of the *Results and Discussion* is extended by the inclusion of some measurement details not previously available, the addition of new comparisons, and a rephrasing in symmetrical terms of what had previously been a clear preference or a conclusion.

For example, the last passage of the first version stated a preference for ferric chloride:

> "The *advantages* of treatment with $FeCl_3$ are reduced energy costs *since* the protein water does not have to be heated to 95-100°; and an excellent nitrogen solubility of the resulting PPC" (11. 61 ff., emphasis added).

Note that the preference is still presented as *reasoned*. In the final version, however, the passage deals with nothing more than the differences and similarities between various precipitation procedures and their outcomes, taking care to balance "positive" outcomes (e.g. higher vitamin C) with "negative" counterparts (e.g. ash):

> "Differences between these precipitation methods include the energy input required for steam (HCl/heat) and ingredient costs (HCl, $FeCl_3$). Compositional differences among the PPC precipitated by various methods included higher crude protein in the HCl/heat precipitate, higher vitamin C and ash in those PPC precipated at ambient temperature (HCl, $FeCl_3$) and higher Fe values in the $FeCl_3$ precipitate . . ." (11. 87 ff.).

Note that the final version's symmetrical presentation and its refusal to *spell out* conclusions does not mean the paper no longer implies a preference. The *Introduction* focused on such dimensions as energy costs and nitrogen solubility, or the suitability of the recovered proteins for human consumption. These dimensions became the criteria of relevance by which important results could be distinguished from the unimportant ones. The recovery procedure favoured by these criteria is clearly the one which the first version of the paper bluntly promoted as an "alternative" to the (discredited) existing methods.

Thus, the final version still argues for a departure from existing practice in favour of an alternative, but no longer *admits* to proposing it. There is still a conspiracy to overthrow that part of the scriptures which promotes heat coagulation, but the attack is not openly announced. Instead, it takes the form of guerrilla warfare, under the cover of dissimulating literary strategies. From the open attack in the first version, we can conclude that this dissimulation is not primarily the work of the authors, but the result of the co-production by critics and reviewers which led to the final version. We can also say that the authors were *forced* into guerrilla warfare by the resistance they encountered; it was not a tactical plot of their own.

This resistance also played a role in a second kind of change found in the final version of the *Results and Discussion*: the comparisons with the results of other studies. These are drawn from the results in an earlier publication on a different protein source by two of the paper's authors, and from the results of a study by Meister and Thompson, to which four new passages refer. This latter study is important because it constitutes the single relevant precedent for the use of ferric chloride as a coagulant, albeit in a different context and with different goals. The study consequently posed the greatest problems in differentiating the new work. To institute their work as an alternative and inject their say into the scriptures of the area, the authors had to ally themselves with their predecessors who, in some respects, had obtained similar results. But at the same time, they had to differentiate between themselves and their predecessors in order to establish their work as relevantly new. The literary resolution of the problem in the first version was to avoid it. The *Introduction* mentions Meister and Thompson twice as a source of specific data to support the authors' proposals, but their work is entirely absent from the rest of the paper. In the final version, Meister and Thompson are mentioned in the *Introduction* once, in passing, but their data are brought into play several times in the *Results*. Characteristically, their role is one of unclear consequentiality:

> "Meister and Thompson (1976) also found $FeCl_3$ to be more effective than HCl as a precipitant of potato protein. They reported that, at pH 3.0, 31 and 36% of the crude protein were recovered by HCl and $FeCl_3$ precipitation, respectively. From these data it is also apparent that Meister and Thompson achieved more effective results with HCl and somewhat less effective results with $FeCl_3$ when compared with the results reported in the present study" (1. 14 ff.).

> "Although laboratory experiments by the authors indicated that slightly less protein would be recovered at pH 4.0 (Fig. 2), Meister and Thompson (1976) showed that $FeCl_3$ precipitation produced maximum recovery at pH 4.0" (1. 32 ff.).

> "The increased ash content associated with HCl precipitation . . . was also observed by Meister and Thompson (1976), who noted that HCl recovered more total solids from the effluent than does precipitation by HCl/heat" (1. 42 ff.).

The final version allots much more space to the preceding study, but most of it, at best, is a weak creditation of the work, displaced to the section on *Results*. The new work shows little interest in gaining the full support of the preceding study, nor in directly addressing the many differences in focus, investigated phenomena, or (implicit) conclusions. If the precedent was largely avoided in the first version, it seems to be ignored, despite its greater presence, in the final one.

This curious accomplishment is again the result of a form of negotiated compromise between the co-producers of the final version, some of whom resisted the authors' interest in differentiating their own work from that of their predecessors. The example suggests a phenomenon I noted in other laboratory writings: beneath its surface structure, the scientific paper enacts a *hidden monodrama*,[28] marked not by the sort of literary plot found in the first version of the *Introduction,* but rather by the author's argument with specific others who have a say in the matters addressed. More simply, much of what is written in a scientific paper is written *against* someone else. Such arguments are present in the reasoning of the laboratory, but seem to be hidden in the final paper.

In our case, the argument was with those who supplied the resource which the authors converted into a scientific paper—that is, with Meister and Thompson. The theme was the compulsory differentiation of the paper's selections from those proposed by Meister and Thompson. Through the resistance of critics and reviewers, the battle for differentiation turned, as we have seen, into a guerrilla war. The surface of the published paper is marked by the hidden fission of interests which characterises the relationship between the authors and those scientists whose resource they draw upon, and from whom they need to differentiate themselves.

The scientific paper presents a codified version of the differentiation which began in the earliest stages of the research, and which appears in the writing and rewriting of the paper as the *hidden strategy* of the text. The point here is that the selections of the laboratory presume not merely a fusion of interests with those for whom the research is launched as a resource, but also a possible fission of interest with those other scientists on whose resource the research itself depended.

We have seen the authors enact this fission in a private monodrama under the cover of the inconspicuous "scientific" frame of the *Introduction* and the symmetric, in-conclusive reasoning of the *Results and Discussion.* And we have seen the fusion of in-terests presumed in the laboratory transform itself into the contingency-deep struc-tured resource-reasoning of the paper's practical frame. The transformation effected in the move from laboratory to paper is both double and thoroughgoing. Exhibit 8 pro-vides a sketch of this process.

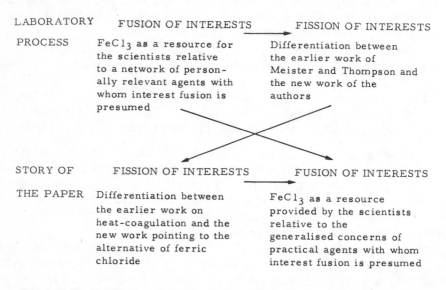

LABORATORY   FUSION OF INTERESTS   FISSION OF INTERESTS

PROCESS   FeCl₃ as a resource for   Differentiation between
               the scientists relative   the earlier work of
               to a network of person-   Meister and Thompson and
               ally relevant agents with   the new work of the
               whom interest fusion is   authors
               presumed

STORY OF   FISSION OF INTERESTS   FUSION OF INTERESTS

THE PAPER   Differentiation between   FeCl₃ as a resource
             the earlier work on   provided by the scientists
             heat-coagulation and the   relative to the
             new work pointing to the   generalised concerns of
             alternative of ferric   practical agents with whom
             chloride   interest fusion is presumed

Exhibit 8: The Proliferation of Interests in the Laboratory and in the Paper, and the Transformations Effectuated as We Move from the Laboratory to the Paper

5.11 The Transformation Function: Are there Rules of Correspondence?

Now that we have variously compared the observations from the laboratory with the first and final versions of the written product, what can we say about the paper's authentic claim to being a research "report"? If the paper is a research report, there must be *rules* of transformation which link it to the work of the laboratory. But what are these rules? What is the link between the scientific text and the laboratory? What are the laws of legitimate purgation and recontextualisation? And how do the transformations we have sketched fit into these rules?

Within a logic of action like that observed in scientific work, the scenes from the laboratory might be described as changes of states brought about intentionally by conscious human beings with reasons and purposes.[29] Clearly, scientific papers do not purport to provide an action description along such lines, including all intentions, states and circumstances of laboratory work. However, it is tempting to assume that a research report intends to provide a summary or *"relevant description"*, limited to supplying necessary information under some criteria of relevance. The search for the rules of transformation, then, can be reformulated as a search for the criteria of relevance.

When we interpret a piece of information, we generally supply those propositions which are presupposed, entailed, or a likely consequence of this information. Thus, a relevant (summary) description should be one which contains only that information which cannot be reasonably presupposed, and is not entailed or a likely consequence of what is said. And a research report, like the scientific paper, would become a description which refers only to those actions, events and phenomena which are immediately relevant for obtaining the paper's technical results. In other words, it would contain only necessary and sufficient information with respect to the results "reported", given whatever knowledge can be presumed in the audience.

Note that this entitles the paper to leave aside the story of the analogical origin of the research in the laboratory. We know that the paper relocates this origin in the *Introduction,* as part of the problem- and resource structure of the present world from which it departs toward the possible. Moreover, in terms of our definition, the *Introduction* is not itself—and need not be—part of the research "reported". Nor are the *Abstracts* and *Summaries,* which pull together some of the paper's arguments, but do not directly address the research.

Given these restricted responsibilities, the criteria of a relevant summary description will apply most to the section on *Methods,* and part of the *Results and Discussion.* We should not expect any unnecessary information from these "report"-sections, such as a "report" on how the precipitation agents used in the experiments were obtained from the storage room, or a "report" on the problems in gaining access to the equipment. The paper is not intended to advise the reader on how to proceed in such matters, but on how to proceed *presuming that such matters can be handled by the readers themselves.* Nor, with our definition, can we expect the paper to spend much time on the tacit knowledge of a speciality area.

But what is the tacit knowledge of a speciality? According to the concerns voiced by the scientists during the first large-scale recovery experiment, the development of foam in the protein concentrates was a major problem. The laboratory response was composed of hurried *ad hoc* decisions—the foam was variously ignored, treated with water, sprayed with a foam detergent, or simply skimmed off the concentrates. I was puzzled by the procedure, and later by the fact that the problem was not even mentioned in the paper:

> Question: "Why didn't you mention the foam which caused you so much trouble?"
>
> Answer: "Well, this is trivial . . . because everyone working in the area knows about the problem. . . . Only outsiders are baffled by it!"

If a paper is to provide a relevant summary, the tacit knowledge in an area must be sufficiently defined, and the information in the paper must correspond to this definition. However, in answering the above question, the scientists suggested that both assumptions may be far from warranted:

> "On the other hand, uncontrolled losses (by removing the foam) may be high, and the composition of the lost part may well be different from that of the remaining product (*I was told that the foam might contain more solid particles*). . . . Furthermore, people use different chemical foam detergents which can change the functional properties of a sample. Then they proceed to measure the functional properties without either taking into account or mentioning the detergent . . ." (5-14/2).

What is "trivial" and what is not seems to have been not at all clear to the scientists, who were challenged by the seemingly innocent problem of foam. Even if we can safely presuppose an awareness of a problem, the ways in which it might be solved by different scientists is not, as we have heard, irrelevant to the results obtained. Why, then, is such information not included in the paper? Many laboratory problems which are left unthematised in the papers can be associated with the development of scientific "know-how" which, as implied in Chapter 2, is a *local* (or even personal) practical knowledge of how to make things work. For every bit of published "method", there seems to be a bit of unpublished know-how which not only reconstructs the recipe sequence of steps in the paper into that of feasible doings within the situational logic of laboratory action, but also provides routines for diagnosing and coping with many unspecified problems.

The point is that this know-how is not a generally available, tacit knowledge of a field which need not be specified in the paper. Even the co-authors of a paper may be left in the dark. For example, after the first runs of recovery experiments, Watkins (the head of the group whose facilities had been used) asked that the procedure be repeated. The scientists took this request to mean that Watkins wished to familiarise his staff (and himself) with the procedure so that they could later use it on their own. I found this surprising, since Watkins was a co-author of the paper in which the procedure was described:

> Question: "But Watkins is your co-author, he has the paper and must have read the procedure!"
>
> Answer: "Yes, but this doesn't mean that they will be able to do the stuff themselves! . . . There is no other reason why they should suddenly want us to repeat the work, (that is) after Watkins read the paper and realised the results are important . . .!" (3-3/1).

What do the scientists say when we ask them directly if the paper includes all the relevant information? To cite one example, the scientists replaced an ether-extraction method of lipid determination by an HCl-hydrolysis technique which yielded significantly different results, but said nothing in the paper about the reason for their choice. I asked whether a scientific reader working in the area could supply the reason himself:

> "He could, in principle . . . but it would require a lot of thinking. And he would have to presuppose that I did a lot of thinking too. . . . In practice, he simply would not know . . ." (9-12/9).

When I asked if it were usually difficult to understand how a previous author had proceeded, I was told:

> "There is some informal communication between the scientists in the U.S., which means that the reason for using a certain procedure can be discovered informally. . . . I do this myself—I call somebody, or write to him, or meet him at a conference. . . ."
>
> *"There is a problem, of course, if one wants to replicate a result or repeat a method. As a rule, however, one does something else anyway. Hence, it is not so interesting to know exactly why and how certain things were done . . ."* (9-12/10, emphasis added).

Lack of journal space was often cited as the reason that current scientific papers do not include all the relevant information on how the laboratory results were obtained. More than once I was told that it was precisely the section on methods which had been cut more and more in the past several decades.[30] This, however, only shifts our problem to the question of why more journal space is not provided for what remains of a research report within the scientific paper. The reader will recall that there is not much space left for a "report" in the first place, given the space that is occupied by *Introduction, Summaries, Abstract, Discussion, References, Acknowledgements,* etc. And the question persists of why the little space that is left in the paper for a "report" on the research is cut off from the reasoned selectivity of this research and isolated from the results it has generated.

In the above quote, the scientists themselves suggest an answer to this question. There may be no need to have all information relevant to the technical success of an outcome, or even relevant to an informed evaluation of the results. Scientific papers may simply not *be* summary descriptions, and our conception of the paper as a concise research "report" in the sense of such a description may be wrong. But what then remains of the rules of correspondence which, we supposed, link laboratory work and scientific paper? Not surprisingly, it is in the writing of the paper that we find a hint as to the process of transformation.

How did the scientists actually proceed when they prepared their text? The first thing to note is that they proceeded in the reverse order to the sequence of events found in the paper. The scientists began by putting together the tables and figures which come last in the paper. These served as the "core" around which the paper was to be constructed. In the present case, the first handwritten version of the paper consisted solely of a series of selected verbal restatements of the contents of these tables and figures, later to become the *Results and Discussion.*

One particular table became the core of the *Methods* section: it contained a flow chart of experimental steps prepared by the scientists for the technicians who were to run the recovery tests. The *Methods* section reads like a recipe giving laboratory steps because it is nothing but a verbal recitation of the flow chart, enriched by names and some equivalent presentations of additional tests. The basic manuscript, consisting of the tables, and *Methods* and *Results* sections, was usually written in one to three days, depending on available time. The *Introduction*, based on another pile of paper (the literature), was written at the end, as was sometimes the case with the concluding remarks of the *Results and Discussion*. These had to be adapted to the core of the paper and frequently a senior co-author "took care" of them. *Abstracts, Summaries* and *References* draw upon other parts of the paper, and were written last.

The core sections of the paper, then, and those most likely to "report" on the research, originate from other writings, just as the *Introduction* derives from the scriptures of the area, and the *Abstract* and *Summaries* from the paper itself. These other writings were the measurement data and laboratory protocols, whose numbers, graphs and photographs we find in the published paper in a cleaned-up, composed, and edited version prepared by the "art shop" of the institute. The writing of the paper begins long before the manuscript is written, through the traces generated during laboratory work.

It follows that the link between the laboratory and the scientific paper cannot be established by rules of cognitive transformation. The scientists who write a manuscript do not recall the research process and then proceed to summarise their recollections. Rather, the link between the paper and the laboratory is provided by the *written traces of laboratory work,* which are continuously generated in the laboratory and at the same time form the source material around which the paper is constructed. The gap which exists between the dynamics of the research process and the literary dramatics of the paper is bridged by a *double mode of production* rather than by cognitive transformation. The scientific paper is the *product of* this double mode of production, not its reflection, or summary description. The instrumental mode of production which results in laboratory measurements involves an almost total decontextualisation, relieved only by the rationales found in the scientists' written notes. The literary mode of production which results in the published paper offers a recontextualisation, but as we have seen, not one which brings back the memory of laboratory work. The transition is, at the same time, a conversion of the written traces themselves. Except in the memory of those who were present during the process, it is an irreversible transition.

5.12 Conclusion: The Process of Conversion and the Idea of an Economy of Change

To conclude, let us consider again the mechanism of conversion invoked several times in the last two chapters. In the transition from laboratory work to the scientific paper, the reality of the laboratory changed. We have seen the situationally contingent, opportunistic logic of research replaced by a generalised context of present and possible worlds, and the interest negotiations of particular agents transformed into a projected fusion of interests of technology, industry, the environment and a human population needing protein. We have seen the reasoned selectivity of laboratory work overruled by formulaic recitations of the doings which emerged from this selectivity, and the measured results of these doings purged of all traces of interdependency with their constructive creation. We have seen the indeterminacy of the laboratory reduced to the careful expression of scientific doubt which the paper allows.

In short, we have observed a conversion into another currency, a transmutation into the totality of another language game. This conversion was itself a process. It started long before the paper was written, through the production of measurement data and other written traces of laboratory work, and continued with the collective enterprise through which these traces became caught, identified, and finally preserved within the double-threaded web of argumentation that distinguishes the finished paper. Without the fabric of reasoning into which the traces are woven in the paper, the numbers and graphs of the laboratory would be without meaning and importance, unidentified and very probably unidentifiable. Given their fixation in a past and a future, in a context of names and relevancies, they are ready for further conversions.

As mentioned before, conversion is not halted by the kind of fixation which the written paper provides. If the paper is read and if some of what it says is "used", it will be inserted into a new fabric of meaning and relevancies, and it will in the process be redefined, modified, analogically transformed or criticised and rejected.

The *Introduction* we read rehearses such future transformations by displaying the work as a resource which converts into assets for a number of practical agents. It presumes a conversion which is not socially corroborated, since the resource-relationships invoked are not matched by corresponding social interactions. Yet it points to a mechanism of social connection which is interesting in itself since it differs from the predominant conception of the social organisation of science as discussed and criticised in Chapter 4, i.e. from the idea that social integration rests upon something which is shared, be it norms, values, or the cognitive paradigms of presumed scientific communities, and from the idea that the relevant mechanism of social integration is a form of quasi-economic *exchange*.

From what we have seen it will be clear that we need not assume shared morals, cognitions or interests in order to account for social cooperation. No identity of values or viewpoints needs to be postulated in order to account, say, for the cooperation between union members whose jobs are threatened and the union representatives who defend these jobs. It is sufficient to assume an invoked fusion of interests by which the threatened jobs of the workers become, for the union representative, a threat to the size of union membership. In the present case, we need not assume that scientists respond favourably to some research results because they share with the authors the criteria of relevance and standards of evaluation which impose a certain "rational" selection. It is sufficient to assume a *temporary* fusion of interests through which scientists respond to results as a resource convertible into results of their own. Social action is interconnected not because of what is shared, but because of what is transmitted from one locus of action to another, transformed, and reintegrated, or because of a continued *process of conversion* which consists of the circulation *and* transformation of social objects.

It is this idea of a process of conversion which needs to be distinguished from the mechanism of quasi-economic exchange encountered in Chapter 4. In the process of conversion, the circulation of objects involves not their equivalence, but their difference. It is a process in which these objects are, continuously and asymmetrically, *reconstructed* from a preceding object, while their *equivalence* to or *difference* from these preceding objects is at the same time *negotiated*. In economic terms, what is postulated here is an *economy of change* rather than of exchange, a process in which equivalence is superimposed on disequivalence, and in which disequivalence means conversion as well as perversion.

Why perversion? The transfiguration in a fairy tale of a wizard into a mouse is at the same time a disfiguration of the wizard. The conversion to a new faith, a new language, or a new level of organisation is a perversion with respect to the old faith, the original language, or the preceding level of organisation. The economy of change is at the same time an economy of conversion *and* perversion. The products of science are continuously transfigured and disfigured as they circulate in transscientific fields. As they move from the scientist's desk to the office of a politician, they change into a policy argument. As they move to an industrial enterprise, they turn into a tool in the process of industrial production. In the hands of another scientist, they convert into a source of continued thematisation of selectivity.

Under all these circumstances, they undergo a recontextualisation and reconstruction similar to what we found in the writing of the paper. Analogical reasoning itself can be seen as nothing but a form of recontextualisation through which a previous scientific object is turned into a new object.

The examples of analogical reasoning given in Chapter 3 describe changes of location of a result, a concept, or an "idea", accompanied by a transformation of context and subsequently, by the transferred object itself. Compared with the source, the outcome of the process includes distortion, mutilation, or in general terms, perversion. Compared with the work observed in the laboratory, the written paper is, as we have seen, a first complete perversion. Indeed, writing itself is an apt medium for such perversion.

Yet without the disequivalence, which we can choose to call perversion or conversion, depending on the point of reference, how would we conceive of social or more specifically, scientific change? This disequivalence results from the indeterminacy inherent in social action, from the degrees of freedom to which we traced back (in Chapter 1) the possibility of scientific development. The last chapters of this book have led us to consider this disequivalence not only as a correlate of scientific change, but also as a correlate of social interdependency and connection as found in the resource-relationships that traverse transscientific fields. We have said that resources which cannot be converted (or perverted), remain socially *ad hoc,* which means that they do not lend themselves to the fusion or fission of interests of social agents, and consequently to the continuation and interconnection of social action. A scientific product which cannot inscribe itself, or impose itself, as a resource to be converted into the ongoing enterprises of other social agents will be neglected and ignored. Hence, this conversion is actively sought in the laboratory and manifests itself in the script of a resource conversion, which the scientific paper represents.

To consider the process of conversion illustrated by the transformation of laboratory selectivity into scientific papers as a basic mechanism of social connection, is to put the analogical transformations within science discussed in Chapter 3, on an equal footing with the transformations which connect scientists and non-scientists in transscientific fields. It allows us to understand the decision translations of the laboratory which connect to these fields, as anticipating these transformations. And it prompts us to substitute for the scientific communities we have long presupposed in social studies of science, the inhomogeneous networks of relationships apparent in actual laboratory interaction.

The fission and fusion of interests which marks these relationships is decided *in* the process of conversion, not before or apart from this process. With the present conception, conflict and cooperation are variable outcomes of social practice rather than basic features of this practice which we need to presuppose. The cooperation found in the circulation of scientific products hinges upon the convertibility of these objects. The continuity of social action is a continuity of disequivalence and change. We know from other areas of social reality that such disequivalence flows naturally from the circulation of social objects and is usually interpreted in the sense of perversion.[31] It is easy to see how it *must* flow naturally from the circulation of social objects in a reality to which time and space have been restored, in a reality which is composed of *local, contextual* breeds of social action. To be connected, the local, contextually contingent practices of science are bridged by processes of transformation imposed by the presumption and negotiation of equivalence and difference.

The continued transformation of social objects noted in other areas of social life is also pervasive in science, where it is at the same time the most and least surprising to find it: most surprising, because the idea of a conversion (or perversion) illuminates the local character of scientific practice, a practice which has, for a long time, served as our paradigm of *non-local* universality; least surprising, because change is most visibly instituted in science, and the conversion of scientific objects is the germ of their change; most surprising, because science thrives on a presumed *equivalence* between the "facts" of nature and the fabrications of the laboratory, and between the fabrication of the laboratory and the written product of a scientific paper; least surprising, because science itself has postulated disequivalence and the indeterminacy upon which it rests as the source of progress and development.

The point illustrated by science is that underlying the problem of continuity is one of discontinuity; underneath the surface of equivalence, is disequivalence; and underlying the circulation of social objects, is their transformation. It is this transformation which we have associated with the continuation of social action, and which we have considered to be a mechanism of social integration. Science illustrates that the perennial problem of social order may not be a problem of "order", but rather a problem of transformation, and of social change.

Notes

1. As claimed, for example, by Hofstadter (1955), who explored and developed distinctions between scientific and artistic uses of language. For some recent analyses of the writings of social science and philosophy, see Silverman (1974), Bourdieu (1975b) or Gusfield (1976). See also Stehr and Simmons (1979), who deal with discourse structures in these areas on a more general level, and Woolgar (1976a) and O'Neill (1981) who address some production properties of historical writing. See also Lepenies (1978) on the scientist as writer, and the storage of psychological traditions in public literature.

2. For some rare analyses of papers in natural science, see Latour and Fabbri (1977), Bastide (1981) and my own Greimasean analysis of the presently studied paper (Knorr and Knorr, 1978). Mullins summarised some rhetorical resources in natural science papers (1977), and O'Neill and Lynch as well as Morrison deal with methodological issues referring to natural science texts. The last two papers appear in a forthcoming volume on the analysis of science texts, edited by O'Neill (1981). Other investigations into the process of publication are by Gilbert and Mulkay (1980) and Woolgar (1980), as well as Bazerman (1979).

3. For a summary of these literary strategies, see Bourdieu (1975b).

4. For one such investigation of "style" in scientific writing, see Aaronson (1977).

5. While the publishing of scientific work in journals began some 300 years ago, when the *Journal des Scavans* and *Philosophical Transactions* were founded in 1665, Roy MacLeod says (in a written communication) that the standardisation of certain features of scientific papers only dates back to the end of the last cen-

tury. The question left open here, of course, is why and how such standardisation came about, and what it meant. Clearly, the kind of standardisation we find today, which combines persuasion with respect for the objectivity of science, still allows a degree of freedom. This becomes clear when scientists argue about how to put things in a paper, depending on the journal they have chosen.

6. Cicourel has repeatedly argued the importance of this point with a view to sociological "reports", for example interview- and questionnaire data (e.g. 1974). See also the respective arguments in his work on discourse and text (e.g. 1975).

7. cf. Bourdieu (1975b: 4-8).

8. Personal communication.

9. I am aware of only one published paper on the question, which addresses it in terms of the transformation of research findings into scientific knowledge on a general, theoretical level. See Gilbert (1976).

10. In the present analysis, I will depart from my previous attempts to apply existing models of discourse analysis (Knorr and Knorr, 1978). Such models are scarce, and will not necessarily help us here. The model of account analysis, as described by Harré, considers speech and texts which precede, accompany and follow action as "produced to ensure the twin goals of intelligibility and warrantability" (1977: 291). While the warrants which scientists propose for their results will be a natural part of our analysis, the issue of meaningfulness as such, or the formal organisation of discourse, cannot occupy us here.

The dramaturgical mode is best exemplified by Gusfield's study of a text (1976). It draws upon literary criticism to analyse the action of a text in terms of the dramatic tension created by a plot and its dénouement. The dramaturgical model is similar to the structural model of narrative discourse developed by Propp for Russian fairy tales (1968) and extensively modified by Greimas. The best introduction to the approach is found in Greimas and Landowski (1979). See also Greimas and Courtés (1979).

Both the dramaturgical and the structural approaches are well suited to certain parts of the scientific paper, and ill at ease with the rest. Greimas reduced Propp's elaborate classification of functions and agents found in the fairy tale to a core structure which consists of the transformation of a need through the transfer of a valued object from an addressor to an addressee by a subject helped by an ally and hindered by an opponent. While the basic function of need-transformation can be retained for those parts of the scientific paper which summarise the "story", it appears inappropriate for the sections on Methods and Results. The same holds for the notion of a plot and its dénouement in the dramaturgical metaphor.

Furthermore, as noted by Morrison (1981), with approaches such as Greimas story grammar, it is the model, and not the material, which specifies what an event turns out to be. Rather than forcing a close correspondence between our texts and any one of the above approaches, we will draw upon the various interpretations when they seem appropriate, but consider the text itself as our main source of information.

11. "Complete" means nothing more (nor less) than that the beginning of the research effort (as identified by the scientists) occurred during the period of observation, and that I have been able to follow the subsequent course of action through the writing of the manuscript and beyond.

12. By which I mean they were co-editors of certain journals, and held official positions in the respective societies.

13. cf. Pickering (1980: 27 f.).

14. This is not to say that an assertion of quantity or quality is the *only* information conveyed in every single sentence. However, even in cases where some other information seems to predominate, the argument includes some quantitative (e.g. economic) aspect. See for example 11. 38-41, in which alternative methods of processing are introduced by reference to an *economic* analysis performed on these methods.

15. Gusfield's suggestion—based upon an analysis of research on drunk driving—that the (dramatic) action of the paper occurs "in the unfolding of the story" is not supported here. In the present case, as in others I have looked at, the dramatic metaphor can only be reasonably applied to the *Introduction*. See Gusfield (1976). One possible explanation for this apparent discrepancy may be a difference between social scientific writing and the style preferred by the "hard" sciences.

16. cf. Lacan (1966: 11-61). Bourdieu identified the same pattern in Heidegger's writings. See Bourdieu (1975b: 115).

17. It will be interesting to know that a recent comparison of Wittgenstein's *Notebooks* with the *Prototractatus* and the *Tractatus* showed a similar reshuffling of original statements in the final version (personal communication). For the respective paper, see M. Pavicić (1977).

18. According to Bourdieu (1975b).

19. Version 4 is preceded by a handwritten discussion of figures and tables, which would become the core of the *Results and Discussion* of the paper. It was followed by a version which includes the typewritten supplement of a Methods section, an Introduction and a title page, and curiously, a reduced version of the Results

section. Version 3 was supplemented by more detailed information, and was the first version typed by a secretary. Version 4, again corrected, was the first to leave the original author's office.

20. For a general discussion of conversational "implicatures" and the recognition that a contribution to discourse is relevant under what Grice calls a "cooperative principle", see Grice (1975).

21. Based on interviews and comments, I am convinced that none of the authors felt the world food problem was one of protein at the time the paper was written. In fact, the senior author voiced grave hesitations on several occasions. Note, however, that these hesitations did not prevent the authors from implying that the world would substantially benefit from more available protein.

22. In some countries, industrial firms which discharge protein waste into public water are required by law to remove the protein because of the potential environmental hazard.

23. Compare, in this respect, the analysis of a more basic scientific paper done by Bastide (1981). In an earlier version of the paper, Bastide demonstrates the emergence of new semiotic objects via the progressive transformation of a biological phenomenon from the state of a conceptual possibility to that of proven existence, from which a new demand to conceive the mechanism which generates the phenomenon leads to a new conceptual possibility.

24. The only reference we find to the effort is a handwritten note added to page 10 of the first version of the paper (see Appendix 1). It reads, "The iron content of this concentrate could be reduced to 1% Fe(dm)", but did not survive subsequent modifications.

25. In his theory of narrative structure, van Dijk uses this term for any description in which all sentences refer to the performance of a course of action. A complete action description would include intentions, purposes, reasoning, procedures, etc. See van Dijk (1974: 29, 41).

26. Even though these interests are connected to decision translations in the laboratory, as argued in Chapter 4, and hence *are* relevant for the kind of results which are constructed.

27. Compared, for example, with an observer's detailed notes. Clearly there is no absolute end to the story one could tell about an ongoing action like that of the laboratory.

28. I use the notion here to refer to an author's private enactment of an argument with a cast of characters which tends to reduce itself to a single adversary who may not appear in this role anywhere else.

29. For a logic of action relevant to written accounts of action, see van Dijk (1974). Cf. Collins (1974, 1975) on tacit knowledge.

30. The interested reader might want to look at some very old, yet relevant articles occasionally quoted by the scientists. Compared with the paper analysed here, these articles provide elaborate narratives of what happened in the laboratory. See Thomas (1909) or Hindhede (1913).

31. Take, for example, the "perversion" of rules through their application (see the examples in Chapter 2), or the continued reinterpretation and modification of a law as it circulates to the site of its enactment. Cicourel's study of juvenile delinquency (1968) is a most illuminating illustration of such "perversions" of laws as practised by police departments. In the case of rules and laws, there is a special premium on the equivalence of the practice which refers to the rules and laws, just as there is in the case of (scientific) data which refer to some reality they represent.

Chapter 6

The Scientist as a Symbolic Reasoner, Or "What do we Make of the Distinction Between the Natural and the Social Sciences?"

Es dämmert jetzt vielleicht in fünf, sechs Köpfen, dass Physik auch nur eine Welt-Auslegung und Zurechtlegung . . . und nicht eine Welt-Erklärung ist.[1]

Friedrich Nietzsche

6.1 The Two Sciences

A well-known danger associated with an interest in the "cognitive" operations of science is that of slipping into idealism and subjectivism, of which we hear again and again in the contests between cognitive and non-cognitive perspectives.[2] Yet there is an equal, if opposite, peril in considering the object as objective and the subject as a distortion of the object.[3] We may lock the environment *into* a subject as well as *out*. Suppose, now, that we begin with neither subject nor object, but with the concept of scientific practice illustrated in previous chapters.

The elements of this practice have been discussed in detail: the local, contextually contingent character of scientific operations; their situatedness in transscientific fields which appear to be traversed and sustained by resource-relationships; the continued transformation and recontextualisation which is part of the realisation and circulation of scientific objects, as well as a mechanism of social connection; and finally, the decision-impregnated, socially-negotiated selectivity of scientific objects which results from these operations. The world of objects displays itself as an upshot of this scientific practice, meaningful and relevant only *within* the social constitution we have characterised, but at the same time not locked into subjective cognitions.[4] For it is precisely the selective constitution of scientific objects which is negotiated, imposed and deposed in this practice, and which is itself at stake in the discourse crystallised in scientific operations.

However, one consequence of such a step is to blur the increasingly popular distinction between the natural or technological sciences on the one hand, and the social or cultural sciences on the other. If the natural world, like the social one, is seen as selectively constructed *within* social practice, if it is a world impregnated with social decisions akin to the social reality with which we are familiar, then we may have to reconsider a dichotomy which relegates the symbolic and socially selective solely to the sciences of man.

To be sure, this distinction between the two sciences has not been proposed by empirical studies of science, but has proliferated mainly within methodological discussions centred around the inadequacy of certain measurement orientations for the study of the social world. Such orientations were called positivistic, and identified with a model of scientific method set by the natural sciences.[5] In fact, new rules of social science method have been developed, displayed and defended in a constant dispute over the standard provided by this model, and a departure from this standard has been the declared goal of an indigenous social methodology.

Not surprisingly, perhaps, the standard itself has been paid little attention in the dispute. While the "positivistic" conception is vigorously rejected as a model for social science methodologies, it is taken more or less at face value in reference to the natural and technological sciences (Garfinkel's depiction of "scientific" rationalities mentioned in Chapter 1 is but one small example). Philosophical investigations which have directly questioned this model as a correct description of the natural sciences are generally ignored or declared irrelevant to the discussion.[6] The same holds true for recent attempts in the social study of science to document aspects of the social construction of scientific reality.[7] In fact, the social study of science itself seems to have a split personality in this regard: while we are inclined to accept the thesis of the theory-ladenness of observation in the natural sciences without much hesitation, we are disinclined to question a dichotomy which relegates interpretative qualities exclusively to the sciences of man.[8]

Note that we are not referring to some narrowly defined social side of science to be found in specific areas. Both the philosophical arguments and the observational material presented here focus, as emphasised, on scientific reasoning as indicative of the technical productions of research. The argument is not that natural and technological scientists act like everyone else when they talk to their peers or fight with their superiors in the organisational hierarchy, but that their *methods* and procedures are sufficiently akin to those of social science to cast doubt on the common distinction between the two sciences.

It should also be noted that the effort here is to reconsider the distinction, and not to reject it outright. Given the relatively recent (and sometimes preliminary) nature of the available material, we must be content merely to raise, and not to settle issues. I would hope that the argument thus far has contributed to this goal.

Yet one aspect of the distinction between the two sciences which warrants further consideration is the question of whether the practice of natural and technological science can be distinguished from the symbolic, interpretative, "hermeneutic" practice of the social sciences, and of social life itself. I hold that it cannot. In fact, my goal is to underline the *essential similarity* between the two modes of production of knowledge which have become so painstakingly separated.

The basis of this similarity lies in the socially situated, contextual features of the manufacture of knowledge which were discussed earlier, as well as in the symbolic, interpretative qualities we shall get to later on. Given this similarity, it is time to reconsider the customary distinctions between the two sciences which ascribe to the one what they deny to the other. And given this similarity, it may be time to acknowledge scientific method as just another version of social life. To be sure, this separation was directed against a supposed "unity of the sciences" which postulated that, in the final analysis, all sciences are like physics. But if the mode of production in the natural and technological sciences is sufficiently different from the model upon which the principle of the unity of the sciences is based, there may be nothing absurd, improper or un-productive about denouncing the separation.

6.2 The Universality of Interpretation and Understanding

The basic distinction between the natural and social sciences, as found in more recent discussions of social methodology,[9] is sufficiently well-known that it need not be repeated here in detail. At its most general level, the distinction rests upon the assignment of a symbolic quality to social rather than natural life, and the attribution of an interpretative, dynamic and interactional quality—sometimes identified with hermeneutics[10]—to social rather than natural science method. While several lines of argument have been derived from these qualities, each seems to endorse the assumption that the difference between the social and the natural worlds is that the latter does not constitute itself as meaningful. Its meanings, the argument goes, are produced by men in the course of their practical lives, while social life is produced by the active constitution and reconstitution of meanings by the subjects themselves.

In recent discussions of the methodological status of the social sciences, there is often a tendency to let this distinction remain. However, as Dilthey[11] has pointed out, different regions of "fact" do not "exist", but are constituted by a certain methodology and epistemology. Hence, a circumscription of the object domain is not sufficient cause for a logically cogent delimitation of the two sciences. Dilthey himself considered the re-enactment of meaning on the part of the observer or social scientist to be the basis of the interpretative approach to social reality he advocated. But his characterisation was later rejected because it led to subjectivism.

In his criticism of Dilthey, Gadamer (1965) has shown that interpretation is not a question of entering the preconstructed meanings of social life through individual empathy, but one of mediating and translating between two traditions. His "universality of hermeneutics" refers to the fact that enquiry involves tradition-bound theoretical presuppositions in the social *and* natural sciences. Nowadays, we are more familiar with this contention in the form of three distinctive lines of argument, all linked to the notion of interpretation:

1. The first centres around the *denial of brute facts*. In essence, it holds that data beyond the challenge of rival interpretations are unattainable by science.
2. The second refers to the *circularity* of interpretation. It implies that any interpretation of an event or text ultimately depends on yet another set of interpretations, thus leading to an infinite regress of meaning.
3. The third can perhaps best be described in terms of Wittgenstein's notion of a *language game*. It conceives of interpretation as a condition for the possibility of data in general, and emphasises the interconnection and interdependency of various levels of interpretation.

Rather than argue the relevancy of these lines of argument for a methodology of the social sciences, let us consider whether the natural sciences can be justifiably characterised by denying the existence of brute observation, by referring to the circularity of their interpretations, or by assuming that their various traditions take on the character of a language game.

Least concrete—and hence, most difficult to establish or discard—is the notion of a language game. The main thrust of Kuhn's work (1962), of course, is to argue that normal scientific search is locked into paradigmatic traditions constituted by systems of hierarchically structured assumptions and conceptions which are sufficiently different between traditions to resemble internally coherent but mutually incommensurable language games. This thesis hinges significantly on the role played by scientific observation as an independent arbiter of scientific theories, as well as on the question of whether scientific theories can be fully defined independent of tradition-bound assumptions and pre-interpretations. Thus, it ultimately hinges on whether we can assume the existence of some form of "brute" fact in the natural sciences, and on whether scientific theories are exempt from cycles of interpretation.

Debates bearing on the question of circularity have been raging in the philosophy of science for quite some time, and the results seem to indicate that interpretative regress is by no means limited to the social sciences or the humanities. For example, logical investigations of the nature of the "rules of correspondence" between observational statements and theoretical hypotheses have shown that the former are not strictly deducible from the latter.[12] Consequently, observations relevant to the evaluation of a certain theory can only be established on the basis of certain assumptions. Furthermore, this process is not one of simple, bivariate correlation, for observation (and the measurement of observation) involve, as another level of pre-interpretation, a series of background theories which themselves need definite justification.[13]

Finally, it has been shown that we cannot require theories in the natural sciences to be fully interpreted, except in relation "to our overall home theory". Our only recourse is to "paraphrase in some antecedent, familiar vocabulary". In practice, says Quine, we terminate the regress of background languages "by acquiescing in our mother tongue and taking its words at face value" (1969: 49). In sum, we seem to be confronted with a situation in which interpretations (observational "facts") can only be explained and justified by reference to other interpretations on which they partly depend (theories), and by reference to their relation to the whole, our overall "home theory"—an exact definition of an interpretative cycle called hermeneutic in the cultural sciences.[14]

The theory-ladenness of perception corresponding to the rejection of brute facts (the first line of argument mentioned above) appears as just one component of this interpretative cycle in the natural sciences. As stressed by Taylor (1976), theories of perception which claim that natural science observation allows access to brute facts are largely a thing of the past. Attempts to convert the theory of brute facts into a theory of an independent observation *language* have been challenged most spectacularly by Feyerabend (e.g. 1975).

Feyerabend's thesis of the "theory-ladenness" of observation is amply documented by historical material, and it is neither the first nor the only claim in this direction. As we know, Hanson, Kuhn and Toulmin have derived similar conclusions from their investigations of the history of science.[15] Nevertheless, we cannot say that the issue has been resolved among philosophers of science. In fact, given what we know about conceptual change in general, it seems likely that the issue of theory-ladenness will not be settled by the leaders in the dispute, but will be overruled by actual developments within the philosophy of science. The signs of such a development are already quite strong: recent work in the area exemplified by Hesse, Stegmüller and Sneed neither neglects, bypasses nor explains away the problem. For example, Hesse explicitly incorporates some conception of the meaning variance of observational terms in her logic of scientific inference.[16]

6.3 The Curious Distinction Between Interested Action and Symbolic Action

Given these developments in the philosophy of science, isn't it justifiable to adopt the idea of the universality of interpretation, and to postulate a notion of scientific enquiry which allows for the symbolic, pre-interpreted character of observation? With respect to the assumption of meaning variance and its consequences, it might well be. But interpretation has also been denied to natural science enquiry by eliminating both interpretation and the negotiation of meaning from conceptions of scientific *action* in general. Curiously enough, the symbolic (and the social as well) have been expelled from scientific action in precisely those conceptions which otherwise argue that science is grounded in human interest and practice. In other words, not those traditional epistemologies against which the thesis of theory-ladenness fought its way, but their critical counterconceptions, the theories of knowledge proposed by Habermas and Heidegger.

Let us first turn to Habermas, whose conception of enquiry in the natural and social sciences, developed mainly in his methodological writings,[17] has been highly influential in the debate on positivism and the discussion of hermeneutics. The basic distinction promoted by this conception in between *work (Arbeit)*[18] and *interaction.* According to Marx, action is the synthesising activity of man which "regulates the metabolism (of man's interaction with nature) *and* constitutes a world". Habermas splits the two components of Marx's notion of action into separate categories.[19] *Interaction* is defined as *communicative* action, or action governed by "binding, consensual norms". It rests upon the grammar of language games, or upon the intersubjectivity of the mutual understanding of intentions. In this sense, communicative action is hermeneutic, for the reality it establishes is constituted in frameworks that are the forms of life of communicating groups. *Work,* on the other hand, is *instrumental* and not communicative action.[20] It is action governed by technical rules based upon empirical knowledge, and it results in conditional predictions about observable events. While the hermeneutic procedures of communicative action organise schemata of world interpretation for which there are no other grounds than further interpretations, instrumental action organises means to an end whose success depends on the validity of technical rules—that is, on empirically true and analytically correct propositions.

The naturalistic cast of scientific enquiry challenged by the work on the theory-ladenness of observation is reinstituted in Habermas' notion of instrumental action. According to Habermas, society is differentiated into subsystems in which one or the other type of action is primarily institutionalised. The paradigm of communicative action is the cultural sciences; hermeneutic processes of enquiry are linked here to a "practical" interest in maintaining the intersubjectivity of mutual understanding.[21] In contrast, the paradigm of instrumental action is the subsystem of the natural and technological sciences, which are governed by technical rather than practical interests. The claim is that modern science has developed "within a methodological frame of reference that reflects the transcendental viewpoint of possible technical control" to produce knowledge which "through its form" is technically exploitable.[22]

As with Peirce, to whom Habermas defers here, this means that science approaches (rather than contemplates) nature in a specific way; i.e., potential operative verification is presupposed in the conception of scientific problems, and predicates are constituted with regard to the system of reference of possible instrumentation.[23] In Habermas' terms, instrumental action which corresponds to this approach has the following characteristics:[24]

1. Language is no longer embedded in interaction, but attains "monologic closure" in the relationship of a subject (the scientist) confined to an object (nature).
2. Action is severed from communication and reduced to the solitary act of the purposive-rational utilisation of means.
3. Individual experience is eliminated in favour of the repeatable experience of the results of instrumental action.
4. Theory and experience are divorced; operations of measurement permit a reversible univocal correlation of operatively determined events and systematically connected signs (the theories).

Note that this characterisation of instrumental action as institutionalised in the natural and technological sciences goes beyond Peirce and his idea that scientific enquiry presupposes potential operative verification. It gives concrete meaning to the "transcendental" interest in technical control, which would otherwise bear little relevance to the empirical investigation of science. However, this concrete meaning paints a picture of science in which enquiry becomes a monologic, closed, solitary game against nature in which theory and experience are first separated and then correlated. The stakes are set in terms of mastery and control, but the game is not a social one. Just as nature is "salvaged out of history", so the symbolic lurking behind Habermas' notions of interaction, communication and experience is salvaged from the enquiry of natural and technological science. Hermeneutics and interpretation are once again confined to the social and cultural science.

The specific character Habermas attributes to the natural and technological sciences finds its precedent in the writings of Heidegger.[25] Habermas parallels different cognitive interests with different forms of action, and has them institutionalised in different subsystems of society. For Heidegger, the context of significance of everyday practice has absolute priority, and the theoretical attitude he postulates for science is founded upon a technical interestedness which he locates in practice. Heidegger holds that meaning arises from the "technicity" of practical action; that is, we give things meaning in our everyday concerns by interacting with them and by using them. We do not first perceive them as physical objects and then assign them functions on the basis of the properties we have isolated. Rather, we manipulate objects in terms of their presupposed functions in a referential context of significance and instrumentality.

If this technicity has absolute priority, then knowing as a form of observing and a form of quest after the nature of things becomes possible only if we refrain from manipulation and utilisation; or, in Heidegger's terms, if there is a deficiency in our concernful dealings with the world. Only by stepping out of a local context of instrumental activities can we first approach the properties of objects as properties independent of the objects they characterise. For example, we can move from talking about a particular hammer which is heavy to a discussion of the properties of heaviness.

However, this stepping out of a practical context has nothing to do with passive contemplation. "Nature" as revealed by science requires a specific mode of concern[26] with regard to practice, a theoretical interest which constrasts with the instrumental-technical involvements of everyday life. But this concern is both deficient and derivative: the instrumentality of things in everyday life is more fundamental than their identity as substances with determinate properties, and the practical interconnectedness of things can never be fully accounted for by scientific explanations of the combinations of these substances.

This brief sketch of Heidegger's conception of science draws attention to some of the differences between Habermas' and Heidegger's notions of "practice" and "technical". For Habermas, practice is linked to the Greek model of an interest in the good life, and to the ideal of mutual understanding through communication, while "techne" is linked to work or instrumental action.[27] For Heidegger, the technical (in the sense of instrumental significance) is the defining characteristic of practice itself.

But our brief sketch also points up an interesting similarity in their respective conceptions of science. Both Heidegger and Habermas attempt to expose what they consider to be a fundamental error in various philosophical and sociological conceptions related to science—namely, the belief that true knowledge of the world is to be gained by means of detached, disinterested, objective reflection.[28] For both Heidegger and Habermas, facticity presupposes interestedness: scientifically relevant facts are not objective features of the world which we merely discover, but the products of culturally and historically specific human interests and achievements.

Yet, while science is seen to be founded upon human practice via interests, it is not considered to be *part* of this practice. For practice is marked not only by interests, but also by a specific mode of interpretation and understanding. Heidegger links this hermeneutic of everyday life to structures of significance and care in which things have presupposed meanings we can never fully disclose. Habermas locates its basis in the structure of communicative acts.[29] Both of them constitute science as something different from and contrasted to this practice. While in this sense science is for the first time founded upon the interest structure of human practice, it is simultaneously excluded from the structures of meaning and significance which this practice displays.

As might be expected, this separation of meaning and interest requires some effort. Heidegger, for example, made it the point of his conception to show how the meaningfulness of the world and the interest taken in it are intrinsically interconnected and *cannot* be separated in practical life. How, then, can the separation be argued in the case of science? Presumably, the answer lies in the fact that neither Heidegger nor Habermas holds that science is directly oriented by human interests. Remember that these interests are held to be transcendental; or, in Heidegger's case, ontologically anchored in the structure of human Being. Thus, if scientific facts are the products of culturally and historically specific human interests, those interests are at least one fundamental step removed from actual scientific practice, to which they need not directly disclose themselves. Despite the fact that science presupposes specific human interests, actual scientific practice can remain free not only from the meaning structures of everyday life, but from its interest structures as well.

With Heidegger, the step into ontology results in a negatively defined science derived from the interpretations, interests and instrumentalities of everyday life. Of course, the picture we get of science as an abstract "theoretical" study of isolated properties of ob-

jects is founded on nothing more than the *decontextualisation* from which it was derived. As we have seen (Section 6.2), a study of the context of scientific theories would
quickly draw attention to the networks of presuppositions through which even the most
abstract study of isolated properties is sustained. A look at scientific theorising would
return to science the basis of meaning and significance without which no scientific enquiry, whether theoretical or not, can proceed. And a glimpse at the process of scientific experimentation might even find at work in science the same kind of technicity
Heidegger postulates for practical action. Short of such a recontextualisation based on
a study of science, Heidegger's derivations from practical action through abstractions
result in a picture which is not only peculiar, but simply inadequate.

With Habermas, such a recontextualisation is at least partly supplied through the notion of instrumental action he associates with the transcendental interest in technical
control. Through the notion of instrumental action, Habermas establishes a link between the fundamental nature of his technical interest and actual scientific practice:
surely we would expect a form of *action* to somehow manifest itself in the scientist's
dealings with nature as observed in the laboratory. However, when we actually look at
the laboratory, we find none of the monologic, presuppositionless (with respect to the
meaning of signs) and formally rational behaviour Habermas postulates for science.

On the other hand, if we reject the notion of instrumental *action* and solely accept
the idea of a transcendental interest in technical control, we do not learn much new.
Deprived of its concrete correlate and historical genesis in specific societies, the notion
of transcendental interest in technical control seems to achieve no more than a return to
the thesis that *homo faber*—and not the Greek ideal of man contemplating nature—accounts for the anthropological origin of science.

6.4 The Symbolic and the Laboratory

Habermas leaves us no other choice than to take seriously the notion of instrumental
action as a model of the actual form of scientific enquiry. The thrust not only of his
theory of knowledge, but also of his theory of social evolution hinges upon the differentiation of distinctive forms of action and their institutionalisation in different subsystems of society.[30] Strictly speaking, the thesis of instrumentality refers only to the
core of technical activities in the laboratory, and not to every action of a scientist. As
emphasised before, we are not talking about the commonly acknowledged social side
of science, but about what has been called its cognitive aspect; that is, the scientist's
technical or "intellectual" operations. We are not concerned with a scientist's
organisational quarrels, nor with their career strategies, in which Habermas could
scarcely deny the element of symbolic interaction and interpretation.[31]

But what about the scientist's experimental manipulations? Can we eliminate the
symbolic form of interaction and communication (and the cycles of interpretation
upon which Habermas and others base them) from the context of "cognitive"
laboratory operations? A model which claims (as does Habermas') that scientific enquiry is typically, basically, or ideally instrumental action, rather than symbolic interpretation and communication, suggests that we can. However, even a brief look at the
laboratory provides evidence that interpretation is as much part of the scientists'
technical or cognitive operations as it is of everyday interaction. The examples
presented throughout this book incorporate such evidence. Let us return for a moment

to the reasoning of the laboratory, and to specifically illustrate its interpretative quality.

What would we expect the evidence for an interpretative, "hermeneutic" character of laboratory enquiry to look like, given what we know about interpretation in historical enquiry, in the understanding of action-meaning by the sociologist or in anthropological investigation? According to Taylor (1976: 153), the object of interpretation presents itself as "confused, incomplete, cloudy, seemingly contradictory—in one way or another, unclear". It is "describable in terms of sense and nonsense, coherence and its absence" like the symbolic objects which constitute a text. In the laboratory, these symbolic objects are provided by the constant generation of measurement traces; that is, by graphs, figures, printouts, diagrams, and the like. They are also provided by such living experience as a colour change, the consistency of a mixture, the appearance of a test animal, or the smell of a chemical reaction.

Both the seemingly objectified results of a measurement procedure and the objects of living experience require interpretation. They must first be recognised as an instance of something, and thus assimilated into an everyday term or scientific concept by means of which we have heard they are subject to interpretation. Second, and perhaps more important, the scientist must "make sense" of these recognitions. This may begin to happen the moment an instance is recognised as something, in those cases where simple descriptions in standard observation terms do not fit clearly and thus require conscious decision-making or identification procedures. But the main question is to establish the "meaning" of some recognised instance in the context of the concerns of the situation, just as a social scientist has to establish the meaning of a specific utterance with respect to the general concerns of the interview.

The scientist mentioned in Chapter 3 who exclaimed, "The stuff has gone white", provided an example of a relatively unproblematic recognition of an instance in observational terms. His later remark that "the protein was precipitated" establishes at least a partial meaning to "The stuff has gone white" in the respective context. If there was anything incomplete, cloudy or confused in regard to these statements, it was not immediately apparent. But what, then, do we make of entries in the official laboratory protocol book such as encountered in the last chapter, in which we read:

> "A dry run using reagents only and the sep funnel, proceeded smoothly. However, problems were encountered when the first material, 286-6A . . also 6B, C was attempted. A murky, possibly imaginary interface appeared only after abt. 1½ hrs., separating an opaque, purplish upper layer which did not clear from a blackish lower layer. Further, the 'interface' could not be seen moving when the outlet was opened to drain off the lower fraction. Lastly, filtration of the extract (drawn from the top of the sep funnel) proved impractical: the cotton plug was overloaded with particulate matter almost immediately. . . ."

Quite obviously, the technician who wrote this note found it difficult to establish "what happened" to her material in observational terms. And from the rest of the entry, it is equally clear that the group in general had even more difficulty interpreting the occurrence within the context of the experiments under way. Needless to say, many events in the natural or technological scientist's laboratory are found to be every bit as "unclear" as the objects of intepretation Taylor postulates for the social sciences. If anything, quantitative measurements or analogical displays pose an even greater challenge to identification and secondary interpretation. Let us look at the example of

René, the chemist/mathematician plunging through his data:

Question: "And when you got your data on the relation between moisture and stability, the optimum was immediately apparent?"

Answer: "It wasn't immediately apparent, as a matter of fact. It was a quibble . . . (*inaudible; tries to find a plot*). Actually, what happened was, quickly, was that we plotted stability measured by some curve, it does not matter by what, as a function of temperature, and we found something that looked . . . (*searches again; cannot find it*). We plotted water content at two temperatures, and one was uh, (*writes on blackboard*) something like that, and one was something like (this), so one could draw a line, say . . . O.K., this is zero degrees and this is 95 degrees, it was something like this. Now let's just look at it, like that, because this uh, that . . . that was the first clue, that is how good the data were, you see . . . most people would say O.K., well that's about (it), you know . . . one is high and one is low, so that, O.K., what is an anomaly there . . . it looks as though this thing is going this way (*points it out*), and it turns out in fact that *that* is in fact what it does, but we only had a peak here. But if you wanted to be careless about the observation, you could easily say *that's* a straight line and *that's* a straight line."

Question: "Why did you not see it as a straight line?"

Answer: "Because I don't . . . because I, uh . . . most people *do* . . . I am always looking for something, some anomaly . . . O.K., that said that there is a premise, the premise is that there is a local isotherm . . . they reflect different kinds of things. . . . We looked at the physical chemistry, nuclear magnetic resonance, electron spin reasonance, X-ray defraction to try to show that in fact . . . that this was not just . . . that these were *real,* that these were not artifacts, they represented real differences. And I think . . . people are still questioning some of it, but I think uhm . . ." (8-5/3).

For a datum to appear as a "real difference" obviously requires some processes of interpretation, negotiation and mobilisation of contextual information. Like the ethnographer in a foreign culture, the scientist in the laboratory is confronted with noise and unlimited uncertainties from which she makes sense by drawing upon concepts and procedures which for the moment remain unquestioned. As in ethnography, the uncertainties relevant here appear on the level of recognition, identification and making sense of data and observations. It should come as no surprise, then, that scientists are familiar with the pay-offs which living experience can provide in this sensemaking process—a benefit which some social scientists seem to have forgotten.

In one case I observed, a scientist physically manipulated six different protein samples before taking his measurements. Struck by a difference in "the feel" of samples treated in standard fashion by a conventionally employed method, he became "suspicious" of the method. As a result, he varied the method in order to achieve samples of equal "feel", translated into the respective quantitative measurements. This allowed him to dispute, via publication, a method "almost universally" in use for "at least thirty years". When questioned, he said that "certain things can only be realised

if you do the experiments yourself". the same kind of experiments had been conducted
six months before with the help of a student, but since the scientist had "never looked
at the stuff" himself, he gained no profitable "ideas", and "could not make any sense
of the data" obtained by the student.

6.5 The Feedback Thesis

Let us assume that the scientific laboratory is indeed the locus in which "what is the
case" is dynamically constituted—and deconstituted—by the scientist's sense-making
activities, just as social situations are the locus in which meaning is socially constituted
in interaction. Let us further assume that these sense-making activities have more in
common with "understanding", as an act in which experience and theoretical ap-
prehension are fused, than with "explanation", as the "application of theoretical
propositions to facts that are established independently, through systematic observation."[32] Finally, let us grant that circularity and the pre-interpretation of observation
and experience mark not only the social and cultural, but also the natural and
technological sciences.

There remains yet one more line of argument to look at: that causal relations in the
social and cultural sciences are "malleable in the light of the development of human
knowledge", which means that, in principle, they can be recognised by men, and thus
incorporated into their actions in such a way as to transform them. Such feedback
alterations are a direct consequence of what Giddens calls the "double hermeneutic"
of social science—that is, the fact that it applies its (second level) concepts to the first
level constructs through which social actors have already preconstructed the social
world.[33] In Giddens' formulation,

> "The concepts and theories produced in the natural sciences quite regularly filter
> into lay discourse and become appropriated as elements of everyday frames of
> reference. But this is of no relevance, of course, to the world of nature itself;
> whereas the appropriation of technical concepts and theories invented by the
> social scientists can turn them into constituting elements of that very 'subject
> matter' they were coined to characterise, and by that token *alter* the context of
> their application."

Nagel has made it a point to argue that such "self-fulfilling" or "self-negating"
predictions are not unique to the social sciences, since observations about a series of
events in the natural sciences can also influence the course of those events. However,
Giddens stresses that such indeterminacy is "logically distinct" from the social
sciences, where "the point of the matter is that 'indeterminacy' . . . results from the incorporation of knowledge as a means to the securing of outcomes in purposeful conduct.".

There seem to be two assumptions on which this and other formulations of the feedback thesis rely. First, that human beings possess a *causal agency* not found in natural
reality; and second, that there is a level of *conceptual mediation* (consciousness) in
social reality through which this causal agency is stimulated to respond with actions
which alter the course of events. Of course, it is not the point to debate here whether
conscious reflection or conceptual mediation are distinctively human features, but we
can argue against limiting causal agency to human beings.

Then, too, the thesis raises questions in regard to consciousness. First, it is not in the least clear that *all* behavioural reaction to knowledge-based interference with the course of social events involves a level of conscious reflection. Presumably, if that were the case, the "consciousness-raising techniques" used by political groups would be utterly redundant. Second, it goes almost without saying that being conscious of a situation does not *automatically* trigger a behaviourally relevant response, and the conditions under which it does or does not are far from clear.

We might speculate that one minimum requirement for a reflection-based response is that the state brought to one's attention be disliked. Yet this dislike would have to be made causally effective in the face of the various social, psychological and material constraints that affect any change in a course of action. Our own practical experience in social life suggests as well that consciousness and reflection are but *one* kind of variable open to manipulation in the complex process of ongoing events, and not the *sine qua non* of their symbolic change and variation.

Furthermore, it can be argued that, if social reality is symbolic, the fact that any interference with it (e.g. through communication), as well as any potential course-of-event changing response (via reflection), will *also* be symbolic refers to nothing more than the specificity of tools, problems and procedures to a particular domain. However, such specificity in no way stops short of the natural sciences. After all, nobody claims that the reality of physical bodies and that of beehives are one and the same in the otherwise "unified" natural sciences, or that they require the same kind of tools and procedures of investigation.

What matters, perhaps, is that some previously given conjunction of events can be changed through *appropriate* interference with those events under specifiable conditions. If we accept such a formulation, the fact of human consciousness and its required specificities may be distinctive to some social sciences. But at the same time, they are the *equivalent* of instinct-triggered responses and their required specificities in biological disciplines, or the operation of forces between physical bodies and the specificities *they* require. This reduces our grand model of distinction between the two sciences to the long-standing notion that various sciences and specialities construe their object domains differently as specific domains, and that they operate—and are called upon to operate—accordingly.

If the reference to consciousness is not necessarily compelling, what about the assumption of causal agency to which we referred earlier? We might even suggest that it is precisely the idea of causal agency which lies behind the whole consciousness argument, since the latter is usually combined with some reference to action or an active response. For the social scientist, the idea of action as self governed, interpreted agency (in contrast to behaviour) has been familiar at least since Max Weber. In contrast to this concept of agency, the classical paradigm in the natural sciences defines events such that they appear directly juxtaposed to any conception of action.

As summarised by Bhaskar (1978: 79 ff., 87), this paradigm assumes (1) that causation is external to events; (2) that matter is passive; (3) that fundamental entities are atomic; (4) that there is no internal structure and pre-formation of entities; and (5) that qualitative diversity is secondary. Bhaskar claims that the idea that the source, trigger, or stimulus of events in natural science is always *extrinsic,* and that the objects of natural science are patients rather than agents "is a pure prejudice" that can be traced back to a mechanical world view long outdated in physics. Such a view must be replaced by a conception of events as "things" possessing powers and liabilities, which may have behaved in ways they actually did not behave.[34] Accordingly, statements of *laws* must be seen as "statements about the tendencies of things which may not be actualised, and may not be manifest to men".

But if "laws" in the natural and technological sciences are no longer seen as statements about *constant* conjunctions of events or experiences, the thesis which holds that there *are* no such constant conjunctions of events in social life *because* of an agent causality distinctively different from that of the natural world also misses the point. Let me cite in somewhat more detail a conception of a natural world which acknowledges the causal agency of its objects, giving credit to modern developments in the physical and biological sciences:[35]

> "Reflect, for a moment, on the world as we know it. It seems to be a world in which all manner of things happen and are done, which we are capable of explaining in various ways, and yet for which a *deductively justified prediction is seldom, if ever, possible.* It seems, on the face of it at least, to be an incompletely described world of agents. A world of winds and seas, in which ink bottles get knocked over and doors pushed open, in which dogs bark and children play; a criss cross world of zebras and zebra-crossings, cricket matches and games of chess, meteorites and logic classes, assembly lines and deep sea turtles, soil erosion and river banks bursting. Now none of this is described by any laws of nature. More shocking, perhaps, *none of it seems even governed by them.* It is true that the path of my pen does not *violate* any laws of physics. But it is not *determined* by any either. Laws do not describe the patterns or legitimate the predictions of any kinds of events. Rather, it seems they must be conceived, at least as regards the ordinary things of the world, as *situating limits and imposing constraints on the types of action possible for a given kind of thing*" (emphasis added).

If causal agency is not to be limited to actors in the social world, then course-of-event changing reactions in response to interference with these agents no longer serves as a distinctive feature of social life, and historicity (in the sense of agency-caused changes in courses of events) will have to be allowed for in nature. If natural laws are thought of as specifying the conditions and limiting the possibilities of types of relevant actions, and not as constant conjunctions of actual events, then the apparent lack of such constant conjunctions of events in social life is no longer a distinguishing characteristic between the social and natural worlds.

On the contrary, a conception of social "laws" as specifying the conditions and limiting the possibilites of types of social action seems quite compatible with all the distinctive features commonly attributed to social as against natural reality, e.g., the "uniqueness" of social events or the "historical and cultural variability" of empirical generalisations mentioned above; or the "unpredictability" of social events and the need to adapt procedures and social techniques to concrete fields of action.[36] Such compatibility is confirmed by analogies which compare *natural* laws to the *rules* of a game, and empirical events to its actual play on some particular occasion (cf. Anscombe, 1971: 21).

These analogies remind us of Winch's famous thesis that social reality must be explained in terms of rules rather than natural laws as traditionally conceived (1958). If the laws of nature have to be understood as "normic and transfactual" statements *analogous* to rules,[37] how would Winch's demarcation of the social sciences—which rests upon a presumed essential difference between normic social rules and factual natural laws—have to be remodelled? Much depends, of course, on further specification of the rule-like character of natural laws. For example, can we think of these rules as a function of some given and possibly long-lasting state of a specified universe of events which is itself subject to agency-effectuated change, in contrast to previously accepted invariance-ideas?

But as I have already suggested, the point here is not to attack the problem of an adequate epistemological conception of statements concerning regularities in the natural and social sciences, nor to attempt to re-settle the question of the distinction between the two worlds. Nor can the present discussion argue for a re-unification of the respective fields of research with respect to their concrete methods and techniques. What *is* at stake here is a reconsideration of the routinely made and ritually cited distinction between the natural and the social sciences in light of new conceptions concerning natural science research and methodology. Above all, my point is to argue that, in technical matters, the scientific reasoner is a *symbolic reasoner* whose selections are sustained by the interpretations which constitute both the living and the frozen discourse (in the scriptures and instruments) of an area.

Notes

1. It has now begun to dawn in five, perhaps six minds, that physics, too, is merely an interpretation or arrangement of the world . . . and not an explanation.

2. For recent examples of such controversies, see the dispute between cognitive anthropology and Harris (1968) as a representative of behaviourism, or Gellner's denunciation of ethnomethodology as a new kind of California idealism—an outcome, it seems, of his earlier polemics against Winch (1973). See also Gellner (1980).

3. For the most comprehensive challenge to this position in social studies of science, see Bloor (1976).

4. As we have seen before, Suppe holds that no position which in some way advocates the symbolic character of natural science procedure by claiming a meaning variance in observational terms is necessarily committed to idealistic or scepticist consequences. Of course, Suppe does not advocate a social conception of the production of knowledge as a viable alternative. See Suppe (1974: 196).

5. As one example, see Giddens' (1974) summary of the dispute over positivism and sociology.

6. For example, Giddens (1976: 155 ff.) reviews some of these results, but only to reemphasise the original distinction between the natural and social sciences.

7. For example, see Krohn (1972), Mendelsohn (1977) and the collection of studies published in Volumes 1 and 4 of the *Sociology of the Sciences Yearbook,* edited by Mendelsohn, Weingart and Whitley (1977) and Knorr, Krohn and Whitley (1980). Volume 4 is particularly relevant to the research process.

8. See the conclusions drawn by O'Neill (1979).

9. Paradigms for such discussions can be found in Harré and Secord (1972), Filmer *et al.* (1972), or Giddens (1976). Some basic articles from the philosophy of social explanation are found in Ryan (1973).

10. From here on, the notion of hermeneutics will be used in this general sense, rather than the more specific one of a methodological approach contrasted with others, such as phenomenology, or that of a specific technique of text-analysis contrasted with other techniques, such as semiotic procedures.

11. Cited in Habermas (1971: 141). See also Volume 5 of Dilthey's *Collected Papers* (1913-58).

12. For a discussion of the nature of the rules of correspondence, see Nagel (1961).

13. cf. Quine (1969: 69 ff.) and Lakatos (1970: 99).

14. e.g. Taylor (1976: 164).

15. See Hanson (1958), Toulmin (1961, 1972), and Kuhn (1970). Hanson has analysed historical cases in terms of Gestalt switches, such as Wittgenstein's "duck-rabbit" switch, Toulmin has used the model of

mutations of scientific theories, and Kuhn has elaborated the thesis of incommensurability in connection with the idea of a paradigm switch.

16. Hesse's book *The Structure of Scientific Inference* (1974) begins with the assumption that primary recognitions do *not* provide a stable and independent list of primitive observation predicates. Sneed treats the problem of incommensurability between two theories as a problem of incommensurable theories presupposed by the theories in question. See J. D. Sneed (1971). Stegmüller's conception of the problem of theory-ladenness can be found in *Rationale Rekonstruktion von Wissenschaft und ihrem Wandel* (1979: 27 ff.).

17. cf. Habermas' essay on the social sciences (1970a), and his *Knowledge and Human Interests* (1971). The views advanced in these volumes do not represent the final result of his efforts to develop a critical social theory. Further developments are available to English-speaking readers in *Communication and the Evolution of Society* (1979). However, the books mentioned earlier *do* contain the most explicit account of his theory of knowledge in the natural and technological sciences, which has been largely ignored in his later works.

18. The notion of labour, although not commonly used in English translations of Habermas, would be more appropriate here, since it directly refers to the "productive Eros" (Baudrillard) of Marxist theory in which labour is an "ontological concept of human existence as such". See Herbert Marcuse, "On the Concept of Labour" (1973: 11 ff.).

19. Habermas (1971, particularly Part 3, 189 ff.).

20. In the original formulation of "Technology and Science as 'Ideology' ", reprinted in *Toward a Rational Society* (1970b: 91 ff.), work is said to consist of "either instrumental action or rational choice or their conjunction". In *Knowledge and Human Interests,* instrumental action seems to *include* an element of purposive-rational choice (as will become clear from its second characteristic mentioned below). Finally, in *Communication and the Evolution of Society,* Habermas supplies a more elaborate classification of types of action, juxtaposing instrumental and social action; the latter included symbolic (expressive) action, *communicative* action oriented toward reaching understanding, and *strategic* action oriented toward the actor's success and corresponding to the "utilitarian model of purposive-rational action" (pp. 40 ff.). While Habermas points out that his previous analyses of labour and interaction "have not yet adequately captured the most general differentiating characteristics of instrumental and social (or communicative) action", it is clear that the basic dichotomy and the grounding of natural and technological sciences in *instrumental* action (as roughly defined by the characteristics summarised here) remains valid throughout his later work.

21. cf. Habermas (1971: 176).

22. cf. Habermas (1970b: 99). "Transcendental" is explained here as referring to the form of knowledge produced by scientists, in contrast, for example, to the content of knowledge, or the subjective intentions of scientists.

23. Peirce's example is that of a diamond's "hardness". The predicate is constituted with regard to other stones that are rubbed against the diamond. The diamond hardness remains independent of the rubbing, yet we can only attribute such "hardness" with regard to possible instrumentation. cf. Peirce (1931-35, Vol. 5: 457 and Vol. 7: 340).

24. cf. Habermas (1971: 191 ff.).

25. The particular reference here is to the ideas Heidegger promoted in *Being and Time* (1962). Much of my understanding of these ideas owes to Dreyfus' interpretation of Heidegger's existential phenomenology, as presented in seminars at the University of California, Berkeley in 1977.

26. For an example of Heidegger's existential conception of science, see pp. 408 ff. (1962).

27. Habermas derives his conception of instrumental action from Peirce. See particularly pp. 113 ff. (1971).

28. Heidegger questions the idea that it is possible or desirable to make explicit (i.e., in some sort of belief system) the implicit assumptions which constitute the background against which knowledge is gained. He radicalises pragmatist philosophy by making the involved, practical viewpoint superior to the theoretical, detached point of view. And he emphasises social context, rather than the individual, when he holds (with Wittgenstein) that philosophical problems can only be (dis)solved by a return to the study of everyday social practices. In their recourse to pragmatism and their emphasis on the social organisation of meaning in everyday life (hermeneutics), Heidegger and Habermas are strikingly similar.

29. Which, in recent writings, he analyses in terms of Searle's theory of speech acts. See Searle (1969).

30. This theory of evolution is outlined in a series of essays in Habermas (1979).

31. Of course, the separation between these social activities and something purely technical is itself problematic, as outlined in Chapter 1.

32. See Dilthey (1913-58, Vol. 5: 143) and Habermas (1971: 144) for these terms.

33. The idea of a double hermeneutic, and the point about first and second level constructs, dates back to

Schutz. cf. Giddens, (1976: 153 ff.).

34. cf. in particular Harré (1970) and Harré and Madden (1975).

35. Taken from Bhaskar (1978: 105).

36. The last thesis is more often found in discussions of problems of application in the social sciences than in epistemological debates. For example, see Lazarsfeld and Reisz (1975). The thesis seems to rest upon a mistaken conception of what goes on in the natural sciences, since the whole problem of technology *is* one of developing knowledge *adequate to* a particular field of action.

37. cf. Bhaskar (1978: 92).

Chapter 7

Conclusion:
The Major Theses of the Book

Let us summarise in brief the major theses of the book by pointing once more to the distinctive conceptions advanced in the preceding chapters. First, we have said that the "cognitive" operations of scientific enquiry display themselves to an empirical epistemology as *constructive* rather than descriptive, and we have explicated constructivity in terms of the decision-laden character of knowledge production. Note that we have linked the selectivity embodied in the products of science to a social process of negotiation situated in time and space rather than to a logic of individual decision-making. Second, we have pointed to *indeterminacy* and to *contextual contingency* —rather than non-local universality—as inherent in scientific procedure. We have associated this contextual contingency with an opportunistic logic of research and considered indeterminacy as constitutive of—rather than destructive of—the idea of scientific change. Third, we have illustrated the *analogical reasoning* which orients the opportunistic logic of research, and considered the circulation of ideas through analogy as part of the process of recontextualisation and transformation. Fourth, we have postulated that *variable transscientific fields* traversed and sustained by resource-relationships rather than professional membership groups such as "scientific communities" constitute the webs of social relations in which the scientists situate their laboratory action. Fifth, we have illustrated in the case of the scientific paper the process of *conversion* (or *perversion*) with which the circulation of scientific objects must be associated in a reality marked by local, contextual, socially situated breeds of action. And we have argued that this process of conversion can be seen as a mechanism of social connection—mediated by the fission and fusion of interests—which operates in transscientific fields. Finally we have challenged, on the basis of what has been learned from an empirical epistemology of knowledge, the distinction as customarily drawn between the sciences of man and those of the natural world. We have reviewed the lines of argument which disclose scientific reason as symbolic, interpretative reason, and we have claimed that the question of the *unity of the sciences* may warrant reconsideration.

As outlined in the *Introduction,* the major theses of the book are grounded in an anthropological investigation of knowledge production. I have said that the thrust of the approach lies in the promise it holds of a *sensitive*—in contrast to a frigid—*methodology,* which I take it will be fruitful in social studies of science. I consider the results obtained so far as the first step to an anthropology of knowledge to which future studies will have much to contribute, both in the other areas of research and in practical knowledge and technique. Needless to say, in present "technological" societies a hegemony over that which counts as knowledge appears to be held by the

152

sciences, whatever the subject matter. The present book is an essay of the nature of knowledge-production and reproduction as exemplified by these sciences.

Appendix 1

The First Official Version of the Scientific Paper, Including the Corrections Suggested by a Senior Co-Author

3

1 <u>Introduction</u>

2 Potato ·· tuber(s), henceforth called potato(es), contain an average of 2.1%

3 crude protein (N × 6.25) on a fresh weight basis and provide the

4 world with 6 million metric tons of protein per year (Markakis,1975).

5 Since most of the protein (about 1/3 of the crude protein) of potato

6 juice is coagulable it has potential as an egg white substitute in

7 some food systems (Rosenau et al.,1976).

8 Nitrogen balance studies with human adults have shown potato protein

9 to be superior to most major plant proteins, approaching the value

10 of whole egg (Kofranyi and Jekat,1965; Jekat and Kofranyi,1970;

11 Meister and Thompson, 1976).

12 Potato processing plant waste effluents such as from potato starch,

13 granules, chips and French fries factories, represent a tremendous potential

14 source of valuable protein. About 268, × 10⁻ metric tons of potato protein

15 (crude protein) are utilized in the U.S. for food processing (Agri-

16 cultural Statistics,1976). According to Kramer and Krull (1977) only

17 20 - 30 % of the vegetable plants is utilized directly for human

18 consumption in the U.S.A. If the remaining 70-80 % of the material

19 could be converted into nutrients, total nutritional resources

20 could be vastly increased and at the same time the waste disposal

21 problem could be minimized. For instance 25,000 metric tons of potato

154

22   ~~protein could be recovered~~ from the wastes of the starch mills

23   /∧ ~~of~~ the Netherlands (De Noord,1975) and 2,000 metric tons in Austria

24   (Wohlmeyer,1974). Potato prot . . see pag 4

3a

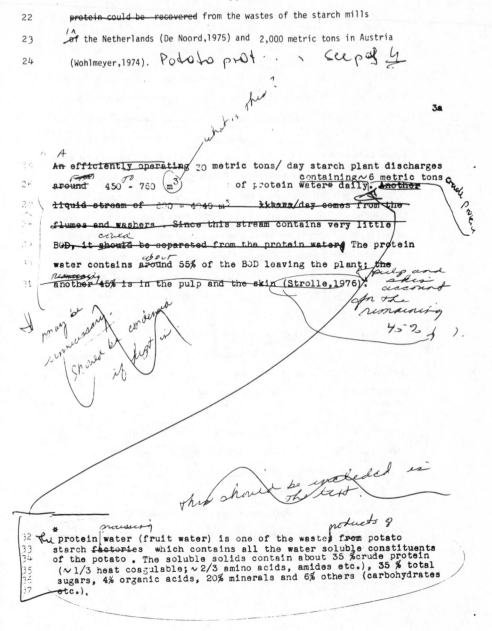

A

An ~~efficiently operating~~ 20 metric tons/ day starch plant discharges

around 450 - 760 (m³)   : of protein water# daily. containing ~6 metric tons ~~Another~~

~~liquid stream of 200 - 1049 m³   liters/day comes from the~~

~~flumes and washers . Since this stream contains very little~~

~~BOD, it~~ could ~~be separated from the protein water.~~ The protein

water contains about ~~around~~ 55% of the BOD leaving the plant; the

~~another 45% is in the pulp and the skin~~ (Strolle,1976). pulp and skin account for the remaining 45%).

this should be included in the text.

32   *Tu protein|water (fruit water) is one of the wastes products of ~~from~~ potato
33   starch ~~factories~~ which contains all the water soluble constituents
34   of the potato . The soluble solids contain about 35 %crude protein
35   (~1/3 heat coagulable; ~2/3 amino acids, amides etc.), 35 % total
36   sugars, 4% organic acids, 20% minerals and 6% others (carbohydrates
37   etc.).

The Manufacture of Knowledge

38 In 1971 Stabile et al. presented an economic analysis of alternative

39 methods for processing potato starch effluents such as concentration

40 by evaporation, protein recovery by heat treatment, ion exchange,

41 biological treatment and combinations of these alternative methods.

42 At the time of this study only concentration of effluents by evaporation

43 appeared economically feasible. Rosenau et al. calculated about

44 $ 2.16 per metric ton of processed potato to cover profit, capital

45 costs and operational expenses if starch, pulp and protein is recovered.

46 It is interesting to note that test plants in the U.S.A. have produced

47 about 18.1 metric tons of potato per acre (4047 m^2). This yields about

48 1.82 metric tons of starch (worth ~ $ 520), 0.73 metric tons of pulp

49 (~ $ 64) and 0.73 metric tons of 50% protein meal (~ $ 160). In

50 comparison, soybeans produce about 0.32 metric tons of protein per

51 acre and alfalfa about 1.09 metric tons. Potato proteins are recovered

52 commercially from potato starch wastes in different European countries

53 (Anon.,1957; Huchette and Fleche,1976; Vlasblom and Peters,1958).

54 The most common way to coagulate potato protein is by heat precipitation

55 (mainly 95 to 100°C) with or without adjusting the initial pH of the

56 waste effluents (Knorr,1977; Strolle et al.,1973). Hydrochloric acid,

57 sulfuric acid and polyphosphoric acid are mainly used for the pH

58 adjustment (pH 3.5 - 5.5). From a cost point of view as well as

59 considerations of adding phosphoric acid or sulfuric acid to public

60 water, hydrochloric acid would be preferred (Meister and Thompson,1976).

61 A common occurence of heat coagulated potato protein concentrates is

62 the resulting low nitrogen solubility (~5 - 10%). Good solubility

63 of PPC could markedly expand potential applications of proteins (Kinsella

64 1976).

5

... ... with ... ... systems
... ... precipitation can conceivable
... ... carcinogenic products

Another important disadvantage of heat coagulation are the energy costs
for concentration and heating of the diluted waste effluents*.

Ferric chloride which is used in seawage work could be another possible
coagulant for the recovery of PPC. It is relatively inexpenive, has
acidic properties and the trivalent iron ion is a good nucleating site
for large floc formation (Daniels,1974). Another advantage of ferric
chloride is that the waste effluents do not have to be heated. The iron
recovered with the protein could add to the nutritional significance
of a recovered product. Meister and Thompson (1976) showed at laboratory
scale that FeCl$_3$ compared at room temperature favorable with hydrochloric
acid.

The aim of this work was to find an alternative precipitation method
resulting in a yield comparable to that of protein recovered by means
of the most commonly used acid/heat treatment method, while
achieving a more acceptable quality of the PPC needed for the
application in human foods.

Materials and Methods
=====================

Preparation of Protein Water

Because of the inconvenience of transporting a dilute solution and because
possible compositional changes, it was decided to simulate processing water
in the pilot plant. to compare different precipitation
methods. 1.1 metric tons of Russet Burbank potatoes (crude protein
content = 2.5% , total solids = 23%) were used. They were loaded into

* typical wastes from potato starch factories contain about 5% solids

9   a modified drag chain feeder (Model A632-44,Arnold Dryer Company,

10) *and* metered into a 98 cm diameter vertical hammermill ..

11 with swinging hammers (Owens Mfg.Co.,Verdon,Nebraska) followed by

12 a Morehouse mill (Model 350, Morehouse Ind.Inc.,Los Angeles,Ca.)

13 The slurry was diluted with water (about 1:1) *(v/v ?)* and centrifuged at 3,200

14 x g ~~by using~~ *in* a horicontal decanter type flow centrifuge (Type P-3000 S,

15 Sharples Co.,Philadelphia,Penn.)to remove the starch. The crude

16 protein content *and total solids* of the resulting protein water ~~was~~ *were* 1.2 % and ~~the~~

17 ~~concentration of total solids~~ 2.2%, *respectively ; the pH was 5.6.*

18 **Preparation of PPC** *(original pH of protein water ?)*

19 The protein water was divided *(pH ?)* *equally into three portions of — litres each ?* ~~in equivalent parts~~ (figure 1).

                    FIGURE I

20 *was adjusted to 3.0 and 4.8 with 2N HCl.*   pH ~~values of 4.8 and 3.0 were adjusted~~ by using 2N HCl. ~~One~~ *The other* batch

21 was adjusted to pH 3.0 ~~by using~~ *with* a 28% aqueous solution of $FeCl_3.6H_2O$.

22 The two batches at pH 3.0 were stirred (Model AG 100, Lightnin

23) in a holding tank for one hour at 20 ±2°C ~~and the~~

24 precipitate ~~was~~ *were* recovered by using a high speed, disk type, solids

25 discharging centrifuge, with 31 cm bowl diameter and RCF_{max} = 14,500 xg

26 (Model BRPX-207 S, De Laval Separator Co.,Poughkeepsie,N.J.). The

27 batch ~~with the pH level of~~ *adjusted to pH* 4.8 was stirred for 15 minutes and ~~then~~ *then*

28 heated by steam injection (Model M 5000, Strahman,   )

29 (Edwards et al.,1975). The heat coagulate was pumped into an open

30 topped stainless steel ~~coagulation~~ tank, (Mohno pump type 3SO,Robbins

31 & Myers Inc.,Springfield,Ohio)

32 ~~And then~~ *and then* it ~~was pumped~~ through a plate type heat exchanger (Model SC-

33 -3196,Creamery Package Co.,Chicago,Ill.) ~~and~~ *in which it was* cooled to 25 ±2°C. For the

34 of these precipitates the solids discharging centrifuge was

35 also used. The pH of the protein concentrates was then adjusted

36 to 7 and the concentrates spray dried at an inlet temperature

37 of the air of 210 - 220°C and an outlet temperature of 105 - 110°C

38 (conical-type laboratory model, Bowen Eng.Inc.,North Branch,N.J.   )

39 Analytical procedures

40 The standard AOAC (AOAC,1975) methods were used for the determination

41 of total solids, nitrogen, crude fat, total sugar, ash, carbohydrate

42 and Vitamin C.Amino acids were determined using the methods descibed

43 by Kohler and Palter (1967). The Analytical Methods for Atomic

44 Absorption Spectroscopy (Analytical Methods,1973) were used for the

45 determination of calcium, iron, magnesium and sodium. Trichlor-

acetic acid was used for the determination of coagulable protein

(Finley and Hautala,1976). Nitrogen solubility was evaluated

48 after Betschart (1974), water absorption capacity after Sosulski (1962)

49 and fat absorption capacity after Lin et al.(1974). For the

50 determination of the whipping properties the method described by

51 Lawhon et al.(1972) was used. The examination of bread texture

52 is described by Knorr (1977). All determinations were done in

53 2 to 5 replications.

1 Results and Discussion

2 Figure 2 shows the relationship between coagulable protein (Nx6.25)

3 remaining in solution and pH for the various precipitation methods

4 used. Is shown in Figure 2.

Figure 2

8

5   ~~In table I a comparison of the results of the pilot plant experiments~~   8
                                                                    are given   table B.
6   ~~As given for the different precipitation methods is shown~~
                  laboratory   a   ed
     ~~The results~~ of experiments on laboratory scale show that $FeCl_3.6H_2O$
                                                   with respect to
     compared favorable with HCl+heat treatment in the amount of coagulable
                                                   (Fig. 2)
9   protein recovered from the protein water. By using a trichloracetic acid/heat
                                                                        in
10   method   (Finley and Hautala,1976) 37 ± 2% of the crude protein of the
                                     was $FeCl_3$ at pH 3 recovered 40 ± 9. of
11   protein water ~~could be~~ recovered. ~~40 ± 1% were coagulable with $FeCl_3$ at pH3~~
     the crude protein   whereas, Hcl/heat   treat
12   (108 % of the trichchloracetic acid/heat coagulable protein) and 35 ± 2%   coag
                                                                            ~ment~   ~ulated~
13   ~~with HCl/heat treatment~~ (95% of the trichloracetic acid coagulable protein)
                                    provided   (table 3)
     ~~The data of the~~ pilot plant studies gave similar results. All of the
                                                             20 ± 2%   proves to
     coagulable protein ~~could be~~ precipitated by $FeCl_3$ ~~treatment~~ at RT and ~be defined~
                                   when   the
     with HCl/heat treatment. ~~By~~ using HCl at RT as coagulant only 62% of the
                                  psw +
     coagulable or 23 % of the crude protein ~~could be~~ recovered. ~~The amount of~~
                                                            was
17   hydrochloric acid and iron(III)chloride hexahydrate to adjust the pH
18   of the protein water is calculated per kg recovered protein (dm) and also
19   given in table I.]

                      TABLE 1
                                                              PPC was
                                                                     (1.0 kg $FeCl_3.6H_2O$
     The amount of $FeCl_3.6 H_2O$ is relatively high. One   decreased
                                                              way This could be
22   ~~this value is~~ by increase of the pH level for the precipitation to 4.0
     without   slightly   protein is
23   ~~This pH gives only~~ less V recovered ~~protein~~ than ~~what was obtained~~
                                                                  at pH 3.0.
24   at pH 3.0,   only 0.9 kg $FeCl_3.6H_2O$ / kg protein are ~~needed~~. required
                                  expect   could indicate
25   Experiments ~~which~~ are under way ~~let~~ V that most of the iron used
                                                                  - Rather weak
     can be recycled by separation of the precipitated $Fe(OH)_2$.   statement
                                                                      could delete
     ~~The results of proximate analyses of the spray dried PPC (table 2) indicate~~

                      TABLE 2
                                          in   precipitate
28   ~~amount of~~ 78.2 % crude protein (N x 6.25) ~~for~~ the HCl/heat ~~treatment~~
29   65.6 % for the HCl and 57.5 % for the $FeCl_3.6H_2O$ treatment. The ash
30   content is about 25 % for the proteins precipitated at RT. One explanation
31   for the high ash concentration of these PPC is the higher adsorption capacity

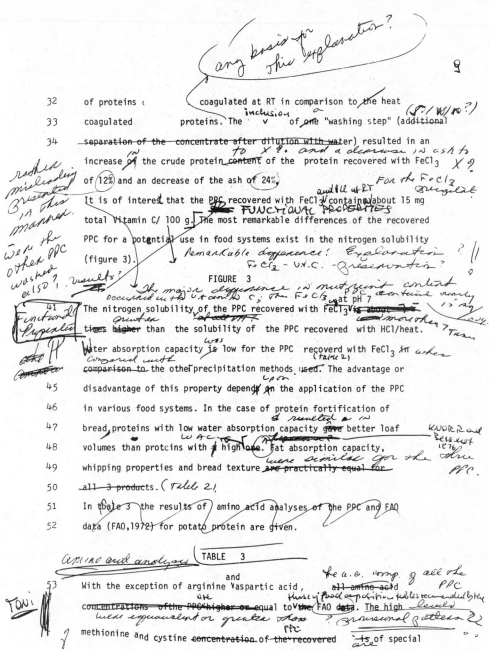

any basis for this explanation?

32 of proteins (coagulated at RT in comparison to the heat *(S⋅/W/R?)*

33 coagulated proteins. The *inclusion of a* ~~v of one~~ "washing step" (~~additional~~

34 ~~separation of the~~ concentrate after ~~dilution with water~~) resulted in an

rather misleading presented in this manner.

increase ~~of~~ the crude protein ~~content~~ of the protein recovered with $FeCl_3$ *to X %. and a decrease in ash to* *X ?*

of 12% and an decrease of the ash of 24%. *For the $FeCl_3$*

were the other PPC washed also? results?

It is of interest that the PPC recovered with $FeCl_3$ contains about 15 mg *and HCl at RT* *surgical*

total Vitamin C/ 100 g. The most remarkable differences of the recovered ~~FUNCTIONAL PROPERTIES~~

PPC for a potential use in food systems exist in the nitrogen solubility

(figure 3). *Remarkable difference! Explanation ? $FeCl_3$ - vit.C. - preservation ?*

FIGURE 3

The major difference in nutrient content occurred with vitamin C; the $FeCl_3$ PPC contains nearly 15 mg

41 The nitrogen solubility of the PPC recovered with $FeCl_3$ ~~is about 7~~ *2* *more than*

Functional Properties

number of all pH ? ~~times higher~~ than the solubility of the PPC recovered with HCl/heat.

Water absorption capacity ~~is~~ *was* low for the PPC recovered with $FeCl_3$ *in* ~~in~~ *compared with (table 2)* ~~comparison to~~ the other precipitation methods used. The advantage or

45 disadvantage of this property depends *upon* on the application of the PPC

46 in various food systems. In the case of protein fortification of

47 bread, proteins with low water absorption capacity ~~gave~~ better loaf *& resulted in*

KNORR and Betschart 1976

48 volumes than proteins with ~~a high one.~~ Fat absorption capacity,

49 whipping properties and bread texture ~~are practically equal for~~ *were similar for the three PPC.*

50 ~~all 3 products.~~ (Table 2)

51 In table 3 the results of amino acid analyses of the PPC and FAO

52 data (FAO,1972) for potato protein are given.

amino acid analyses TABLE 3

and

53 With the exception of arginine *& aspartic acid, the a.a. comp. of all the PPC all amino acid* ~~concentrations of the PPC higher or equal to the~~ FAO data. The high *were equivalent or greater than*

methionine and cystine ~~concentration of the~~ recovered PPC ~~is~~ of special

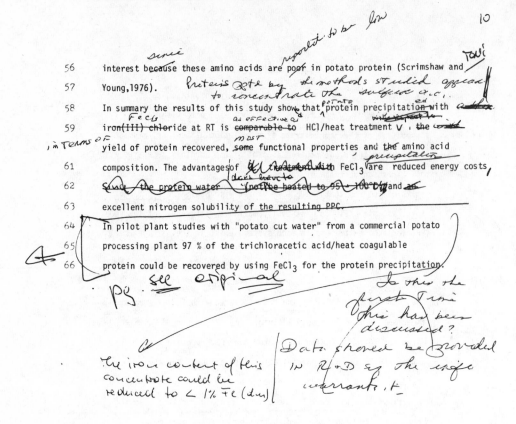

56   interest because these amino acids are poor in potato protein (Scrimshaw and

57   Young, 1976).

58   In summary the results of this study show that protein precipitation with

59   iron(III) chloride at RT is comparable to HCl/heat treatment, the

     yield of protein recovered, some functional properties and the amino acid

61   composition. The advantages of FeCl$_3$ are reduced energy costs

62   the protein water (not the heated to 95 - 100°C) and

63   excellent nitrogen solubility of the resulting PPC.

64   In pilot plant studies with "potato cut water" from a commercial potato

65   processing plant 97 % of the trichloracetic acid/heat coagulable

66   protein could be recovered by using FeCl$_3$ for the protein precipitation.

Appendix 2

The Final, Published Version
of the Scientific Paper

POTATO PROTEIN CONCENTRATES: THE INFLUENCE OF
VARIOUS METHODS OF RECOVERY UPON YIELD,
COMPOSITIONAL AND FUNCTIONAL CHARACTERISTICS

Berkeley, CA 94710

Received for Publication October 4, 1977

ABSTRACT

Potato processing effluents represent a potential source of valuable protein as well as a major waste disposal problem. Potato protein is commonly recovered by heat (in excess of 90°C) with pH adjustment between 3.5 and 5.5. The present study compared yield, and some compositional, and functional characteristics of potato protein concentrate (PPC) recovered with either HCl or $FeCl_3$ (pH 3.0, 20–22°C), or HCl/heat (pH 4.8, 98–99°C). Under pilot plant conditions, recoveries of 22.7, 36.7, and 37.5% of the crude protein (N × 6.25) were obtained with HCl, $FeCl_3$, and HCl/heat, respectively. Crude protein content of the PPC precipitated by HCl, $FeCl_3$, and HCl/heat were 65.6, 57.5, and 78.2% respectively. Ash and vitamin C values were higher in those PPC recovered at room temperature, with Fe content being highest in the PPC recovered with $FeCl_3$. The nitrogen solubility of the $FeCl_3$ precipitate, at pH 7.0, was 1.5 and more than 7 times that of the HCl, and HCl/heat precipitates, respectively. Whipping capacity of PPC was not influenced by precipitation method. The most favorable fat absorption and water absorption capacities were exhibited by the HCl and HCl/ heat precipitates, respectively.

1
2
3
4
5

INTRODUCTION

Potato tuber(s), henceforth termed potato(es), contain an average of 2.1% crude protein on a fresh weight basis. Annual, world-wide production of potato protein is ≃ 6 million metric tons (Markakis 1975). In the U.S., approximately 268,000 metric tons of crude potato protein

163

6   (N X 6.25) are available annually (U.S. Dept. of Agr. 1976). A portion
7   of this potato protein is in the form of processing waste effluents
8   resulting from the manufacture of potato starch, flakes, granules, chips
9   and french fries. Approximately one-third of the crude protein in the
10 waste effluent (potato juice) may be recovered with heat or a trichlora-
11 cetic acid/heat treatment.
12   Potato protein is recovered from the effluents of potato starch manu-
13 facture in various European countries. Quantities such as 2,000 and
14 25,000 metric tons of potato protein are potentially available annually
15 in Austria and The Netherlands, respectively (De Noord 1975; Huchette
16 and Fleche 1976; Vlasblom and Peters 1958; and Wohlmeyer 1974).
17 The waste effluent from potato starch plants contains 2–5% solids, and
18 accounts for $\simeq$ 55% of the BOD leaving the plant. A typical composi-
19 tion of the soluble solids is: 35% crude protein, 35% total sugars, 20%
20 minerals, 4% organic acids, and 6% others.
21   There has been interest in the recovery of potato protein during the
22 past 60 years, and several methods have been reported. Generally, these
23 methods consist of heat coagulation, heat coagulation with pH adjust-
24 ment, pH adjustment alone with HCl, H_3PO_4, $FeCl_3$, or H_2SO_4, ion
25 exchange chromatography, and reverse osmosis. Proponents of heat
26 coagulation (Strolle et al. 1973; Vlasblom and Peters 1957; and Xander
27 and Hoover 1959) most commonly use temperatures in excess of 90°C.
28 When pH adjustment is used, it is usually between 3.5 and 5.5. Meister
29 and Thompson (1976) demonstrated, in laboratory experiments, that
30 $FeCl_3$ compared favorably with HCl as a precipitant of potato protein.
31 Ion exchange chromatography has been used to recover protein, amino
32 acids and potassium from potato waste streams (Heisler et al. 1972),
33 and Porter et al. (1970) studied the use of reverse osmosis for potato
34 protein recovery.
35   Heat coagulation is the most commonly used method to commer-
36 cially recover potato protein. The energy costs of concentrating and
37 heating the dilute waste effluent are a disadvantage of this method. In
38 addition, heat coagulated protein is, generally, quite insoluble, which
39 could limit some potential food applications. Of those acids used for
40 pH adjustment, HCl is preferred in terms of cost and potential hazards
41 to the public water supply. With the use of $FeCl_3$ as the precipitant, any
42 Fe recovered with the protein could add to the nutritional value of the
43 final product.
44   The amino acid balance of potato protein is quite favorable. Nitrogen
45 balance studies with human adults have shown potato protein to be
46 superior to most major plant protein, with its nutritive value approach-
47 ing that of whole egg (Kofranyi and Jekat 1965; Jekat and Kofranyi
48 1970; and Meister and Thompson 1967).

49   An economic analysis of alternative methods for processing potato
50   starch effluents was conducted by Stabile *et al.* (1970). At that time,
51   the authors concluded that concentration of effluents by evaporation
52   appeared to be the only economically feasible method. An up-dated
53   economic analysis may be warranted in light of increased energy costs.
54   The purpose of this study was to compare the effectiveness of HCl,
55   FeCl$_3$, and HCl combined with heat, as precipitants of potato protein
56   in the laboratory, as well as under pilot plant conditions, and to evalu-
57   ate some compositional, nutritional and functional characteristics of
58   the protein concentrates recovered by these three methods.

1   MATERIALS AND METHODS

2   Preparation of Potato Protein Concentrate

3   Potato processing water was simulated in the pilot plant. Washed
4   Russet Burbank potatoes (1.1 metric tons), containing 2.5% crude pro-
5   tein (N × 6.25) and 23% total solids, were used. The potatoes were
6   loaded into a modified drag chain feeder (Model A 632-44, Arnold
7   Dryer Co., Milwaukee, Wisc.) where 0.2% (w/w) NaHSO$_3$ was added to
8   inhibit darkening of the potatoes. The potatoes were then metered into
9   a 98 cm diameter vertical hammermill with swinging hammer (Owens
10   Mfg. Co., Verdon, Neb.) followed by a Morehouse Mill (Model 350,
11   Morehouse Ind. Inc., Los Angeles, CA). The slurry was diluted with
12   water ($\simeq$ 1:1 v/v) and insoluble solids were removed by centrifugation
13   at 3,200 G in a horizontal flow, decanter type centrifuge (Type P-3000
14   S, Sharples Co., Philadelphia, Penn.). The resulting supernatant, pH 5.6
15   contained 1.2 and 2.2% crude protein and total solid, respectively.
16   The aqueous solution containing the soluble protein (protein water)
17   was equally divided into three portions and processed as outlined in
18   Fig. 1. Two batches were adjusted to pH 3.0 and 4.8, respectively, with
19   2N HCl. The third was adjusted to pH 3.0 with a 28% (w/w) aqueous
20   solution of FeCl$_3 \cdot 6H_2O$. The two batches at pH 3.0 were stirred
21   (Model Ag 100, Mixing Equipment Co. Inc., Rochester, N.Y.) in a
22   holding tank for 1 hr at 20–22°C. The precipitates were recovered by
23   using a high speed, disk-type solids discharging centrifuge, with 31 cm
24   bowl diameter and a RCF$_{max}$ of 14,500 G (Model BRPX-207 S, De
25   Laval Separator Co., Poughkeepsie, N.J.). The batch adjusted to pH 4.8
26   was stirred for 15 min and then heated by steam injection to 98–99°C
27   (McDaniel Suction Tec, Dairy Industries Inc., Foster City, CA) as des-
28   cribed by Edwards *et al.* (1975) The heated coagulum was then pumped

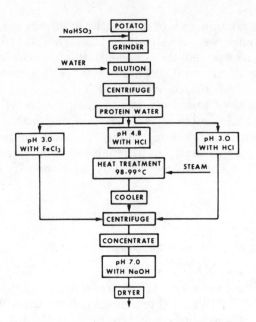

FIG. 1. SIMPLIFIED FLOW DIAGRAM FOR
THE RECOVERY OF POTATO PROTEIN
CONCENTRATES IN THE PILOT PLANT
PROCESS

29 (Moyno pump type 380, Robbins & Myers Inc., Springfield, Ohio)
30 through a plate type heat exchanger (Model Sc-3196, Creamery Package
31 Co., Chicago, Ill.) where it was cooled to 24–26°C. The solids discharg-
32 ing centrifuge was used for the collection of this precipitate.
33   After collection by centrifugation the total weight of the concen-
34 trates was determined and samples were taken for Kjeldahl analysis.
35 The yield was calculated as the amount of crude protein in the concen-
36 trates as a percent of the total amount in the protein water (see Table
37 1). The pH of each of the precipitated protein concentrates was
38 adjusted to pH 7 with 2N NaOH. The concentrates were then spray
39 dried at an air inlet temperature of 200–210°C and an outlet tempera-
40 ture of 105–110°C (Conical-type, laboratory model, Bowen Engineer-
41 ing Inc., North Branch, N.J.).
42   One experiment was conducted in the pilot plant on "potato cut
43 water" obtained from a commercial potato chip processing plant. The
44 effectiveness of the three precipitation methods, i.e. HCl, $FeCl_3$ and
45 HCl/heat, was evaluated.

Table 1. Recovery of potato protein concentrates in the pilot plant by various methods

	Precipitation Method		
	HCl at RT pH 3.0	FeCl₃ at RT pH 3.0	HCl/Heat pH 4.8
	--	-- % --	--
Recovery of Crude Protein	22.7	36.7	37.5
Recovery of TCA/heat Insoluble Protein	61.5	99.4	102.0

46   Methods for Analysis and Functional Properties

47   The standard AOAC methods (AOAC 1975) were used for the deter-
48   mination of total solids, nitrogen, crude fat, ash and vitamin C. Total
49   sugars were determined by the method of Potter *et al.* (1968) and total
50   carbohydrates (in terms of glucose) were assayed according to the pro-
51   cedure of Dubois *et al.* (1956). The method of Kohler and Palter
52   (1967) was followed for determining amino acid composition. Pro-
53   cedures outlined in Analytical Methods for Atomic Absorption Spec-
54   troscopy (Analytical Methods 1973) were used for the determination of
55   calcium, iron, magnesium and sodium. Trichloracetic acid (TCA)/heat
56   treatment, as reported by Finley and Hautala (1976), was employed to
57   determine TCA coagulable protein of the protein water. For the deter-
58   mination of coagulable protein of the protein water at different pH
59   levels (see Fig. 2) the pH was adjusted with 2N HCl and 28% (w/w)
60    $FeCl_3 \cdot 6H_2O$ solution at room temperature and filtered after 60
61   minutes through an S & S 576 filter paper. The nitrogen content of the
62   filtrate was determined by Kjeldahl analysis. In the case of HCl/heat
63   treatment the pH was adjusted and then the protein water was heated
64   to 95°C for 10 min, cooled to room temperature and filtered after 50
65   min. A previously described method was used to evaluate nitrogen solu-
66   bility (Betschart 1974). Water absorption capacity, fat absorption
67   capacity, and whipping capacity were determined using minor modifica-
68   tions of the methods of Sosulski (1962), Lin *et al.* (1974) and Lawhon
69   *et al.* (1972), respectively, as described by Betschart and Kohler (1975).
70   All experiments, with the exception of nitrogen solubility, were con-
71   ducted at the initial pH attained. The means of laboratory experiments
72   are the result of from 2 to 5 replications. Pilot plant data are based
73   upon a single run with analyses of these samples carried out in from 2
74   to 5 replications.

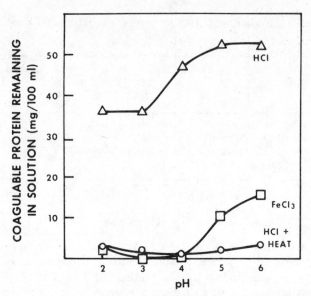

FIG. 2. RELATIONSHIP BETWEEN TCA HEAT INSOL-
UBLE PROTEIN REMAINING IN SOLUTION AND PH
FOR THE DIFFERENT PRECIPITATION METHODS

RESULTS AND DISCUSSION

Protein Recovery

Laboratory experiments showed that $FeCl_3$ compared favorably
with HCl/heat treatment at pH 2–4 with respect to the amount of
coagulable protein recovered from the protein water (Fig. 2). At pH 5
and 6 HCl/heat was the most effective precipitation method studied.

By the use of TCA/heat, in combination, 37 ± 2% of the crude
protein in the protein water was recovered (termed coagulable protein).
Recoveries of crude protein by HCl, $FeCl_3$, and HCl/heat precipitation
methods were 23 ± 1, 40 ± 1, and 35 ± 2%, respectively. These recoveries represented 62, 108, and 95% of the coagulable protein by
HCl, $FeCl_3$, and HCl/heat precipitation, respectively. Thus, at pH 3.0
$FeCl_3$ was more effective than HCl in recovering potato protein concentrate (PPC). Meister and Thompson (1976) also found $FeCl_3$ to be
more effective than HCl as a precipitant of potato protein. They reported that, at pH 3.0, 31 and 36% of the crude protein were recovered
by HCl and $FeCl_3$ precipitation, respectively. From these data it is also
apparent that Meister and Thompson achieved more effective results

19 with HCl and somewhat less effective results with $FeCl_3$ when com-
20 pared with results reported in the present study.
21   Results obtained in the pilot plant with simulated waste effluent
22 indicated that $FeCl_3$ and HCl/heat were equally effective in recovering
23 protein (Table 1), with HCl recovering significantly less crude protein.
24 Quantities of protein recovered by HCl and $FeCl_3$ were 62 and 99%,
25 respectively, of the TCA/heat coagulable protein. The recovery of PPC
26 by various methods was also studied in the pilot plant with commercial
27 "potato cut water." Thus, results were similar to those obtained with
28 simulated potato processing water. By using $FeCl_3$ as a coagulant, 97%
29 of the TCA/heat coagulable protein could be recovered.
30   The quantity of $FeCl_3 \cdot 6H_2O$ required to precipitate PPC was 1.6 kg
31 per kg protein (dm). By raising the precipitation pH to 4.0, 0.9 kg
32 $FeCl_3 \cdot H_2O$ would be needed per kg protein. Although laboratory
33 experiments by the authors indicated that slightly less protein would be
34 recovered at pH 4.0 (Fig. 2), Meister and Thompson (1976) showed
35 that $FeCl_3$ precipitation produced maximum recovery at pH 4.0.

36 **Composition**

37   Proximate analyses of the spray dried PPC revealed that the crude
38 protein contents of the HCl, $FeCl_3$, and HCl/heat precipitates were
39 65.6, 57.5, and 78.2%, respectively. In addition to the differences in
40 protein content of the PPC recovered by various methods, major com-
41 positional differences were observed for ash, vitamin C, iron and
42 sodium (Table 2). The increased ash content associated with HCl preci-
43 pitation at room temperature was also observed by Meister and
44 Thompson (1976), who noted that HCl recovered more total solids
45 from the effluent than does precipitation by HCl/heat. The PPC precipi-
46 tated at ambient temperatures with HCl and $FeCl_3$ would be more
47 appropriate for human consumption if ash values were reduced. Vita-
48 min C content (15–18 mg/100 g) was significantly higher in those PPC
49 recovered at room temperature, whereas the $FeCl_3$ precipitate was
50 markedly higher in iron than the other two precipitates.

51 **Functional Properties**

52   With the exception of whipping capacity, those functional properties
53 of PPC evaluated were markedly influenced by method of precipitation.
54 Nitrogen solubility of PPC recovered at room temperature was much
55 higher than that of the HCl/heat precipitate (Fig. 3). At pH 6 and
56 above, the nitrogen solubility of $FeCl_3$ precipitate was superior to that
57 precipitated by HCl; at pH 7, it was >7 times that of the HCl/heat

Table 2. Analyses and select functional properties of potato protein concentrates[a]

Composition/Property	Precipitation method		
	HCl at RT	FeCl$_3$ at RT	HCl/heat
	% Dry matter[b]		
Total solids (%)	93.7	94.7	95.4
Nitrogen	10.5	9.2	12.5
Crude fat	2.3	1.3	2.4
Ash	24.5	25.1	7.2
Total sugars	3.6	2.6	1.3
Total Carbohydrates	7.2	7.1	7.1
Total Vitamin C (mg/100 g)	18.1	14.9	0.01
Calcium	0.14	0.04	0.14
Iron	0.10	4.32	0.12
Magnesium	0.20	0.11	0.10
Sodium	4.25	3.85	1.53
Functional Properties	Percent		
Nitrogen solubility (pH 7)	56.0 ± 0.1[c]	87.5 ± 2.1	11.5 ± 0.7
Water absorption capacity (pH 7)	214 ± 3	86 ± 5	273 ±6
Fat absorption capacity (pH 7)	234 ± 16	188 ± 10	110 ± 10
Whipping Capacity Foam (% Volume increase pH 7)	568 ± 40	524 ± 9	523 ± 9

[a]Means of 2 to 5 replications
[b]% dry matter unless otherwise indicated
[c]Means ± standard deviation

58 precipitated PPC (Table 2). Increased nitrogen solubility indicates that
59 the PPC were less serverely denatured during processing, and would
60 more likely be functionally active in food systems in which protein
61 solubility was a prerequisite.
62   Water absorption capacity was highest in the HCl/heat precipitate
63 which had been most severely heated during precipitation, whereas fat
64 absorption capcity was the lowest in this precipitate (Table 2). The high
65 water absorption of heat precipitated plant proteins vs those recovered
66 with HCl at room temperature has also been reported for alfalfa leaf
67 protein concentrate (Betschart and Kohler 1975). HCl precipitation
68 produced the PPC with the most favorable fat absorption capacity. The
69 spray dried PPC precipitated by HCl were light and fluffy, with greyish
70 beige overtones. That precipitated at room temperature was the lightest
71 in color, whereas the FeCl$_3$ precipitate had a light green cast.
72   These data on functionality within simple, model systems provide an
73 indication of potential functionality in food systems.

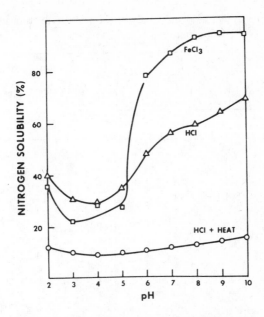

FIG. 3. RELATIONSHIP BETWEEN NITRO-
GEN SOLUBILITY AND PH OF DIFFERENT
POTATO PROTEIN CONCENTRATES

74   Amino Acid Analyses

75   With the exception of arginine, aspartic and glutamic acids, the
76   amino acid composisition of the HCl/heat treatment PPC was
77   equal or greater than that reported by FAO (1972) for potato protein
78   (Table 3). The higher levels of methionine and cystine in PPC are of
79   interest since these amino acids were previously reported to be low in
80   potato protein (Scrimshaw and Young 1976). When compared with
81   FAO (1973) Provisional Amino Acid Scoring Pattern, the PPC contain
82   quantities of amino acids equal to or greater than the suggested levels
83   for all the essential amino acids (except tryptophan which was not de-
84   termined).
85   In summary, $FeCl_3$ and HCl/heat treatment recovered similar
86   quantities of potato protein, whereas HCl at room temperature was the
87   least effective method. Differences between these precipitation
88   methods include the energy input required for steam (HCl/heat) and
89   ingredient costs (HCl, $FeCl_3$). Compositional differences among the
90   PPC precipitated by various methods included higher crude protein in
91   the HCl/heat precipitate, higher vitamin C and ash in those PPC precipi-

Table 3. Amino acid analyses of potato protein concentrates recovered by various methods

Amino Acid	HCl	FeCl₃	Precipitation Method HCl/Heat	Potato Protein FAO (1972)
		—	g/16 g N	—
Lysine	6.02	6.46	6.79	5.28
Histidine	2.04	2.03	2.11	1.76
Arginine	4.40	4.76	4.74	5.28
Aspartic Acid	12.83	13.37	11.08	13.12
Threonine	4.27	4.43	4.86	3.84
Serine	4.15	4.49	4.90	3.52
Glutamic Acid	11.67	11.58	10.47	17.60
Proline	3.35	3.70	4.11	3.84
Glycine	3.51	3.86	4.14	3.52
Alanine	4.01	3.91	4.41	4.00
Cystine	1.41	1.74	1.47	0.94
Valine	5.50	5.89	6.24	5.76
Methionine	2.09	1.96	2.70	1.12
Isoleucine	4.53	4.76	5.20	3.84
Leucine	7.20	7.41	8.53	6.24
Tyrosine	4.17	4.30	4.74	2.72
Phenylalanine	4.67	4.82	5.34	3.36

92   tated at ambient temperatures (HCl, FeCl₃) and higher Fe values in the
93   FeCl₃ precipitate. In terms of functionality, PPC precipitated by all
94   three methods possessed similar whipping capacity. Differences
95   included greater nitrogen solubility for the FeCl₃ precipitate, with the
96   highest water absorption capacity and fat absorption capacity exhibited
97   by the HCl/heat and HCl precipitates, respectively. The ultimate selec-
98   tion of a precipitation method for potato protein will depend upon an
99   analysis of the nutritional and antinutritional, economic, engineering,
100 compositional and functional parameters, within the constraints of the
101 end product use of the PPC.

Reference to a company and/or product named by the Department is only for purposes of information and does not imply approval or recommendation of the product to the exclusion of others which may also be suitable.

References

AARONSON, S. (1977) Style in Scientific Writing, *Current Contents, Life Sciences* **20**: 6.15.

AGASSI, J. (1973) Methodological Individualism, in J. O'NEILL (ed.), *Modes of Individualism and Collectivism,* London: Heinemann.

ANDREWS, F. (ed.) (1979) *Scientific Productivity. The Effectiveness of Research Groups in Six Countries,* Cambridge, England: Cambridge Univ. Press and Paris: Unesco.

ANSCOMBE, G. E. (1971) *Causality and Determination,* Cambridge, England: Cambridge Univ. Press.

APOSTEL, L. *et al.* (1979) An Empirical Investigation of Scientific Observation, *Communication and Cognition, Special Issue on Theory of Knowledge and Science Policy:* 3-36.

ASHBY, W. R. (1962) Principles of the Self-Organizing System, in H. VON FOERSTER & G. W. ZOPF (eds.), *Principles of Self Organisation,* New York: Pergamon.

ATLAN, H. (1979) *Entre le cristal et la fumée. Essai sur l'organisation du vivant,* Paris: Seuil.

BACHELARD, G. (1934) *Le nouvel esprit scientifique,* Paris: Presse Universitaire de France.

BACHRACH, P. and BARATZ, M. S. (1963) Decisions and Non-Decisions: An Analytical Framework, *American Political Science Review* **57**: 632-42.

BAR-HILLEL, Y. (1954) Indexical Expressions, *Mind* **63**: 359-79.

BARNES, B. (1977) *Interests and the Growth of Knowledge,* London: Routledge & Kegan Paul.

BARNES, B. and DOLBY, R. G. (1970) The Scientific Ethos: A Deviant Viewpoint, *Archives européennes de sociologie* **11**: 3-25.

BARNES, and LAW, J. (1976) Whatever Should Be Done with Indexical Expressions, *Theory and Society* **3**: 223-37.

BARNES, S. B. and MACKENZIE, D. A. (1979) On the Role of Interests in Scientific Change, in R. WALLIS (ed.), *On the Margins of Science: The Social Construction of Rejected Knowledge, Sociological Review Monograph* **27**, Keele: Univ. of Keele.

BASTIDE, F. (1981) Le Foie Lavé. Approche sémiotique d'un texte des sciences expérimentales, in J. O'NEILL (ed.), *Science Texts. Recent Developments in the Sociology of Science,* London: Routledge & Kegan Paul.

BAZERMAN, C. (1979) Academic Discourse. Some Features of Writing in the Physical Sciences, the Social Sciences and the Humanities, CUNY: Baruch College.

BEN-DAVID, J. (1971) *The Scientist's Role in Society,* Englewood Cliffs, NJ: Prentice Hall.

BERGER, P. and LUCKMANN, T. (1967) *The Social Construction of Reality,* London: Allen Lane.

BERNABE, J. and PINXTEN, R. (eds.) Diversification within Cultural Anthropology. *Communication and Cognition Monographies, Communication and Cognition,* Vol. 7(3/4), Geneva.

BHASKAR, R. (1978) *A Realist Theory of Science, Sussex,* England: Harvester Press.

BLACK, M. (1962) *Models and Metaphors,* Ithaca, NY: Cornell Univ. Press.

BLOOR, D. (1976) *Knowledge and Social Imagery,* London: Routledge & Kegan Paul.

BLOOR, D. (1978) Polyhedra and the Abominations of Leviticus, *The British Journal for the History of Science* **11**: 245-72.

BLUME, S. S. and SINCLAIR, R. (1973) *Research Environment and Performance in British University Chemistry. Science Policy Studies* No. 6, London: H.M.S.O.

BOHM, D. (1957) *Causality and Chance in Modern Physics,* London: Routledge & Kegan Paul.

BÖHME, G. (1975) The Social Function of Cognitive Structures: A Concept of the Scientific Community Within a Theory of Action, in K. KNORR, H. STRASSER & H. G. ZILIAN (eds.), *Determinants and Controls of Scientific Development,* Dordrecht, Holland: D. Reidel.

BÖHME, G., DAELE, W. VAN DEN and KROHN, W. (1973) Die Finalisierung der Wissenschaft, *Zeitschrift für Soziologie* **2**: 128-44.

BÖHME, G., DAELE, W. VAN DEN and KROHN, W. (1977) *Experimentelle Philosophie. Ursprünge autonomer Wissenschaftsentwicklung,* Frankfurt/Main: Suhrkamp.

BÖHME, G., DEALE, W. VAN DEN and WEINGART, P. (1976) Finalization in Science, *Social Science Information* **15**: 307-30.

BÖHME, G. and ENGELHARDT, M. VON (eds.) (1979) *Entfremdete Wissenschaft,* Frankfurt/Main: Suhrkamp.

BOURDIEU, P. (1972, 1977) *Esquisse d'une théorie de la pratique,* Geneva: Librairie Droz. English translation, revised and enlarged; *Outline of a Theory of Practice,* Cambridge, England: Cambridge Univ. Press, 1977.

BOURDIEU, P. (1975a) The Specificity of the Scientific Field and the Social Conditions of the Progress of Reason, *Social Science Information* **14**(6): 19-47.

BOURDIEU, P. (1975b) L'Ontologie politique de Martin Heidegger, *Actes de la Recherche en Sciences Sociales* **5-6**: 65-79 and 109-56.

BRENNER, M. (ed.) (1980) *Social Method and Social Life,* London: Academic Press.

BRENNER, M., MARSH, P. and BRENNER, M. (eds.) (1978) *The Social Contexts of Method,* London: Croom Helm.

BUNGE, M. (1967) Technology as Applied Science, *Technology and Culture* **8**: 329-47.

CALLON, M. (1975) L'opération de traduction comme relation symbolique, in M. ROQUEPLO (ed.), *Les incidences des rapports sociaux sur la science,* Paris: CORDES.

CALLON, M. (1980) Struggles and Negotiations to Define What is Problematic and What is Not, in K. KNORR, R. KROHN, and R. WHITLEY (eds.), *The Social Process of Scientific Investigation. Sociology of the Sciences,* Yearbook Vol. 4, Dordrecht, Holland: D. Reidel.

CALLON, M., COURTIAL, J. P. and TURNER, W. (1979) *Les actions concertées chimie macromoléculaire. Socio-logique d'une agence de traduction,* Paris: École Nationale Supérieure des Mines.

CALLON, M. and VIGNOLLE, J. P. (1977) Breaking Down the Organization: Local Conflicts and Societal Systems of Action, *Social Science Information* **16**: 147-67.

CAMPBELL, D. (1974) Evolutionary Epistemology, in P. A. SCHILPP (ed.), *The Philosophy of Karl Popper,* La Salle, IL: Open Court Publ.

CAMPBELL, D. (1977) Descriptive Epistemology: Psychological, Sociological and Evolutionary, William James Lectures, Harvard Univ., Spring.

CICOUREL, A. (1964) *Method and Measurement in Sociology,* New York: The Free Press.

CICOUREL, A. (1968) *The Social Organization of Juvenile Justice,* New York: Wiley.

CICOUREL, A..(1973) *Cognitive Sociology. Language and Meaning in Social Interaction,* Harmondsworth, Middlesex: Penguin.

CICOUREL, A. (1974) Interviewing and Memory, in C. CHERRY (ed.), *Pragmatic Aspects of Human Communication,* Dordrecht, Holland: D. Reidel.

CICOUREL, A. (1975) Discourse and Text: Cognitive and Linguistic Processes in Studies of Social Structure, *Versus: Quaderni di Studi Semiotici* Sept-Dec: 33-84.

CHUBIN, D. E. and MOITRA, S. (1975) Content Analysis of References: Adjunct or Alternative to Citation Counting, *Social Studies of Science* **5**: 423-41.

COLE, G. (1979) Classifying Research Units by Patterns of Performance and Influence: A Typology of the Round 1 Data, in F. ANDREWS (ed.), *Scientific Productivity. The Effectiveness of Research Groups in Six Countries,* Cambridge, England: Cambridge Univ. Press and Paris: Unesco.

COLE, J. R. and COLE, S. (1973) *Social Stratification in Science,* Chicago: Univ. of Chicago Press.

COLEMAN, J. (1971) *Resources for Social Change: Race in the United States,* New York: Wiley.

COLLINS, H. M. (1974) The T.E.A. set: tacit knowledge and scientific networks, *Science Studies* **4**: 165-86.

COLLINS, H. M. (1975) The Seven Sexes: A Study in the Sociology of a Phenomenon or the Replication of Experiments in Physics, *Sociology* **9**: 205-24.

COOPER, W. (1966) *The Struggles of Albert Woods,* Harmondsworth, Middlesex: Penguin.

CRANE, D. (1965) Scientists at Major and Minor Universities: A Study of Productivity and Recognition, *American Sociological Review* **30**: 699-714.

CRANE, D. (1972) *Invisible Colleges,* Chicago: Univ. of Chicago Press.

CRAWFORD, E. and PERRY, N. (1976) *Demands for Social Knowledge: The Role of Research Organizations,* London: Sage.

Critical Inquiry (1978) Special Issue on Metaphor, Vol. 5.

CROZIER, M. and FRIEDBERG, E. (1977) *L'acteur et le système,* Paris: Seuil.

CUNNINGHAM, S. D., CATER, C. M. and MATTIL, K. F. (1977) Rupture and Protein Extraction of Petroleum Grown Yeast, *Journal of Food Science* **40**: 732-35.

Deadalus (1978) Limits of Scientific Inquiry, Special Issue, Spring.

DENZIN, N. K. (1969) Symbolic Interactionism and Ethnomethodology: A Proposed Synthesis, *American Sociological Review* **34**: 922-34.

DERRIDA, J. (1976) *Of Grammatology,* Baltimore: Johns Hopkins Univ. Press

DIJK, T. VAN (1974) *Philosophy of Action and Theory of Narrative,* University of Amsterdam: Department of General Studies.

DILTHEY, W. (1913-58) *Abhandlungen zur Grundlegung der Geisteswissenschaften,* in G. MISCH (ed.), *Gesammelte Schriften,* Vol. 5, Göttingen: Vandenhoeck & Ruprecht.

DOMBROWSKI, H. D., KRAUSE, U. and ROOS, P. (eds.) (1978) *Symposium Warenform-Denkform. Zur Erkenntnistheorie Sohn-Rethels,* Frankfurt/Main: Campus.

DUNHILL, P. and LILLY, M. D. (1975) Protein Extraction and Recovery from Microbial Cells, in S. TANNENBAUM & D. I. WANG (eds.), *Single Cell Protein II.* Cambridge, MA: M.I.T. Press.

EDGE, D. (1979) Quantitative Measures of Communication in Science: A Critical Review, *History of Science* **17**: 102-34.

EDGE, D. O. and MULKAY, M. J. (1976) *Astronomy Transformed,* New York: Wiley.

ELKANA, Y. and MENDELSOHN, E. (eds.) (1981) *Cognitive and Historical Sociology of Scientific Knowledge. Sociology of the Sciences,* Yearbook Vol. 5, Dordrecht, Holland: D. Reidel.

ENGELHARDT, M. VON and HOFFMAN, R. W. (1974) *Wissenschaftlich-technische Intelligenz im Forschungsbetrieb. Eine Empirische Untersuchung zu Arbeit, Beruf und Bewusstsein,* Frankfurt/Main: Europäische Verlagsanstalt.

ENGELHARDT, M. VON and HOFFMAN, R. W. (1979) Entfremdete Wissenschaftler? Das Verhältnis der naturwissenschaftlich-technischen Intelligenz zu anderen Gruppen von Lohnabhängigen, in G. BÖHME & M. VON ENGELHARDT (eds.), *Entfremdete Wissenschaft,* Frankfurt/Main: Suhrkamp.

FEYERABEND, P. (1962) Explanation, Reduction, and Empiricism, in H. FEIGL & G. MAXWELL (eds.), *Scientific Explanation, Space and Time, Minnesota Studies in the Philosophy of Science,* Vol. 3, Minneapolis: Univ. of Minnesota Press.

FEYERABEND, P. (1970) Against Method. Outline of an Anarchistic Theory of Knowledge, in M. RADNER & S. WINOKUR (eds.), *Analyses of Theories and Methods of Physics and Psychology, Minnesota Studies in the Philosophy of Science,* Vol. 4, Minneapolis: Univ. of Minnesota Press.

FEYERABEND, P. (1975) *Against Method,* London: New Left Books.

FILMER, P., PHILIPSON, M., SILVERMAN, D. and WALSH, D. (1972) *New Directions in Sociological Theory,* London: Routledge & Kegan Paul.

FOERSTER, H. VON (1960) On Self-Organizing Systems and their Environments, in M. C. YOVITS & S. CAMERON (eds.), *Self-Organizing Systems,* New York: Pergamon.

FOUCAULT, M. (1975) *Surveiller et punir. Naissance de la prison,* Paris: Gallimard.

FOUCAULT, M. (1977) *Histoire de la sexualité. 1. La volonté de savoir,* Paris: Gallimard.

FOUCAULT, M. (1978) Vérité et pouvoir, *L'Arc* **70,** *Special Issue on La crise dans la tête*: 16-26.

FRAASEN, B. VAN (1977) *The Argument Concerning Scientific Realism,* Los Angeles: Univ. of Southern California.

GADAMER, H. G. (1965) *Wahrheit und Methode,* Tübingen: J. C. B. MOHR.

GALTUNG, J. (1967) *Theory and Methods of Social Research,* Oslo: Universitetsforlaget.

GARFINKEL, H. (1967) *Studies in Ethnomethodology,* Englewood Cliffs, NJ: Prentice Hall.

GASTON, J. (1973) *Originality and Competition in Science,* Chicago: University of Chicago Press.

GASTON, J. (1978) *The Reward System in British and American Science,* New York: Wiley.

GELLNER, E. (1973) *Cause and Meaning in the Social Sciences,* London: Routledge & Kegan Paul.

GELLNER, E. (1980) *Spectacles and Predicaments: Essays in Social Theory,* Cambridge, England: Cambridge Univ. Press.

GIDDENS, A. (ed.) (1974) *Positivism and Sociology,* London: Heinemann.

GIDDENS, A. (1976) *New Rules of Sociological Method,* London: Hutchinson.

GILBERT, N. (1976) The Transformation of Research Findings into Scientific Knowledge, *Social Studies of Science* **6:** 281-306.

GILBERT, N. and MULKAY, M. (1980) Contexts of Scientific Discourse: Social Accounting in Experimental Papers, in K. KNORR, R. KROHN & R. WHITLEY (eds.), *The Social Process of Scientific Investigation, Sociology of the Sciences,* Yearbook Vol. 4, Dordrecht, Holland: D. Reidel.

GOFFMAN, E. (1961) *Encounters,* Indianapolis: Bobbs-Merrill.

GOFFMAN, E. (1972) The Neglected Situation, in P. P. GIGLIOLI (ed.), *Language and Social Context,* Harmondsworth, Middlesex: Penguin.

GOFFMAN, E. (1974) *Frame Analysis. An Essay on the Organization of Experience,* New York: Harper & Row.

GOMBRICH, E. (1960) *Art and Illusion,* New York: Pantheon Books.

GOODMAN, N. (1966) *The Structure of Appearance,* New York: Bobbs Merrill.

GOODMAN, N. (1968) *Languages of Art,* Indianapolis: Bobbs Merrill.

GOULDNER, A. (1976) *The Dialectic of Ideology and Technology,* New York: Seabury Press.

GOULDNER, A. (1979) *The Future of Intellectuals and the Rise of the New Class,* New York: Seabury Press.

GRATHOFF, R. (1975) On Normality and Typicality in Everyday Life. *Sociological Analysis and Theory* **5:** 81-106.

GRATHOFF, R. (1979) Über Typik und Normalität im alltäglichen Milieu, in W. SPRONDEL & R. GRATHOFF (eds.), *Alfred Schutz und die Idee des Alltags in den Sozialwissenschaften,* Stuttgart: Ferdinand Enke.

GREIMAS, A. J. and COURTÉS, J. (1979) *Sémiotique. Dictionnaire raisonné de la théorie du langage,* Paris: Hachette.

GREIMAS, A. J. and LANDOWSKI, E. (1979) *Introduction à l'analyse du discours en sciences sociales,* Paris: Hachette.

GRICE, P. (1975) Logic and Conversation, in P. COLE & J. MORGAN (eds.), *Syntax and Semantics,* Vol. 3, *Speech Acts,* New York: Academic Press.

GURVITCH, G. (1971) *The Social Frameworks of Knowledge,* Oxford: Basil Blackwell.

GUSFIELD, J. (1976) The Literary Rhetoric of Science, *American Sociological Review* **41:** 16-34.

HABERMAS, J. (1970a) *Zur Logik der Sozialwissenschaften,* Frankfurt/Main: Suhrkamp.

HABERMAS, J. (1970b) *Toward a Rational Society,* Boston: Beacon Press.

HABERMAS, J. (1971) *Knowledge and Human Interests,* Boston: Beacon Press.

HABERMAS, J. (1979) *Communication and the Evolution of Society,* Boston; Beacon Press.

HAGSTROM, W. O. (1965) *The Scientific Community,* New York: Basic Books.

HANSON, N. R. (1958) *Patterns of Discovery,* Cambridge, England: Cambridge Univ. Press.

HARRÉ, R. (1970) *Principles of Scientific Thinking,* London: Macmillan.

HARRÉ, R. (1977) The Ethnogenic Approach: Theory and Practice, in L. BERKOWITZ (ed.), *Advances in Experimental Social Psychology,* Vol. 10, New York: Academic Press.

HARRÉ, R. (1978) Models in Science, *Phys. Educ.* **13:** 275-78.

HARRÉ, R. (1979) *Social Being,* Oxford: Basil Blackwell.

HARRÉ, R. and MADDEN, E. H. (1975) *Causal Powers: A Theory of Natural Necessity,* Totowa, NJ: Rowman and Littlefeld.

HARRÉ, R. and SECORD, P. (1972) *The Explanation of Social Behaviour,* Oxford: Basil Blackwell.

HARRIS, M. (1968) *The Rise of Anthropological Theory. A History of Theories of Culture,* New York: Crowell.

HARVEY, B. (1980) The Effect of Social Context on the Process of Scientific Investigation, in K. KNORR, R. KROHN and R. WHITLEY (eds.), *The Social Process of Scientific Investigation, Sociology of the Sciences,* Yearbook Vol. 4, Dordrecht, Holland: D. Reidel.

HEIDEGGER, M. (1962) *Being and Time,* New York: Harper & Row.

HEMPTINNE, Y. DE (1979) A Cybernetic Analysis of Governmental Mechanisms for Policy Making in Science and Technology, *Communication and Cognition, Special Issue on Theory of Knowledge and Science Policy:* 317-35.

HEMPTINNE, Y. DE and ANDREWS, F. M. (1979) The International Comparative Study on the Organization and Performance of Research Units: An Overview, in F. M. ANDREWS (ed.), *Scientific Productivity. The Effectiveness of Research Groups in Six Countries,* Cambridge, England: Cambridge Univ. Press and Paris: Unesco.

HESSE, M. (1970) *Models and Analogies in Science,* Notre Dame, IN: Univ. of Notre Dame Press.

HESSE, M. (1974) *The Structure of Scientific Inference,* Berkeley: Univ. of California Press.

HINDHEDE, M. (1913) Studien über Eiweissminimum, *Skandinavisches Archiv für Physiologie* **30:** 97-182.

HINTIKKA, J. (1976) *The Semantics of Questions and the Questions of Semantics. Acta Philosophica Fennica,* Vol. 28(4), Amsterdam.

HINTIKKA, J. (1979) Towards an Interrogative Model of Scientific Inquiry, *Communication and Cognition, Special Issue on Theory of Knowledge and Science Policy:* 208-20.

HIRSCH, J. (1971) *Wissenschaftlich-technischer Fortschritt und politisches System,* Frankfurt/Main: Suhrkamp.

HOFSTADTER, A. (1955) The Scientific and Literary Uses of Language, in L. BRYSON *et al. (eds.), Symbols and Society,* New York: Conference on Science, Philosophy and Religion in their Relation to the Democratic Way of Life, Institute for Religious and Social Studies.

HOLZNER, B. and MARX, J. (1979) *Knowledge Application. The Knowledge System in Society,* Boston: Allyn and Bacon.

HUGHES, T. (1979) Electric Light and Power, Paper presented at the "History and Sociology of Science Colloquia", Philadelphia: University of Pennsylvania, Department of History and Sociology of Science.

HUSSERL, E. (1962) Die Frage nach dem Ursprung der Geometrie als intentional-historisches Problem, in W. BIEMEL (ed.), *Die Krisis der europäischen Wissenschaften und die transzendentale Phänomenologie. Husserliana, Gesammelte Werke,* Vol. 6, The Hague: Martinus Nijhoff.

JACOB, F. (1977) Evolution and Tinkering, *Science* **196:** 1161-1166.

JOHNSTON, R. (1976) Contextual Knowledge: A Model for the Overthrow of the Internal/External Dichotomy in Science, *Australia and New Zealand Journal of Sociology* **12:** 193-203.

JURDANT, B. (1979) Socio-Épistemologie des hautes énergies. Questions de méthode, Strasbourg: Groupe d'Étude et de Recherche sur la Science de l'Université Louis Pasteur.

KERVASDOUÉ, J. DE and KIMBERLY, J. (1977) Are Organizations Culture-Free? The Case of Hospital Innovation in the US and France, Paper presented at the Conference "Cross Cultural Studies on Organizational Functioning", Honolulu.

KINSELLA, J. E. and SHETTY, K. J. (1978) Yeast Proteins: Recovery, Nutritional and Functional Properties, in M. FRIEDMAN (ed.), *Nutritional Improvement of Food and Feed Proteins,* New York: Plenum Publ. Corp.

KNORR, K. D. (1973) Methodik der Völkerkunde, in *Enzyklopädie der geisteswissenschaftlichen Arbeitsmethoden,* Vol. 9, München: R. Oldenburg.

KNORR, K. D. (1977) Producing and Reproducing Knowledge: Descriptive or Constructive?, *Social Science Information* **16:** 669-96.

KNORR, K. D. (1979a) Tinkering Toward Success: Prelude to a Theory of Scientific Practice, *Theory and Society* **8:** 347-76.

KNORR, K. D. (1979b) Contextuality and Indexicality of Organizational Action: Toward a Transorganizational Theory of Organizations, *Social Science Information* 18: 79-101.

KNORR, K. D. (1980) Anthropologie und Ethnomethodologie: Eine theoretische und methodische Herausforderung, in W. SCHMIED-KOWARZIK & J. STAGL (eds.), *Theorie der Ethnologie und Kulturanthropologie,* Berlin: D. Reimer.

KNORR, K. D. and KNORR, D. (1978) From Scenes to Scripts: On the Relationship Between Research and Publication in Science, Research Memorandum 132, Vienna: Institute for Advanced Studies.

KNORR, K. D., KROHN, R. and WHITLEY, R. (eds.) (1980) *The Social Process of Scientific Investigation. Sociology of the Sciences,* Yearbook Vol. 4, Dordrecht, Holland: D. Reidel.

KOESTLER, A. (1969) *The Act of Creation,* London: Pan Books.

KORNHAUSER, W. (1962) *Scientists in Industry; Conflict and Accommodation,* Berkeley: Univ. of California Press.

KROHN, R. (1972) *The Social Shaping of Science,* Westport, CO: Greenwood Press.

KROHN, R. (1977) Scientific Ideologie and Scientific Process: The Natural History of a Conceptual Shift, in E. MENDELSOHN, P. WEINGART & R. WHITLEY (eds.), *The Social Production of Scientific Knowledge. Sociology of the Sciences,* Yearbook Vol. 1, Dordrecht, Holland: D. Reidel.

KUHN, T. S. (1962, 1970) *The Structure of Scientific Revolutions,* Chicago: Univ. of Chicago Press, 2nd enlarged edition, 1970.

KUHN, T. S. (1971) Notes on Lakatos, in R. C. BUCK & R. S. COHEN (eds.), *Boston Studies in the Philosophy of Science,* Vol. 8, Dordrecht, Holland: D. Reidel.

KÜPPERS, G., LUNDGREEN, P. and WEINGART, P. (1978) *Umweltforschung - die gesteuerte Wissenschaft?* Frankfurt/Main: Suhrkamp.

LACAN, J. (1966) *Les écrits,* Paris: Seuil.

LAKATOS, I. (1970) Falsification and the Methodology of Scientific Research Programmes, in I. LAKATOS & A. MUSGRAVE (eds.), *Criticism and the Growth of Knowledge,* Cambridge, England: Cambridge Univ. Press.

LAKATOS, I. (1976) Understanding Toulmin, *Minerva* 14: 126-43.

LAKATOS, I. and MUSGRAVE, A. (eds.) (1970) *Criticism and the Growth of Knowledge,* Cambridge, England: Cambridge Univ. Press.

LANGE, H. (1972) *Wissenschaftlich-technische Intelligenz. Neue Bourgeoisie oder neue Arbeiterklasse?* Köln: Pahl-Rugenstein.

L'ARC (1978) La crise dans la tête, Special Issue on Intellectuals, Vol. 70.

LATOUR, B. (1979) Le dernier des capitalistes sauvages. Interview d'un biochemiste, Paris: Conservatoire des Arts et Métiers.

LATOUR, B. (1980a) Is It Possible to Reconstruct the Research Process? Sociology of a Brain Peptide, in K. KNORR, R. KROHN & R. WHITLEY (eds.), *The Social Process of Scientific Investigation, Sociology of the Sciences,* Yearbook Vol. 4, Dordrecht, Holland: D. Reidel.

LATOUR, B. (1980b) The Three Little Dinosaurs or a Sociologist's Nightmare, *Fundamenta Scientiae* 1: 79-85.

LATOUR, B. and FABBRI, P. (1977) Pouvoir et Devoir dans un article des sciences exactes, *Actes de la Recherche en Sciences Sociales* 13: 81-95.

LATOUR, B. and WOOLGAR, S. (1979) *Laboratory Life. The Social Construction of Scientific Facts,* Beverley Hills: Sage.

LAZARSFELD, P. and REISZ, J. (1975) *An Introduction to Applied Sociology,* New York: Elsevier.

LEMAINE, G., MACLEOD, R., MULKAY, M. and WEINGART, P. (eds.) (1976) *Perspectives on the Emergence of Scientific Disciplines,* The Hague: Mouton and Chicago: Aldine.

LEMAINE, G. and LECUYER, B.-P. (1972) *Les voies du succès,* Paris: CNRS/EPHE (Groupe d'étude et de recherche sur la science).

LEPENIES, W. (1978) Der Wissenschaftler als Autor. Über konservierende Funktionen der Literatur, *Akzente* 2: 129-47.

LEPENIES, W. (1981) Anthropological Perspectives in the Sociology of Science, in Y. ELKANA & E. MENDELSOHN (eds.), *Cognitive and Historical Sociology of Scientific Knowledge. Sociology of the Sciences,* Yearbook Vol. 5, Dordrecht, Holland: D. Reidel.

LOFLAND, J. (1976) *Doing Social Life. The Qualitative Study of Human Interaction in Natural Settings,* New York: Wiley.

LUHMANN, N. (1968) Selbststeuerung der Wissenschaft, *Jahrbuch für Sozialwissenschaft* 19: 147-70.

LUHMANN, N. (1971) *Soziologische Aufklärung. Aufsätze zur Theorie sozialer Systeme,* Opladen: Westdeutscher Verlag.

LUHMANN, N. (1975) *Soziologische Aufklärung, Bd. 2. Aufsätze zur Theorie der Gesellschaft,* Opladen: Westdeutscher Verlag.

LUHMANN, N. (1977a) Differentiation of Society, *Canadian Journal of Sociology* 2: 29-53.

LUHMANN, N. (1977b) Theoretische und praktische Probleme der anwendungsbezogenen Sozial-wissenschaften, in Wissenschaftszentrum Berlin (ed.), *Interaktion von Wissenschaft und Politik,* Frankfurt/Main: Campus.

LUHMANN, N. (1981) *Essays of Niklas Luhmann,* New York: Columbia Univ. Press.

LUKES, S. (1978) *Essays in Social Theory,* London: Macmillan.

LYNCH, M. (1979) Technical Work and Critical Inquiry: Investigations in a Scientific Laboratory, Paper presented at the Conference "The Social Process of Scientific Investigation", Montreal: McGill Univ., Dept. of Sociology.

MARCH, J. G. and OLSEN, J. P. (1976) *Ambiguity and Choice in Organizations,* Bergen: Universitetforlaget.

MARCH, J. and SIMON, H. (1958) *Organizations,* New York: Wiley.

MARCSON, S. (1960) *The Scientist in American Industry,* Princeton, NJ: Princeton Univ., Industrial Relations Section.

MARCUSE, H. (1973) On the Philosophical Foundation of the Concept of Labor in Economics, *Telos* **16:** 9-37.

McKEGNEY, D. (1979) The Research Process in Animal Ecology, Paper presented at the Conference "The Social Process of Scientific Investigation", Montreal: McGill Univ., Dept. of Sociology.

MEANS, G. and FEENEY, R. (1971) *Chemical Modification of Proteins,* San Francisco: Holden-Day.

MEDAWAR, P. (1969) *The Art of the Soluble,* Harmondsworth, Middlesex: Penguin.

MEHAN, H. and WOOD, H. (1975) *The Reality of Ethnomethodology,* New York: Wiley.

MELTZER, L. (1956) Scientific Productivity in Organizational Settings, *Journal of Social Issues* **12:** 32-40.

MENDELSOHN, E. (1977) The Social Construction of Scientific Knowlege, in E. MENDELSOHN, P. WEINGART & R. WHITLEY (eds.), *The Social Production of Scientific Knowledge, Sociology of the Sciences,* Yearbook Vol. 1, Dordrecht, Holland: D. Reidel.

MENDELSOHN,· E., WEINGART, P. and WHITLEY, R. (eds.) (1977) *The Social Production of Scientific Knowledge. Sociology of the Sciences,* Yearbook Vol. 1, Dordrecht, Holland: D. Reidel.

MERTON, R. K. (1957) Priorities in Scientific Discovery, *American Sociological Review* **22:** 635-59.

MERTON, R. K. (1968) The Matthew Effect in Science, *Science* **159**(3810): 56-63.

MEY, H. (1972) *Field-Theory. A Study of its Application in the Social Sciences,* London: Routledge & Kegan Paul.

MEY, M. DE (1980) The Interaction Between Theory and Data in Science. A New Model for Perception Applied to Harvey's Discovery of the Circulation of the Blood, in K. KNORR, R. KROHN & R. WHITLEY (eds.), *The Social Process of Scientific Investigation, Sociology of the Sciences,* Yearbook Vol. 4, Dordrecht, Holland: D. Reidel.

MEY, M. DE (1981) *The Cognitive Paradigm,* Sussex, England: Harvester Press and New Jersey, USA: Humanities Press.

MORIN, E. (1977) *La méthode. 1. La nature de la nature,* Paris: Seuil.

MORRISON, K. (1981) Some Researchable Recurrences in Social Science and Science Inquiry, in J. O'NEILL (ed.), *Science Texts: Recent Developments in the Sociology of Science,* London: Routledge & Kegan Paul.

MULKAY, M. (1974a) Methodology in the Sociology of Science, *Social Science Information* **13:** 107-19.

MULKAY, M. (1974b) Conceptual Displacement and Migration in Science: A Prefatory Paper, *Social Studies of Science* **4:** 205-34.

MULKAY, M. (1976) Norms and Ideology in Science, *Social Science Information* **15:** 637-56.

MULKAY, M. (1979) *Science and the Sociology of Knowledge,* London: George Allen & Unwin.

MULKAY, M., GILBERT, N. and WOOLGAR, S. (1975) Problem Areas and Research Networks in Science, *Sociology* **9:** 187-203.

MULLINS, N. (1977) Rhetorical Resources in Natural Science Papers, Princeton: Institute for Advanced Studies.

MULLINS, N., HARGENS, L., HECHT, P. K. and KICK, E. L. (1977) The Group Structure of Co-Citation Clusters: A Comparative Study, *American Sociological Review* **42:** 552-62.

NAGEL, E. (1961) *The Structure of Science: Problems in the Logic of Scientific Explanation,* London: Routledge & Kegan Paul.

NELKIN, D. (1975) The Political Impact of Technological Expertise, *Social Studies of Science* **5**(1): 35-54.

NELKIN, D. (1978) *Science Textbook Controversies and the Politics of Equal Time,* Cambridge, MA: M.I.T. Press.

NIETZSCHE, F. (1964) On Truth and Falsity in their Ultramoral Sense, in O. LEVY (ed.), *The Complete Works of Friedrich Nietzsche,* Vol. 2, New York: Russell & Russell.

NIETZSCHE, F. (1968) *The Will to Power,* New York: Vintage Books.

NIETZSCHE, F. (1973) Über Wahrheit und Lüge im aussermoralischen Sinn, in G. COLLI & M. MONTINARI (eds.), *Werke. Kritische Gesamtausgabe,* Vol. 3, Part 2, Berlin: de Gruyter.

NOWOTNY, H. (1973) On the Feasibility of a Cognitive Approach to the Study of Science, *Zeitschrift für Soziologie* **2:** 282-96.

NOWOTNY, H. (1979) *Kernenergie: Gefahr oder Notwendigkeit?* Frankfurt/Main: Suhrkamp.

NOWOTNY, H. and ROSE, H. (eds) (1979) *Countermovements in the Sciences. Sociology of the Sciences,* Year-book Vol. 3, Dordrecht, Holland: D. Reidel.

O'NEILL, J. (ed.) (1973) *Modes of Individualism and Collectivism,* London: Heinemann.

O'NEILL, J. (1979) Marxism and the Two Sciences, Toronto: York University.

O'NEILL, J. (1981) Historian's Artefacts. Some Production features in Historical Inquiry, in J. O'NEILL (ed.), *Science Texts: Recent Developments in the Sociology of Science,* London: Routledge & Kegan Paul.

O'NEILL, J. and LYNCH, M. (1981) Some Issues in Formal Analysis and Situated Inquiry, in J. O. NEILL (ed.), *Science Texts: Recent Developments in the Sociology of Science,* London: Routledge & Kegan Paul.

PAVIČIĆ, M. (1977) Logick filozofska rukotvorina g. Wittgensteina, *Ideje* **5:** 36-48

PEIRCE, C. S. (1931-35) *Collected Papers,* C. HARTSHORNE & P. WEISS (eds.), Cambridge, MA: Harvard Univ. Press.

PEIRCE, C. S. (1955) *Philosophical Writings of Peirce,* J. BUCHLER (ed.), New York: Dover Publ.

PELZ, D. and ANDREWS, F. (1966, 1976) *Scientists in Organizations: Productive Climates for Research and Development,* New York: Wiley, Revised and enlarged edition, 1976.

PHILLIPS, D. (1974) Epistemology and the Sociology of Knowledge: The Contributions of Mannheim, Mills, and Merton, *Theory and Society* **1:** 59-88.

PICKERING, A. (1980) The Role of Interests in High Energy Physics: The Choice Between Charm and Colour, in K. KNORR, R. KROHN & R. WHITLEY (eds.), *The Social Process of Scientific Investigation, Sociology of the Sciences,* Yearbook Vol. 4, Dordrecht, Holland; D. Reidel.

PIKE, K. (1967) *Language in Relation to a Unified Theory of the Structure of Human Behavior,* The Hague: Mouton.

PINCH, T. (1980) Theoreticians and the Production of Experimental Anomaly; The Case of Solar Neutrinos, in K. KNORR, R. KROHN & R. WHITLEY (eds.), *The Social Process of Scientific Investigation, Sociology of the Sciences,* Yearbook Vol. 4, Dordrecht, Holland: D. Reidel.

PINXTEN, R. (ed.) (1979) *On Going Beyond Kinship, Sex and the Tribe,* Gent: E. Story-Scientia.

POPPER, K. (1963) *Conjectures and Refutations,* London: Routledge & Kegan Paul.

PRICE, D. DE SOLLA (1970) Citation Measures of Hard Science, Soft Science, Technology and Non-Science, in C. NELSON & D. K. POLLOCK (eds.), *Communication among Scientists and Engineers,* Lexington, MA: D. C. Heath.

PRICE, D. DE SOLLA (1979) The Citation Cycle, Paper presented at the Mid-Year Meeting of the American Society for Information Science, Banff, Canada.

PROPP, V. (1968) *Morphology of the Folktale,* Rev. ed., Austin: Univ. of Texas Press.

PUTNAM, H. (1971) *Philosophy of Logic,* New York: Harper & Row.

QUINE, W. V. O. (1960) *Word and Object,* Cambridge, MA: M.I.T. Press.

QUINE, W. V. O. (1969) *Ontological Realitivity and Other Essays,* New York: Columbia Univ. Press.

RAVETZ, J. (1977) The Expertness of Expert, in E. SEMPER and P. COGGIN (eds.), *Hidden Factors in Technological Change,* Oxford: Pergamon.

RESTIVO, S. (1978) Parallels and Paradoxes in Modern Physics and Eastern Mysticism: I—A Critical Reconnaissance, *Social Studies of Science* **8:** 143-81.

RESTIVO, S. and ZENZEN, M. (1978) A Humanistic Perspective on Science and Society, *Humanity and Society* **2:** 211-36.

ROSE, H. and ROSE, S. (eds.) (1976) *The Political Economy of Science,* London: Macmillan.

ROSSI-LANDI, F. (1975) *Language and Economics,* The Hague: Mouton.

RYAN, A. (ed.) (1973) *The Philosophy of Social Explanation,* Oxford: Oxford Univ. Press.

SALOMON, H. J. (1977) Science Policy Studies and the Development of Science Policy, in I. SPIEGEL-RÖSING & D. DE SOLLA PRICE (eds.), *Science, Technology and Society,* London: Sage.

SCHOEPFLE, M., TOPPER, M. and FISHER, L. (1974) Operational Analysis of Culture and the Operation of Ethnography: A Reconciliation, *Communication and Cognition* **7**(3/4): 378-406.

SCHON, D. A. (1963) *Displacement of Concepts,* London: Tavistock.

SCHUTZ, A. (1943) The Problem of Rationality in the Social World, *Economica* **10**(38): 130-49.

SCHUTZ, A. (1970) Some Structures of the Life-World, in I. SCHUTZ (ed.), *Collected Papers,* Vol. 3, *Studies in Phenomenological Philosophy,* The Hague: Martinus Nijhoff.

SEARLE, J. (1969) *Speech Acts,* London: Cambridge Univ. Press.

SELLARS, W. (1963) *Science, Perception and Reality,* New York: Humanities Press.

SERRES, M. (1974) *Hermes III. La traduction,* Paris: Minuit.

SERRES, M. (1980) *Le parasite,* Paris: Grasset et Fasquelle.

SHAPIN, S. (1979a) Homo Phrenologicus: Anthropological Perspectives on an Historical Problem, in B. BARNES & S. SHAPIN (eds.), *Natural Order,* Beverley Hills: Sage.

SHAPIN, S. (1979b) The Politics of Observation: Cerebral Anatomy and Social Interests in the Edinburgh Phrenology Disputes, in R. WALLIS (ed.), *On the Margins of Science: The Social Construction of Rejected Knowledge, Sociological Review Monograph* **27**, Keele: Univ. of Keele.

SILVERMAN, D. (1970) *The Theory of Organizations,* London: Heinemann.

SILVERMAN, D. (1974) Speaking Seriously: The Language of Grading, *Theory and Society* **1**: 1-15 and 341-59.

SIMON, H. (1945) *Administrative Behavior,* New York: The Free Press.

SMALL, A. W. (1905) *General Sociology,* Chicago: Univ. of Chicago Press.

SMALL, H. and GRIFFITH, B. C. (1974) The Structure of Scientific Literatures I: Identifying and Graphing Specialties, *Science Studies* **4**: 17-40.

SNEED, J. D. (1971) *The Logical Structure of Mathematical Physics,* Dordrecht, Holland: D. Reidel.

SOHN-RETHEL, A. (1972) *Geistige und körperliche Arbeit. Zur Theorie der gesellschaftlichen Synthesis,* Frankfurt/Main: Suhrkamp.

SOHN-RETHEL, A. (1973) Intellectual and Manual Labour: An Attempt at a Materialistic Theory, *Radical Philosophy* **6**: 30-37.

SOHN-RETHEL, A. (1975) Science as Alienated Consciousness, *Radical Science Journal* **2/3**: 72-101.

STEGMÜLLER, W. (1969) Probleme und Resultate der Wissenschaftstheorie und analytischen Philosophie, Vol. 1, *Wissenschaftliche Erklärung und Begründung,* Studienausgabe Teil 2, Berlin: Springer Verlag.

STEGMÜLLER, W. (1979) *Rationale Rekonstruktion von Wissenschaft und ihrem Wandel,* Stuttgart: Philipp Reclam.

STEHR, N. (1978) The Ethos of Science Revisited, *Sociological Inquiry* **48**: 172-96.

STEHR, N. and MEJA, V. (eds.) (1982) *The Sociolopy of Knowledge Dispute,* London: Routledge & Kegan Paul.

STEHR, N. and SIMMONS, A. (1979) The Diversity of Modes of Discourse and the Development of Sociological Knowledge, *Journal for General Philosophy of Science* **10**: 141-61

STORER, N. W. (1966) *The Social System of Science,* New York: Holt, Rinehart & Winston.

STUDER, K. and CHUBIN, D. (1980) *The Cancer Mission, Social Contexts of Biomedical Research,* Beverley Hills: Sage.

SULLIVAN, D., WHITE, H. D. and BARBONI, E. J. (1977) Co-Citation Analysis of Science: An Evaluation, *Social Studies of Science* **7**: 223-40.

SUPPE, F. (1974) The Search for Philosophic Understanding of Scientific Theories, in F. SUPPE (ed.), *The Structure of Scientific Theories,* Urbana, IL: Univ. of Illinois Press.

TAYLOR, C. (1976) Hermeneutics and Politics, in P. CONNERTON (ed.), *Critical Sociology,* New York: Penguin.

THILL, G. (1972) *La Fête scientifique,* Paris: Inst. Cath. de Paris.

THOMAS, K. (1909) Über die biologische Wertigkeit der Stickstoffsubstanzen in verschiedenen Nahrungsmitteln, *Archiv für Anatomie und Physiologie* **4, 5,** and **6**: 219-301.

THOMSON, J. J. (1907) *The Corpuscular Theory of Matter,* London: Archibald Constable.

TOULMIN, S. (1961) *Foresight and Understanding. An Enquiry into the Aims of Science,* London: Hutchinson.

TOULMIN, S. (1967) The Evolutionary Development of Natural Science, *American Scientist* **57**: 456-71.

TOULMIN. S. (1972) *Human Understanding,* Oxford: Clarendon Press.

TOURAINE, A. (1978) Intellectuels d'en haut et intellectuels d'en bas, *L'Arc* **70**: 87-91.

ULLRICH, O. (1979) *Technik und Herrschaft. Vom Hand-Werk zur verdinglichten Blockstruktur industrieller Produktion,* Frankfurt/Main: Suhrkamp.

WATZLAWICK, P., WEAKLAND, J. and FISCH, R. (1974) *Change: Principles of Problem Formation and Problem Resolution,* New York: Norton.

WEBB, E. J., CAMPBELL, D., SCHWARTZ, R. D. and SECHREST, L. (1966) *Unobtrusive Measures: Nonreactive Research in the Social Sciences,* Chicago: Rand McNally.

WEINGART, P. (1976) *Wissensproduktion und Soziale Struktur,* Frankfurt/Main: Suhrkamp.

WEINGART, P. (1979) Science and Technology in a Legitimation-Crisis, Hypothesis and Indicators, *Communication and Cognition, Special Issue on Theory of Knowledge and Science Policy:* 378-93.

WERNER, O. (1969) On the Universality of Lexical/Semantic Relationships, Paper presented at the 1969 American Anthropological Association meetings in New Orleans.

WHITLEY, R. (1972) Black Boxism and the Sociology of Science, in P. HALMOS (ed.), *The Sociology of Science, Sociological Review Monograph* **18**, Keele: Univ. of Keele.

WHITLEY, R. (1975) Components of Scientific Activities, Their Characteristics and Institutionalization in Specialties and Research Areas: A Framework for the Comparative Analysis of Scientific Developments, in K. KNORR, H. STRASSER & H. G. ZILIAN (eds.), *Determinants and Controls of Scientific Development,* Dordrecht, Holland: D. Reidel.

WHITLEY, R. (1977a) The Sociology of Scientific Work and the History of the Scientific Developments, in S. BLUME (ed.), *Perspectives in the Sociology of Science,* New York: Wiley.

WHITLEY, R. (1977b) Changes in the Social and Intellectual Organization of the Sciences: Professionalization and the Arithmetic Ideal, in E. MENDELSOHN, P. WEINGART & R. WHITLEY (eds.), *The Social Production of Scientific Knowledge, Sociology of the Sciences,* Yearbook Vol. 1, Dordrecht, Holland: D. Reidel.

WHITLEY, R. (1978) Types of Science, Organizational Strategies and Patterns of Work in Research Laboratories in Different Scientific Fields, *Social Science Information* 17: 427-47.

WILLIAMS, R. and LAW, J. (1980) Beyond the Bounds of Credibility, *Fundamenta Scientiae* 1: 295-315.

WINCH, P. (1958) *The Idea of Social Science,* London: Routledge & Kegan Paul.

WITTGENSTEIN, L. (1968) *Philosophical Investigation,* Oxford: Basil Blackwell.

WOOLGAR, S. (1976a) Writing an Intellectual History of Scientific Development: The Use of Discovery Accounts, *Social Studies of Science* 6: 395-422.

WOOLGAR, S. (1976b) The Identification and Definition of Scientific Collectivities, in G. LEMAINE, R. MACLEOD, M. MULKAY & P. WEINGART (eds.), *Perspectives on the Emergence of Scientific Disciplines,* The Hague: Mouton and Chicago: Aldine.

WOOLGAR, S. (1980) Discovery: Logic and Sequence in a Scientific Text, in K. KNORR, R. KROHN & R. WHITLEY (eds.), *The Social Process of Scientific Investigation, Sociology of the Sciences,* Yearbook Vol. 4, Dordrecht, Holland: D. Reidel.

YOUNG, R. (1977) Science *Is* Social Relations, *Radical Science Journal* 5: 65-129.

ZENZEN, M. and RESTIVO, S. (1979) The Mysterious Morphology of Inmiscible Liquids: The Discovery and Pursuit of an Anomaly in Colloid Chemistry, Paper presented at the Conference "The Social Process of Scientific Investigation", Montreal: McGill Univ. Dept. of Sociology.

ZIMAN, J. (1968) *Public Knowledge,* Cambridge, England: Cambridge Univ. Press.

ZIMMERMAN, D. and WIEDER, L. (1970) Ethnomethodology and the Problem of Order: Comment on Denzin, in J. DOUGLAS (ed.), *Understanding Everyday Life,* Chicago: Aldine.

ZUCKERMAN, H. (1977) *Scientific Elite: Nobel Laureates in the United States,* New York: The Free Press.

Index of Names

Index of Subjects